BUCOLIC ECOLOGY

BUCOLIC ECOLOGY

Virgil's *Eclogues* and the
Environmental Literary
Tradition

Timothy Saunders

B L O O M S B U R Y
LONDON · NEW DELHI · NEW YORK · SYDNEY

Bloomsbury Academic
An imprint of Bloomsbury Publishing Plc

50 Bedford Square   1385 Broadway
London   New York
WC1B 3DP   NY 10018
UK   USA

www.bloomsbury.com

First published in 2008 by Gerald Duckworth & Co. Ltd.

British Library Cataloguing-in-Publication Data
A catalogue record for this book is available from the British Library.

ISBN: PB: 978-0-7156-3617-6
ePUB: 978-1-4725-2110-1
ePDF: 978-1-4725-2109-5

Library of Congress Cataloging-in-Publication Data
A catalog record for this book is available from the Library of Congress.

Typeset by Ray Davies

Contents

For my parents, Andrew and Penny Saunders,

and for Tanja

Acknowledgements

Many people and institutions have aided me in the writing of this book, and it is a pleasure to acknowledge them here. First and foremost, thanks must go to the Department of Classics at the University of Bristol, where as a doctoral student I planted the seeds for the study I have sought to bring to fruition in the pages to come. Located as they are in a setting that Virgil all but names, the Woodland Road, I can think of no more lively or flourishing an environment within which to throw and receive ideas. Even though barely a tussock of the thesis that resulted has survived its subsequent cropping and evolution into this book, it is still to my supervisor, Charles Martindale, that I would like to express my greatest thanks. It is his example and inspiration that more than anything else has illumined for me the stars by which I continue to try to shepherd, farm and navigate Virgil's works.

I was first challenged to start thinking about how I might turn that thesis into a book by my two examiners, Duncan Kennedy and Joseph Farrell. Each of them took on their role with a generosity, sense of adventure and willingness to engage that more than puts their Virgilian forebear, Palaemon, in the shade. Work on the book itself was greatly enhanced when I received a post-doctoral research fellowship at the University of Tromsø in Norway. Here too I have been especially fortunate in my colleagues and would like thank Helène Whittaker von Hofsten, Peter Jackson and the Border Poetics group in particular for many a long lunch and conversation about Virgil, ecphrasis and all kinds of edgy topics respectively. More broadly, I have benefited greatly from Norway's distinctive academic, as well as topographical, environment. My nascent thoughts on the cosmos were originally presented at a seminar in the Department of Classics at the University of Oslo and I would like to thank all the participants of that seminar, especially Monika Asztalos, Anastasia Maravela-Solbakk, Juan Christian Pellicer and Marianne Soon Ophaug, for their warm welcome, their wealth of ideas and, in short, their seminal role in giving the book as a whole its vital sense of 'lift-off'. I also owe many a 'tusen, tusen takk' to my longstanding friend and colleague, Mathilde Skoie. With her customary verve and zest, and at a time when she had more than enough to be getting on with of her own, she not only read the final draft from start to finish and commented upon it at some length, but was even willing to lug it around half of Europe in the process.

The final typescript has also been greatly improved by the two anonymous readers for the press. Even though their names must remain, like that second figure on Menalcas' cups, just beyond the tip of my tongue, their comments too helped me re-think and re-shape my text on both the micro- and the macro-cosmic scale. Of course, any stray atoms that remain … well, let's just put them down to the joys of random chance.

Finally, I would like to thank my editor, Deborah Blake, for all her help and guidance. Like many others before me, I must also list another of her virtues, one that I had no right to call upon, but for which I am immensely grateful all the same – that of patience.

The thanks I owe to those mentioned in my dedication is of a wholly different kind and I only hope I manage to express it more fully in many other ways besides, well beyond the pages of this book.

Introduction

Virgil's *Eclogues* are bold, innovative, ambitious and playful poems. Virgil himself indicates as much when, at the close of his next work, the *Georgics*, he recalls how he had once played these shepherd songs 'audacious with youth' (*audaxque iuuenta Geo.* 4.565). The audacity of these poems, and with it those other qualities I have listed, is by no means difficult to discern. It lies, for instance, in their innovative lexicon, by means of which they introduce all kinds of objects, epithets, concepts, practices and place names to Latin poetry for the very first time;[1] it lies in their persistent orientation towards the future, with their prophecies of even better songs to come, including the hope that their singer will one day defeat even Orpheus and Linus with his songs;[2] it lies in their daring and often unexpected sense of humour, which is nowhere better exemplified than in *Eclogue* 4, a poem that appears to structure the constitution of the coming new golden age in terms that are reminiscent of no less surprising a configuration than the soul of a cow;[3] and it is signalled not only by the repeated use of the adjective *nouus* ('new') to list the new milk, new poems, new progeny, new nectar, new sun, new wedding torches, new acts of litigation and new spring-time that their singers, addressees and settings variously contemplate, promise, experience and produce,[4] but also by the ongoing difficulties commentators have experienced across the years in trying to reconcile what they think bucolic, or pastoral, poetry ought in practice to be, with what they actually encounter when they come to read the *Eclogues* themselves.[5]

It is, at any rate, this view of the *Eclogues* as bold, innovative, ambitious and playful poems that the present book sets out to promote. It does so, moreover, in the belief that these qualities are seldom more powerfully expressed than through the relationship the *Eclogues* establish between bucolic song and the physical universe. I shall rehearse some of my reasons for thinking this below, but first I should acknowledge that this characterisation of the *Eclogues* is by no means the only one available, nor is it the one that most commonly emerges from nature-based readings of these poems. Indeed, as the critic Paul Alpers has illustrated, such readings tend to attribute to the *Eclogues* what might at first sight seem to be rather more conservative, and certainly more sombre, qualities instead: an overriding sense of nostalgia; a persistent evocation of, and lamentation for, a world that has been lost; and an aura of melancholy (that supposedly quintessential 'Virgilian' property) pervading the whole. There is, of

1

course, no real reason why these two sets of characteristics should necessarily cancel one another out: the *Eclogues'* engagement with the past need not, after all, be any less innovative, or imaginative, than their investment in the future, and their very audacity may consist in part in their insertion of humour at precisely those moments when all else would appear to be joyless and lost.[6] But there nonetheless remains in practice a notable propensity among nature-based readings of the *Eclogues* to prioritise the past over the present and the future, sorrow over laughter and destruction over creation.

Why this might be so is open to interpretation. One possibility is that such a focus places an undue emphasis on the theme of the loss of land, some of the effects of which are registered in *Eclogues* 1 and 9, but only fleetingly, if at all, anywhere else.[7] Another is suggested by Alpers in his books *The Singer of the Eclogues* (1979) and *What Is Pastoral?* (1996). For Alpers there argues that our very interest in the representation of nature and landscape in the *Eclogues*, as well as the assumptions that come with it, 'are largely due to romantic poetry and its transformation of our modes of literature and thought'.[8] He demonstrates, above all, how several of the readings of the *Eclogues* that take nature or landscape as their primary concern reproduce the terms of Friedrich Schiller's essay of 1795-6, 'On Naive and Sentimental Poetry', as a consequence of which they come to regard any poem that is in some way or other about nature as a poem that is thereby about our disconnection from nature as well.[9] Indeed, Alpers himself would seem to be of the belief that the influence and attraction of Schiller's thought has proven to be so great that it is now all but impossible to escape from the shadow of this essay and to offer any account of the *Eclogues* which takes the natural world as its principal theme without attributing to these poems an overriding sense of absence, nostalgia, melancholy and loss.[10] In response to this, he suggests we can avoid such overtly romanticised readings only if we turn our attention to the figure of the herdsman and interpret the depiction of such things as nature and landscape solely in relation to him instead.[11]

My own view is that such a move is neither necessary nor even especially desirable. It is undesirable because the *Eclogues'* engagement with the natural world forms too fundamental a part of their self-definition to be so lightly dismissed; and it is unnecessary because it is by no means the case that every approach to nature available to us today must lead us inexorably back to Schiller's essay. In the chapter on landscape, we shall indeed encounter one configuration of the natural world that can, and frequently has, served to classify the *Eclogues* as forms of 'sentimental' verse, but even in this instance the fit is by no means exact. The other chapters, by contrast, with their focus on the catasterisms, cosmology, geography, topography and atomic structure of these poems, deploy ways of organising and analysing bucolic space that bear even less of an allegiance to the axes of Schiller's thought. As a result, they place rather less

2

emphasis on the *Eclogues'* intermittent concern with absence, melancholy and loss, and rather more on their range and complexity, as well as on their audacity, novelty, ambition and wit.

It is indeed largely in order to emphasise the extent to which 'nature' is a far more capacious thing (and concept) than readings in the Schillerian, and anti-Schillerian, tradition tend to allow that I have organised each chapter around a different way of configuring and interpreting the natural world.[12] One of the effects of this is that, as one chapter proceeds to the next, our field of vision is gradually reduced. We begin among the great expanses of outer space; then we home in on the earth with its countries, settlements, terrains, flora and fauna; and finally we end up all the way down among the atoms. Yet the different versions of nature we thereby encounter, and the different formations the natural world comes to assume as we proceed, are due not only to these simple changes of scale, but are also the result of the different modes of perception each of these shifts of focus necessarily invites. After all, terms such as 'astronomy' and 'cartography' are by no means neutral labels, but they help determine, first, what we might mean by nature whenever we wish to discuss its relationship to poetry; second, how we then define the relationship this version of nature holds towards the kind of poetry in which it is supposed to appear; and, third, how we subsequently come to construe the nature of that poetry as a result. I discuss this issue explicitly and at some length in my chapter on 'landscape', but it applies equally to the other approaches I employ. For even though titles such as 'cosmology', 'geography', 'topography' and 'physics' make use, unlike 'landscape', of both words and practices that have their roots in the ancient world, the disciplines they describe are no longer entirely the same now as they were then.

In general, though, my own understanding of the methods of configuring and examining the natural world identified in each chapter title is intended to be neither too dogmatic nor strict. The first chapter, on 'catasterisms', looks broadly at how Virgil's bucolic poetry aspires on occasion to ascend to the heavens in the form of a star; the second, on 'cosmology', has the structure and representation of the physical universe – and in particular the respective locations, movements and meanings of the planets and other heavenly bodies – as its theme; the third, 'geography' takes the earth as its sphere and focuses especially on the *Eclogues'* use of place names and other sites one might reasonably expect to find on a map; the fourth, on 'topography', assesses the significance of natural features such as mountains, rivers, meadows and trees; the fifth, on 'landscape', assesses the role assigned to the natural world when it is represented and construed in primarily visual terms; while the sixth, on 'physics' understands nature on the microscopic level, as the collection of atoms that constitutes the building blocks of the physical and poetic universe of the *Eclogues* alike.

My aim in employing such a wide variety of frames for approaching and

3

interpreting the natural world in the *Eclogues* is to illustrate just how wide-ranging and pervasive is the relationship between poetry and nature in Virgilian bucolic. To this degree, the argument of the book is cumulative. While each chapter can hopefully be read with some profit on its own, the full extent of the equation I posit between the *Eclogues'* understanding of the structure and workings of the natural world and their structuring and achievement of their poetic programme only becomes truly apparent when bucolic nature is assessed in all its forms, from the greatest sweep of outer space to the smallest atoms. It is therefore by making the whole of this journey from the cosmos to the microcosm that this book seeks to offer fresh and extensive insights into the nature of Virgil's bucolic verse. Its argument in short is that the *Eclogues* turn to the natural world throughout in order to define their nature and place in the literary tradition and that it is through this particular process of self-definition that they express the full extent of their audacity and ambition. For even as these poems recast other songs and texts from the literary tradition as natural features in the physical universe and thereby construct, as it were, an atlas of literary endeavour, they often demonstrate their own aspiration to take their place among the stellar achievements of that tradition, right up there among the stars. More than this, though, by viewing the creation of their own compositions in terms that both reiterate and anticipate the creation of the cosmos, they even suggest that they too can sing songs equal to, or perhaps even greater than, those of Orpheus and, in so doing, can reorganise and redefine the world of literature and nature alike in the course of their singing.

The *Eclogues'* habit of casting themselves and other texts from the literary tradition as heavenly bodies, geographical places, natural spaces and topographical features is by no means without precedent in Greco-Roman literature. On the contrary, it is a common feature of ancient literary theory as well as practice.[13] Nonetheless, these particular poems interweave the properties and processes of poetry and nature to such an extent that it seems appropriate to describe the structure of their production and transmission as a form of 'bucolic ecology'. The word 'ecology' does, of course, need to be treated with a certain degree of caution, not least because the school of criticism which deploys this kind of language the most, ecological literary criticism (or 'ecocriticism' for short), has tended to invest heavily in Romantic modes of representation and thought.[14] As such, the very usage of this word threatens to import back into my account those recognisably Romantic emphases that I, like Alpers, would at least like to temper, if not always entirely keep out.[15] All the same, I have found that the characterisation of an ecosystem as a decentralised network of relations that incorporates a variety of diverse elements fits well with the representation of literary process and transmission in these poems. These include, for instance, the idea that apparently different practices and processes, such as those of nature and poetry themselves, need not avoid one another, but can actively and productively (if not always harmoniously) interrelate. When, for instance, the zoologist Ernst Haeckel coined the word 'ecology' in 1866, he described it as:

> the body of knowledge concerning the economy of nature – the investigation of the total relations of the animal both to its inorganic and to its organic environment; including, above all, its friendly and inimical relations with those animals and plants with which it comes directly or indirectly into contact – in a word, ecology is the study of all those complex interrelations referred to by Darwin as the conditions for the struggle for existence.[16]

Haeckel's recognition that the exchanges which take place within the world of nature might on occasion assume the form of a struggle is certainly one that applies to the exchanges of the *Eclogues* as well. These, after all, frequently take the form of a contest and can result in the loss of pipes, livestock, land and even, potentially, herdsmen's lives.[17] At the same time, the very structure of an ecosystem, which is often supposed not to have a centre,[18] also allows for these different fields to interact and respond to one another in a much more reciprocal manner, in which neither need always claim strict priority over the other. Thus, just as Tityrus 'teaches' (*doces* 1.5) the woods to re-echo the name of Amaryllis in *Eclogue* 1, for instance, so in turn does Menalcas acknowledge at the close of *Eclogue* 5 that his hemlock reed had once 'taught' him (*docuit* 5.87) *Eclogues* 2 and 3.[19]

Above all, though, the value of using a language of ecology to describe the poetry of the *Eclogues* is that it brings to the fore two structuring principles whose presence in these poems we shall encounter time and again: repetition and recursion. The very presence of these two processes promises in itself to offer an alternative configuration of the relationship between literature and nature to that suggested by Schiller. For whereas Schiller's essay tends to treat an ancient text as if it were an untouched place in nature and to assume that, like this kind of environment, that text is liable to fracture and lose its true nature if an alien body, such as a modern reader, were to intrude upon it, an ecological model allows for that text and that place to be changed by any new arrival, without it necessarily being either lost or destroyed in the process. It has the capacity, in other words, to evolve: it is by no means the same text or the same place as it once was, but it still retains something that might be called its 'nature' all the same. Indeed, as we shall see in Chapters 5 and 6 in particular, Virgil's *Eclogues* actively invite and depend upon the participation of new and future readers for their ongoing processes of production and transmission.

The way in which I intend to understand the principle of a literary ecology in this book, then, is similar to that which Bonnie Marranca adopts in her *Ecologies of Theater* (1996). Developing Haeckel's understanding of

5

the workings of an ecological system, Marranca expands upon his definition and applies it to literary texts in the following way:

> I have enlarged this definition to contemplate the world of a work as an environment linked to a cultural (aesthetic) system. Texts themselves are always alive in the world, finding new life in the way they are absorbed into the works of artists through the ages and in the subjectivity of each reader/spectator. A text, then, can be considered as an organism, and a collective of texts, images or sounds an ecosystem.[20]

This manner of configuring the relationship between a text and a reader, as well as between one text and another, evidently imbues the process of literary production and transmission with a recognisably recursive temporality. As we shall see, the *Eclogues* themselves explicitly adopt this kind of repetitive temporal structure. They do so, moreover, not simply by grounding their songs in the cyclical patterns of natural processes, but also by frequently representing both those songs and the physical universe as static, visual objects, whose recursive structures each new reader or singer must inaugurate and set in motion all over again through his or her shaping perception. One manifestation of this involves the ritual scenes of celebration that take place in response to these moments of inauguration and initiation, the recurring, repetitive nature of which I have tried to capture through the term 'bucolic litany'. Another relates to the structure of the book of *Eclogues* as a whole. For on the one hand, the widely-recognised mathematical nature of this structure, which has often led these poems to be described in terms borrowed from architecture, might be taken to entail a somewhat static and rigid entity.[21] Yet because they represent themselves at the very same time as places in nature that both await and invite the engagement of other readers and singers from different times and places, the actual experience of reading the *Eclogues* is in practice far more mobile and dynamic than this. Indeed, it is precisely because these poems represent themselves more specifically as *responsive* places in nature that they take into account the location of any given reader in the world and the text alike (as we shall see again in a moment) and evolve accordingly. Thus, even though the mathematical structure remains and its effects continue to be felt, the book acquires as a result a shifting set of centres of gravity that reflect the position of a reader at any given moment. For this reason, the book of *Eclogues* is by no means a wholly static artefact, yet, by the same token, neither does it map out a clear linear progression. A poem such as *Eclogue* 7, that is, is not simply one more staging post along the road from *Eclogue* 1 to *Eclogue* 10, but rather, for as long as it is the poem currently being read, it establishes the very shape and delineation of the universe within which all the other eclogues are, for the moment at least, to be placed and perceived.

Be that as it may, the attention an ecological approach pays to the presence of such processes as repetition and recursion in the poetic programme of the *Eclogues* marks an obvious break from that adopted in Schiller's essay, which promotes instead a clear and seemingly unbridgeable barrier between ancient texts and modern readers. Through its active inclusion of new and potentially destabilising elements in the form of later readers, texts and events, moreover, this ecological understanding of literary process also distances itself from those versions of pastoral and bucolic that would seek to attribute to these literary kinds a view of nature as a stable, fixed entity that is variously unresponsive to, or incapable of sustaining the intrusion of, such 'artificial' influences as historical time or political process.[22] Instead, as Marranca's outline of ecocritical practice suggests, one can think of readers as inhabiting and conveying distinctive environments in themselves, which then come to interrelate with those of the text in the process of reading. Indeed, I try to illustrate how this characterisation of the act of reading is very much in play in the opening lines of *Eclogue* 8, in which the narrator invites his addressee to listen in to the herdsmen Damon and Alphesiboeus, whether this particular dignitary is currently navigating the rocks of great Timavus or hugging the shore of the Illyrian sea.[23] It should also be acknowledged that readers bring with them different ways of looking at nature as well, and quite how they do so can depend, for instance, on whether they are soldiers, land surveyors or would-be herdsmen, all of whose perspectives are catered for in the *Eclogues* themselves. It makes a difference, that is, whether we conceive of the natural world of these poems as a landscape, a topography or as places on a geographical map, since each of these frameworks cuts up the literary and conceptual space of Virgilian bucolic in different ways. As has already been mentioned, it is in response to this that each chapter of this book adopts one or other of these approaches in turn.

Given the role I have just awarded to the particular environment within which any individual reading of the *Eclogues* is to take place, it is perhaps only right that I should end by saying a few words about the setting within which I have produced my own. This book has been written in its entirety in the small city of Tromsø in the far north of Norway. Lying as it does roughly 350 km above the Arctic Circle, with its two months of permanent daytime in the summer and two months of equally unbroken night in the winter, Tromsø offers a somewhat uncompromising vantage point for a survey of this kind. While I am tempted to argue from this that at least some of this book must therefore have been written in a state of heightened illumination, logic (as well as honesty) entails that just as much of it is also then the product of a mind that continued to labour on long after the lights had gone out. I would prefer to leave it to the silent imagination of others, though, to determine which part was written when and which of these two archetypal forces of light and shade has won out in the end.

A final word on terminology. It has long been debated whether the *Eclogues* are best described as instances of 'bucolic' or 'pastoral'. For the purposes of this book, I have opted for the former classification, not least because I think it captures better the particular relationship these poems bear, like Theocritus' *Idylls*, towards ancient forms of epic and love elegy. It would, of course, be wrong of me, given the notion of evolution I deploy and my belief that the *Eclogues* look as much to the future as to the past, to outlaw the use of the term 'pastoral' entirely. But to divest that word of its propensity to reduce much of what it is used to describe to the category of humble, escapist and often trivial verse would require the felling of far more trees than either I or my publisher could in all conscience wish to sanction.

1

Catasterisms

In the ancient world, few forms of poetry were treated with a higher regard than those which dealt, either implicitly or explicitly, with the cosmos. It is therefore a measure of the *Eclogues'* own audacious ambition that they too consistently define themselves in relation to the stars and even on occasion aspire to participate in this most elevated literary category. In the next chapter, we shall look in more detail at some of these acts of celestial self-definition, but first we shall turn to two poems, *Eclogues* 3 and 5, which together introduce and pursue the idea that bucolic poetry has both the ambition and even the capacity to scale the literary heights and become truly cosmological.

Eclogue 3: cups and cosmos

The suggestion that the cosmos might constitute both a topic and a destination for bucolic poetry makes its first sustained appearance in the *Eclogues* in the form of two sets of cups in *Eclogue* 3. Through the terms in which the herdsman Menalcas describes his set in particular, these cups come to act as tokens of cosmological literature (3.36-43):

> pocula ponam
> fagina, caelatum diuini opus Alcimedontis,
> lenta quibus torno facili superaddita uitis
> diffusos hedera uestit pallente corymbos.
> in medio duo signa, Conon et – quis fuit alter,
> descripsit radio totum qui gentibus orbem,
> tempora quae messor, quae curuus arator haberet?
> necdum illis labra admoui, sed condita seruo.

I shall stake cups of beech, the embossed work of divine Alcimedon, upon which, with an easy lathe, a pliant vine has been superimposed, which clothes the berry-clusters spread over the pale ivy. In the middle are two symbols, Conon and – who was the other, who described the whole firmament to the nations with his rod, what times the reaper should keep, what times the curved ploughman? I have not yet brought my lips to them, but keep them stored away.

An analogy between the crafting of these cups and the composition of cosmological literature runs throughout this passage. When Menalcas introduces his set as *caelatum diuini opus Alcimedontis*, for example, two

9

connotations of the word *caelatum* conjoin to usher in this analogy. The first of these connotations, 'chiselled' or 'embossed', suggests an association between carving and inscribing more generally. Yet the intervention of the adjective *diuinus* ('divine') between *caelatum* and the noun it qualifies, *opus* ('work'), also draws this epithet towards its putative 'root' in *caelum* ('heaven') and in so doing endows the inscriptions on these cups with a certain heavenly quality as well.[1] The celestial and literary credentials of these cups are then brought further into relief when Menalcas refers to the two astronomers placed in their middle as *signa*, which can mean 'stars' as well as 'symbols'. This single word on its own therefore replicates in miniature the ongoing exchange in the *Eclogues* between the structures and images of the cosmos on the one hand and those of literature on the other. The conjunction of 'stars' and 'symbols' is especially pertinent here because both of these *signa* evoke literary and cosmological associations alike. Conon, for instance, is the astronomer who, in the mid-240s BC, discovered that the lock of hair Queen Berenice II of Egypt had promised to the gods in exchange for the safe return from war of her husband, Ptolemy III, had ascended into heaven and formed a new constellation. In addition to its initial astronomical (and political) importance, this discovery also acquired a certain literary significance when the Hellenistic poet Callimachus commemorated it in his *Coma Berenices* ('Lock of Berenice'). The second figure, meanwhile, displays several of the trappings of a didactic writer: he possessed a teacher's rod (*radius*), 'described' (*descripsit*)[2] the whole of the firmament with this rod and instructed the nations when to reap and when to plough.[3] Both of these *signa* might therefore be said to represent different traditions of writing about the cosmos, but what they have in common is that both also take on the attributes of the universe they describe: Conon, who discovered a catasterism, has himself been catasterised; for the second astronomer, meanwhile, it is his instrument of didactic instruction that enables him not only to explicate but actively to participate in the workings of the cosmos, since the word for this rod, *radius*, also connotes 'a ray of light' and thus recasts the act of didactic instruction as itself a cosmological event.

This exchange of terms and figures between cosmology and literature is in several respects paradigmatic for the *Eclogues* as a whole. In the immediate context of *Eclogue* 3, however, this interrelationship is by no means to be taken for granted, but is rather precisely what now comes to be at stake in Menalcas' argument with Damoetas. For when Menalcas proposes to place these cups as his stake in the singing contest they are about to hold between them, he is in effect making the case for viewing them as worthy tokens of bucolic song. The word 'token' is appropriate here because Menalcas' description of these cups is itself a response to Damoetas' challenge to him to 'tell with what token you will compete with me' (*tu dic mecum quo pignore certes* 31). Damoetas, though, who for his part has just staked a young cow (*uitula*), is distinctly unimpressed (3.44-8):

1. Catasterisms

Et nobis idem Alcimedon duo pocula fecit
et molli circum est ansas amplexus acantho,
Orpheaque in medio posuit siluasque sequentis;
necdum illis labra admoui, sed condita seruo.
si ad uitulam spectas, nihil est quod pocula laudes.

The same Alcimedon also made two cups for us and he wrapped soft acanthus
around the handles, and he placed Orpheus in the middle and the woods
following; I have not yet brought my lips to them, but keep them stored away.
If you look to the cow, there is nothing to praise in the cups.

In terms of what follows, this puncturing riposte appears to achieve its
goal: the cups are not mentioned again in this eclogue; Menalcas in
response undertakes to meet Damoetas on his own ground ('in no way will
you escape today; I shall come wherever you call' *numquam hodie effugies;
ueniam quocumque uocaris* 49); and, at the close of the contest, the umpire,
Palaemon, refers only to the cow as an appropriate prize (109). Indeed,
even prior to Damoetas' reply, Menalcas would seem to have excluded
these cups from the spatial, epistemological and temporal sphere of this
eclogue alike: in contrast with Damoetas' cow, which is already to hand
('this cow here' _hanc_ *uitulam* 29) and which is milked twice a day and
suckles two calves (*bis uenit ad mulctram, binos alit ubere fetus* 30),
these cups remain untouched and are stored away elsewhere (43); their
owner, Menalcas, is seemingly ignorant of the identity of one of the
figures depicted on them (40); and, also in contrast with Damoetas' cow,
which is placed as a stake in the present moment ('I put down' *depono*
31), the stake represented by the cups is reserved for the future ('I shall
place' *ponam* 36).

The apparent rejection of the cups in this eclogue would seem to entail
that the paradigm of composing cosmological literature is rejected here as
well. In particular, it has been argued that the lofty ideals represented by
these cups are unlikely to be appreciated by two herdsmen who, up to this
point, have been engaged in rather more earthy exchanges of invective and
abuse.[4] To dismiss the cups outright in this way, however, would be to
overlook the extent to which they replicate both the emblems and the
rhetorical strategies of those preceding exchanges. The beech-wood out of
which they are crafted, for example, is a familiar and immediate feature
of these two herdsmen's environment. It was, after all, right where they
are now, 'here at the old beech trees', according to Damoetas a few lines
earlier, that Menalcas had broken Daphnis' bow and arrows in a fit of
pique (*Aut hic ad ueteres fagos cum Daphnidis arcum / fregisti et calamos*
12-13). At the very least, this correspondence between the beech-wood of
the cups and the beech trees of the eclogue's environment suggests that
the cups participate in what one might call the 'ecology' of *Eclogue* 3; but
there is also a further affiliation between these two passages which
indicates they share a common literary heritage as well. For both are

11

indebted in some way or other to *Idyll* 8, a poem which tells of Menalcas'
defeat to Daphnis in a song competition.[5] In that poem too, Menalcas'
opponent first stakes a cow (μόσχος), while Menalcas in response says he
is unwilling to risk anything from his parents' flock, but proposes to wager
an alternative prize – in this case a pipe – instead. And in that poem too,
this alternative stake, like the cups in *Eclogue* 3, is summarily matched
and mocked by his opponent.[6]

Another correspondence between the description of these cups and the
earlier slanging match comes with Menalcas' claim that Alcimedon had
fashioned these vessels on an 'easy lathe' (*torno facili* 38). The only other
occasion on which the adjective *facilis* ('easy') appears in the *Eclogues* is
earlier in this poem, when Damoetas claims that, while Menalcas was
committing a lewd act in a shrine, 'the easy Nymphs laughed' (*sed faciles
Nymphae risere* 9). Whatever else the adjective *facilis* connotes in either of
these two instances, its iteration here and only here in the *Eclogues*
suggests that the response of the bucolic world, signalled in advance by the
laughter of the 'easy' Nymphs, is already capable of accommodating a work
of the kind turned out by Alcimedon's 'easy' lathe. In the case of both *fagina*
and *facilis*, moreover, Menalcas' description of his cups picks up on words
spoken previously by Damoetas and thereby inducts these cups from the
start into the processes and practices of bucolic exchange.

When it comes to his turn, Damoetas demonstrates that he can play this
game as well. His description of his own cups not only mimics and mocks
Menalcas' but it also engages those cups all the more fully in what might
be called the 'economy' of *Eclogue* 3. He achieves this by reverting at one
point in his description to the very language of the placing of stakes that
has brought them here to begin with. For just as Damoetas 'places down'
(*depono* 31) his cow and Menalcas does not dare to 'place down' (*deponere*
32) anything from the flock but 'will place' (*ponam* 36) some cups instead,
so too, according to Damoetas, has Alcimedon 'placed' (*posuit* 46) Orpheus
in the middle of his cups and the woods following him.

So far from being entirely disconnected from their immediate context in
Eclogue 3, then, these two sets of cosmological cups replicate a number of
the terms and images of the ongoing argument in which they appear.
Indeed, through its use of the imperative *dic* ('tell'), the line with which
Damoetas issues his challenge to Menalcas to name his stake, 'tell with
what token you will compete with me' (*tu dic mecum quo pignore certes* 31)
– a phrase that triggers the two descriptions of the two sets of cups – recalls
the very line with which *Eclogue* 3, and thus the bickering of the two
herdsmen, begins:

> MENALCAS: Dic mihi, Damoeta, cuium pecus? an Meliboei?
> MENALCAS: Tell me, Damoetas, whose flock? Is it Meliboeus'?

In this case too, the repetition of a single word points towards a broader set of resonances between the accounts of the cups that follow Damoetas' challenge and the trading of insults that precedes it. The 'tell me' (*dic mihi*) form of address, for instance, frequently introduces a question in Roman comedy and, as such, signals the humorous banter that characterises both the preliminary exchanges of this eclogue and the description of the cups.[7] Whether Menalcas is knowingly playing the fool at this point or not, several features of his presentation of these cups conjoin to make both him and his stake look ridiculous. This is achieved largely through a pronounced incongruity between the objects described and the manner of their description. Line 37, in which the order of words enhances their comic effect, is a case in point. The first surprise comes with the very first word, *fagina*, which here makes its first appearance in this form in extant Latin poetry.[8] Even if the novelty of this word aggrandises the cups to a certain degree, it nonetheless still signifies a relatively lowly and seemingly local material. The second surprise therefore comes right away with the term to which *fagina* stands in apposition: *caelatum*. 'Of beech, a heavenly' is at the very least an unexpected collocation and may once have been a reasonably amusing one as well. Indeed, even if Menalcas' audience is not yet ready to hear the *caelum* in *caelatum*, the second connotation of this word, 'embossed', is just as likely to have them chuckling in their togas, since prior to its appearance here the verb *caelare* had been reserved solely for artworks fashioned out of metal, a far more precious material than wood (substitute the word 'plastic' for 'beech' and you should get the desired effect).[9] Whether he fears this introduction is a touch too subtle, or whether he wishes simply to enhance the eventual bathos, Menalcas now waxes increasingly lyrical: next comes the celestial epithet *diuini* (which, as we have seen, does draw the *caelum* out of *caelatum*) and the noun *opus*, which appears only here in the *Eclogues* and which is usually reserved for a 'work', both literary and literal, of a more august nature.[10]

By this point, Menalcas has his audience on tenterhooks, its interest sufficiently tickled into wanting to know the name of the author of this celestial marvel. Pausing at the so-called 'bucolic diaeresis' (when the end of a word coincides with the end of the fourth foot), to enhance their suspense, Menalcas milks this moment for all it is worth: 'I shall stake cups / of beech, the heavenly-embossed work of the divine ...' – could it be Hephaestus? Daedalus? or even, as in *Idyll* 5, Praxiteles?[11] No, it's just '... Alcimedon'. The somewhat austere readings of the cups that have predominated in modern times might suggest otherwise, but I would wager that, at this moment of sublime bathos, and in response to a name so unknown – or, at least, so *outré*[12] – members of the Roman literati would, in the words of Lucretius, have been shaking their sides with uproarious guffaws and besprinkling their cheeks with dewy teardrops.[13]

A second, comparable moment of bathos comes when, at the very instant he has the opportunity to prove he is not as *indoctus* ('unlearned') as he had earlier accused Damoetas of being (26), Menalcas fluffs his lines and forgets the name of the second figure on his cups. Here too his sense of comic timing, aided once again by a diaeresis between the fourth and fifth feet, contributes to the humour: 'In the middle are two symbols, Conon and ...' (the audience holds its breath) '...' (the audience still holds its breath) '...' (yes?) '...' (the suspense increases) '...' (and then it is punctured) '... um, who was that other?' Above all, though, Menalcas' cups are brought down to size by the comparison they invite throughout between themselves and that other, more illustrious emblem of cosmological poetry: the shield of Achilles from Book 18 of Homer's *Iliad*. The verb *caelatum* in particular recalls the true metalwork of that other literary artefact, which was fashioned of bronze, tin, gold and silver, while the epithet *diuinus* likewise leads one to think not so much of Alcimedon, but of the genuinely divine author of the shield, Hephaestus.

Damoetas, who in the process also manages to prove he is not as 'unlearned' as Menalcas would have us believe, then deflates the value and grandeur of these cups still further in the account he gives of his own set. Like Menalcas, he describes first the bordering motifs and then the symbols that lie at the centre of his cups; but, like a good (or, rather, a better) Alexandrian, he also outdoes Menalcas by compressing each of these descriptions into one line apiece (46-7), by suggesting that such figures and motifs are in any case something of a commonplace (44 and 47) and by asserting that these objects are not even worth as much as a cow (48). In a gesture that indicates he has in any case understood Menalcas' attempt to elevate his beech-wood cups to the stars, Damoetas perhaps also lampoons that same attempt by placing as the images in the centre of his own cups the archetypal cosmological poet Orpheus and the woods in hot pursuit. In sum, he translates the work of Alcimedon's *facilis tornus* ('easy lathe') into something facile and treats its topics as all too easy.

Like the 'easy Nymphs' (*faciles Nymphae*) recalled earlier in the eclogue, therefore, the sounds that arise from Alcimedon's 'easy lathe' are largely those of laughter. Yet the affinity the accounts of the cups bear towards the exchanges that precede them is by no means confined to comedy alone; they share with those exchanges something of the 'black market' approach to the themes and figures of the literary tradition as well. The line with which Menalcas opens the eclogue, for example, not only recollects the characteristic introductions of Roman comedy but, along with Damoetas' reply –

DAMOETAS: Non, uerum Aegonis; nuper mihi tradidit Aegon.
DAMOETAS: No, but Aegon's: Aegon recently handed them over to me.

– it also recalls the opening of *Idyll* 4:[14]

ΒΑΤΤΟΣ: εἰπέ μοι, ὦ Κορύδων, τίνος αἱ βόες; ἦ ῥα Φιλώνδα;
ΚΟΡΥΔΩΝ: οὔκ, ἀλλ᾽ Αἴγωνος· βόσκεν δέ μοι αὐτὰς ἔδωκεν.

1. Catasterisms

BATTOS: Tell me, Corydon, whose oxen are they? Philondas'?
CORYDON: No, but Aegon's; he gave them to me to feed.

The brusque and irreverent manner in which the opening of *Eclogue* 3 reworks the opening of *Idyll* 4 is indicative of this eclogue's treatment of its literary heritage more generally. Through the relationship it bears towards the opening of that idyll, as well as towards *Eclogues* 1 and 2, this preliminary exchange acts more or less as a roll-call of the dispossessed and their dispossessors: Damoetas, who endows the Corydon of *Eclogue* 2 with his pipe,[15] here displaces the Corydon of *Idyll* 4 from his position as the addressee in this line; Meliboeus, who is unknown to the *Idylls*, is the name of the herdsman who heads off into exile in *Eclogue* 1; while Aegon, who is the only character to survive from *Idyll* 4 (hence, perhaps, the repetition of his name), and whose name suggests both a goat and the agonistic nature of the exchanges to come,[16] has 'handed over' his flock to Damoetas (rather than to the, now doubly displaced, Corydon of the idyll). The next twenty lines or so then act out what might be entailed by this verb *tradere* (from which English derives both 'trade' and 'tradition') as they recount a sequence of thefts, ambushes, insults and deceptions, most of which are conveyed by means of an analogous sequence of literary 'borrowings'.[17]

By the time the two herdsmen come to argue over the relative value of Menalcas' cups and Damoetas' cow, then, the irreverent, witty and often audaciously learned way in which they trade in insults and literary figures alike has become normative for this eclogue. In this context, Damoetas' dismissive description of his own set of cups is neither misplaced nor ill-informed but is rather an erudite and amusing tour de force of its kind. In the spirit of the contest to come, he picks up on themes and rhetorical structures promoted by his opponent and then either trumps or denigrates them.[18] We have already seen how the greater concision of his account trumps Menalcas' and there is also at least one other technical aspect in which he outdoes his opponent. For while Menalcas places his description of what lies 'in the middle' (*in medio*) of his cups in the middle of his account of those cups, Damoetas goes one better by placing his own *in medio* at the medial caesura in the central line of his five-line response.[19] His desire to outdo Menalcas, moreover, expresses itself on a thematic level too, since the figure of Orpheus placed in the middle of his cups – and here the language of the placing of stakes does indeed carry over to the placing of artistic images – is intended to trump Menalcas' two astronomers. At the same time, when he mimics one of his opponent's phrases word-for-word, the effect of this imitation is to empty both this phrase itself and the cups to which it applies of any real value.

To this extent, the cups as emblems of cosmological literature are treated with no more respect than the other emblems of poetry traded in this eclogue, such as goats, cows, sheep or, indeed, the Theocritean figures of Menalcas and Damoetas themselves. Rather, like those other emblems,

15

the cups are but another card in the bucolic deck, which can be brought into play at any moment in this contest of barter and banter. At the same time, it is precisely their engagement in this kind of contest that promises to enable these two herdsmen to achieve the kind of cosmological poetry represented on these cups. For in one of their early exchanges, in which Menalcas recalls how Damoetas had tried to steal Damon's goat, Menalcas introduces a question that invokes a particular history of literary and cosmological thefts. When he asks (3.16):

> Quid domini faciant, audent cum talia fures?
> What should masters do, when thieves dare such things?

he is trading in a line from Catullus' translation of Callimachus' *Coma Berenices*. In this line, the poet laments the theft of the lock of hair from Queen Berenice's head (Catullus 66.47):[20]

> Quid facient crines, cum ferro talia cedant?
> What will hair do, when such things [as mountains] yield to iron?

Menalcas' question is sometimes understood to figure the relationship between Virgil (the thief or *fur*) and Catullus (one of the masters, or *domini*, from whom Virgil is stealing).[21] To this extent, it rather fittingly characterises the, somewhat scurrilous, mode of conducting literary transactions that persists throughout these exchanges. At the same time, it also draws out those features of this tale of catasterism that make it particularly receptive to this kind of treatment. For a start, the reference here to Catullus' translation rather than to Callimachus' original dictates that the *Coma Berenices* is smuggled into *Eclogue* 3 already in the form of 'stolen goods'. Likewise, the appearance of a line from that poem in this context helps highlight the fact that the catasterism there described is itself the consequence of an exchange (between Berenice and the gods) and a theft (the lock had disappeared mysteriously from the temple before Conon identified its new location in the heavens).[22] If the appearance of Conon, the discoverer of the *Coma Berenices*, as one of the *signa* on the cups marks the goal for poetry that reaches for the stars, then the preceding exchanges, which also invoke the story of this same catasterism, are precisely the point from which – and, indeed, the means by which – such a journey might begin.

The sequence of responsions between the descriptions of the cups and the exchanges that precede them therefore identifies at least one of the paths by which bucolic poetry might become cosmological poetry. But how far is this path actually pursued, either here in this poem or elsewhere in the *Eclogues*? Menalcas would seem to raise this question himself when he says of his cups that 'I have not yet brought my lips to them, but keep them stored away' (*necdum illis labra admoui, sed condita seruo* 43). This concluding remark, which is subsequently reiterated (and ridiculed) by

Damoetas, continues the portrayal of these cups as conveyors of the cosmological literary paradigm. At the same time, it also suggests that this is a paradigm the two herdsmen have yet to utilise. The first half of the sentence, for instance, 'I have not yet brought my lips to them', would not be out of place if the object referred to was a pipe, a reed or any other bucolic instrument. The implication of each herdsman's admission that he has not yet drunk from his cups, therefore, is that he has not yet played the kind of song promoted by those cups either. The verb *condere*, which appears in the second half of this sentence, achieves a similar effect. Meaning 'to compose' or 'found' a song as well as 'to store away' or 'hide', it withholds the prospect of a bucolic cosmological song even as it raises it.[23]

One obvious interpretation of this line would accordingly seem to be that Menalcas, like Damoetas, has not yet attempted to compose cosmological poetry, but is instead keeping this option back for the future. Looked at in this way, it is striking how these two sets of cups more or less map out the book ends of Virgil's next work, the *Georgics*. The line 'what times the reaper should keep, what times the curved ploughman' (*tempora quae messor, quae curuus arator haberet* 42) constitutes a concise summary of *Georgics* 1, while the story of Orpheus all but brings the fourth and final book to a close. At the same time, a comparison with a similar passage in *Eclogue* 10, in which the past participle form *condita* is also used, would seem to suggest that the trajectory of this verb is not solely towards the future. Rather, just as Gallus there proposes to 'go and modulate to the oat of the Sicilian shepherd songs which I have <u>stored away in</u> [or <u>founded on</u>] Chalcidic verse' (*ibo et Chalcidico quae sunt mihi <u>condita</u> uersu / carmina pastoris Siculi modulabor auena* 10.50-1), so too might Menalcas be hinting that he already has some samples of cosmological verse in his back catalogue. Damoetas' claim that he also owns a similar set of cups, and his insinuation that the themes they depict are somewhat commonplace makes this interpretation all the more plausible. Indeed, the very phrase with which Menalcas claims he has not yet drunk from his cups, but is keeping them stored away, *necdum illis labra admoui, sed condita seruo*, is a fairly close translation of a line the goatherd in *Idyll* 1 employs to describe the single bowl he hopes to give Thyrsis in exchange for the song of the dying Daphnis: οὐδέ τί πω ποτὶ χεῖλος ἐμὸν θίγεν, ἀλλ' ἔτι κεῖται / ἄχραντον ('Not yet has my lip touched it, but it lies unused' *Id.* 1.59-60). When even the words Menalcas uses to describe his cups are well-worn and second-hand (a point highlighted by Damoetas when he repeats this line verbatim in his own account), one cannot help but wonder just how pristine the cups themselves are either.

There are in any case a number of features of these cups that make them appropriate tokens of the song contest to come. As we have already seen, Damoetas' description of his own set seeks to trump and denigrate Menalcas' rendition in a way that anticipates the practices and procedures of their ensuing amoebaean exchange. Likewise, the language of 'placing' – which, as we also saw earlier, binds the description of the cups into the rhetoric of the laying of stakes – from this point on becomes the language of judgement as well: shortly after their argument over the stakes, Damoetas instructs their umpire, Palaemon, to 'place these things deep in your senses' (*sensibus haec imis ... reponas* 54), while Palaemon himself admits at the close that he is unable to 'place' (*componere* 108) the two contestants in order. Through the placement of Orpheus in the middle of Damoetas' cups, then, these objects are posited as possible arbiters of the competition to come as well as putative prizes for it. Indeed, the bid these cups make to represent the exchanges of this eclogue in both these senses makes an even greater investment in the notion of place than this. For if these artefacts really are to claim a broader representative value for the exchanges of *Eclogue* 3, then the logic of the reproduction of the middle of the cups in the middle of their descriptions would suggest that this trajectory should continue to reach out to the middle of the eclogue as well. And sure enough here too, at line 56, we find the chief arbiter, Palaemon, as he sets the scene for the contest to come and establishes a perspective from which it might be judged. Like the cosmos, moreover, this setting and this perspective is one of wholeness and totality: 'and now all the fields, now all the trees are in bloom' (*et nunc omnis ager, nunc omnis parturit arbos* 56).

This putative analogy between the setting for the song contest on the one hand and the cosmos on the other is then continued in the very first line of that contest. There, Damoetas responds to Palaemon's scene-setting and injunction to begin by picking up on the very word *omnis* that Palaemon had repeated twice in the central line of the eclogue cited above: 'The beginning of my muse is from Jove: all things are from Jove' (*Ab Ioue principium musae: Iouis omnia plena* 60). This repetition of *omnis* steeps the word all the more fully in the cosmological paradigm, since it has long been recognised that this line paraphrases the opening of Aratus' astronomical treatise, the *Phaenomena*, a poem which also makes liberal use of the adjective for 'all' or 'everything' (πᾶς) in its opening lines (Aratus 1-4):[24]

Ἐκ Διὸς ἀρχώμεσθα, τὸν οὐδέποτ᾽ ἄνδρες ἐῶμεν
ἄρρητον· μεσταὶ δὲ Διὸς πᾶσαι μὲν ἀγυιαί,
πᾶσαι δ᾽ ἀνθρώπων ἀγοραί, μεστὴ δὲ θάλασσα
καὶ λιμένες· πάντη δὲ Διὸς κεχρήμεθα πάντες.

Let us begin from Zeus, whom we men never leave unmentioned. All the highways are full of Zeus, and all the marketplaces of men, and the sea is full of him and the harbours; we all need Zeus for everything.

As far as the representative status of cosmological allusions and paradigms is concerned, it is worth noting that *omnis* is a word that appears in every one of Virgil's ten eclogues. In regard to *Eclogue* 3 in particular, however, perhaps the most important aspect of this allusion to Aratus is that it could well point back to the unidentified figure placed in the centre of Menalcas' cups. For Eudoxus is one of many candidates posited as the astronomer whose name Menalcas cannot remember and it was his prose *Phaenomena* which Aratus transposed into verse.[25] One might also be able to spot Aratus' own name hidden a few lines later in Menalcas' description of his cups in the word for 'ploughman', *arator* (3.42), but it is perhaps the fact that this figure remains anonymous at all that brings the name 'Aratus' all the more to the fore. For when the opening two lines of the *Phaenomena* state that Zeus will never stay unmentioned, the name that does stay unmentioned – indeed, the name for 'unmentioned' – is quite possibly the author's own: ἄρρητον.[26] Aratus would therefore seem to be an appropriate figure to be hidden both in Damoetas' opening couplet in the competition and in the cosmological cups that are themselves supposedly 'hidden' away (*condita*).

Between the opening of Aratus' *Phaenomena* and Damoetas' lines in *Eclogue* 3, moreover, lies yet another intertext, since Theocritus too alludes to this Aratean passage in the opening couplet of *Idyll* 17: Ἐκ Διὸς ἀρχώμεσθα καὶ ἐς Δία λήγετε Μοῖσαι, / ἀθανάτων τὸν ἄριστον, ἐπὴν ἀείδωμεν ἀοιδαῖς ('From Zeus let us begin and end, O Muses, with Zeus, the best of the immortals, whenever we are singing songs' *Id.* 17.1-2). Theocritus' poem is a celebration of Ptolemy II, in the context of which Ptolemy's mother Berenice is praised as well. Even though this is a different Ptolemy and a different Berenice from the couple celebrated by Callimachus in his *Coma Berenices* and therefore evoked in *Eclogue* 3, this shift from one Ptolemaic generation to another between the idyll and the eclogue duly figures the bucolic succession from the *Idylls* and the *Eclogues* more generally.[27] What is more, the grounding of this relationship in a shared heritage in Aratus' *Phaenomena* suggests that, in addition to generational time, literary time is here being co-ordinated with cosmological time as well.

Just as the opening of the song contest encourages a particular reading of the cups, so too do the cups promote a particular set of readings of the riddles with which that contest is brought to a close (3.104-7):

DAMOETAS:
Dic quibus in terris (et eris mihi magnus Apollo)
tris pateat caeli spatium non amplius ulnas.
MENALCAS:
Dic quibus in terris inscripti nomina regum
nascantur flores, et Phyllida solus habeto.

DAMOETAS: Tell me in which lands (and you will be a great Apollo to me) the space of the sky is not more than three ells.
MENALCAS: Tell me in which lands flowers are born inscribed with the names of kings, and you alone shall have Phyllis.

One does not need to posit a definitive answer to these riddles in order to see how they might relate to the cups.[28] Most obviously, Damoetas' riddle has a clear cosmological dimension: the word *caeli* ('heaven') echoes the *caelatum opus* ('heavenly work') of the cups and, again like the cups, this riddle projects an image of the cosmos encompassed within a small space. Likewise, the rhetorical structure of both these riddles, with their opening *dic* ('tell'), recalls not only the first line of *Eclogue* 3 as a whole, but also the phrase which introduced the descriptions of those cups: *tu dic mecum quo pignore certes* ('tell with what token you will compete with me' 31). What is equally significant about the allusion to Aratus with which the song competition begins and the cosmological content of the first of the two riddles with which it ends, moreover, is that both come from Damoetas. As the herdsman who had rejected the value of the cups as tokens of the contest to come, this at the very least questions the sincerity of those rejections. Indeed, in his account of his own set of cups, Damoetas already indicates not only that he has recognised Menalcas' allusion to Callimachus' *Coma Berenices*, but that he too has read Catullus' translation. For when he opens his response with the words *Et nobis idem Alcimedon* ('for us also the same Alcimedon' 44), he gestures towards one of Catullus' lines about Conon: *idem me ille Conon caelesti in lumine uidit* ('the same Conon saw me in the heavenly light' Cat. 66.7).

In the end, *Eclogue* 3 repeatedly plays with the idea that bucolic poetry such as this has the capacity to inhabit the cosmological paradigm represented by the cups, but at no point does it explicitly or unequivocally embrace that paradigm. The very last word of the poem, for instance, is *biberunt* ('they have drunk'), but whether the image of meadows drinking from streams stands in for the poem's drinking of the cosmological paradigm from the cups or if it simply stands in its stead and leaves the cups untouched replicates rather than resolves the interpretative issues of the eclogue as a whole. In as far as the cups are representative of the transactions bandied about in the first half of the eclogue, it is notable that these transactions are generally unsuccessful. Damoetas' attempted theft of Damon's goat, for instance – which, through an allusion to Catullus' translation of the *Coma Berenices*, triggers an association between bucolic behaviour and an ascent into the cosmos – is on this occasion resisted. In the anecdote that precedes this account of a failed catasterism, moreover, another pre-emptive strike is also made against bucolic poetry's attempt to reach for the stars. For when Damoetas recalls how Menalcas had broken Daphnis' bow and arrows (12), the word he uses for these arrows, *calami*, is reserved elsewhere in the *Eclogues* for the 'reeds' upon which their herdsmen commonly play.[29] Since Daphnis is one of the exemplary exponents of bucolic verse, the breaking of those instruments that might have enabled him to shoot his songs all the higher bears an obvious programmatic significance. Above all, though, it is the opposition these two herdsmen draw between a cow (*uitula*), the metonymic emblem of bucolic poetry, on the one hand, and the cups, those emblems of cosmological composition on the other, that seems to resist any simplistic equation between bucolic and cosmological poetry more generally.

After all, the equivocal role these cups come to play in this eclogue is, as we have seen, largely prefigured in their initial description. Indeed, when Menalcas describes them first as *caelatum opus* ('a heavenly / embossed work') and later as *condita* ('stored away' or 'hidden'), he demonstrates that he is conversant with the etymology of *caelatum* expounded by Varro in his *De Lingua Latina* (5.18).[30] In that work, Varro, citing Aelius, claims that *caelum* ('heaven') was so-called because it was *caelatum* ('raised above the surface') and we have already observed how Menalcas himself draws our attention to this analogy. Varro then goes on to say that *caelare*, 'to rise', might also be defined through contrast with its opposite *celare*, 'to hide'. For in the daytime, Varro explains, heaven 'is hidden, just as by night it is not hidden' (*Sed non minus illud alterum de celando ab eo potuit dici, quod interdiu celatur, quam quod noctu non celatur DLL* 5.18). We shall come to see the relevance of this remark again when we look at a fragment of song from *Eclogue* 9 in the next chapter, but it would appear that Menalcas is playing upon the dichotomy between *caelare* and *celare* here too when he describes his own *caelatum opus* as *condita* ('hidden'). Like the cosmos during the time of day when bucolic poetry most commonly takes place, that is, the cups of *Eclogue* 3 might well remain out of sight, but this does not necessarily mean they are therefore also out of mind.

Eclogue 5: drinking from the cups

If in *Eclogue* 3 the relationship between bucolic poetry and cosmological poetry remains tantalisingly elusive, in *Eclogue* 5 it is vividly enacted. This poem consists for the most part of two complementary songs which together raise Daphnis, the emblematic figure of bucolic poetry, all the way to the stars. In the second of these songs, Menalcas (who here returns from *Eclogue* 3) imagines the annual scenes of celebration that will commemorate Daphnis' deification. Included among the festivities will be altars, olive oil, laughter, wine, dancing and singing, but perhaps the most striking inclusion of all are the cups that Menalcas himself had kept hidden away in the earlier eclogue but now undertakes to put explicitly to use: 'Every year,' he promises, 'I shall set up two cups foaming with fresh milk' (*pocula bina nouo spumantia lacte quotannis / ... statuam*, 67-8).

To ensure we do not miss this reference to *Eclogue* 3 (and we should in any case bear in mind that it is a herdsman of this name who introduces the cups in both these eclogues), Menalcas invites two other figures from that poem to his party: his opponent in the song contest, Damoetas, and one of his opponents in love, Aegon ('Damoetas will sing to me and Lyctian Aegon' *cantabunt mihi Damoetas et Lyctius Aegon* 5.72). By filling his cups with milk, moreover, Menalcas also brings yet another antithetical figure from *Eclogue* 3 into the fold: the cow that had come to milking twice a day. The cosmological paradigm, in other words, is by this stage in *Eclogue* 5 brimming with bucolic. These joyous scenes mark the commemoration of the kind of synthesis between bucolic and cosmological poetry that is wagered as a poetic option in *Eclogue* 3, but not overtly realised there. For the remainder of this chapter, we shall therefore look at how this synthesis is achieved and indicate what it might mean for Virgil's bucolic poetics more generally.

The two complementary songs which together trace the ascent of Daphnis to heaven consistently chart his passage there in relation to the stars. Mopsus sings the first of these songs and begins with the image of Daphnis dead on the ground and his mother calling upon the stars (5.20-3):

> Exstinctum Nymphae crudeli funere Daphnin
> flebant (uos coryli testes et flumina Nymphis),
> cum complexa sui corpus miserabile nati
> atque deos atque astra uocat crudelia mater.

> The Nymphs were lamenting Daphnis, extinguished in a cruel death (you, hazel trees and streams, are witnesses of the Nymphs) when his mother, having embraced the pitiable body of her son, calls upon the gods and the cruel stars.

This vignette describes a complete disassociation between Daphnis and the heavens. Indeed, the picture of his mother embracing his body and calling upon the cruel stars would seem to suggest that he has actively been abandoned by them. The word *exstinctum* ('extinguished') in particular likens Daphnis to a fire, lamp or heavenly light that has been put out.[31] By the end of Mopsus' song, however, the connection between Daphnis and the constellations has been audaciously reaffirmed, with the proud epitaph he orders the shepherds to have inscribed upon his tomb: 'I am Daphnis in the woods, known from here all the way to the stars' (*Daphnis ego in siluis, hinc usque ad sidera notus* 43). Upon the conclusion of Mopsus' song, Menalcas promises to carry on where his companion had left off and raise Daphnis to the stars (*Daphninque tuum tollemus ad astra; / Daphnin ad astra feremus* 51-2). The word with which he begins his song, moreover, and which acts as an epithet for Daphnis is *candidus*. This epithet reverses his initial depiction as 'extinguished' and makes him, in Wendell Clausen's words, 'radiant, like a star' instead.[32] Menalcas then at once places him at the threshold of Olympus, whereupon 'Daphnis sees the clouds and the stars beneath his feet' (*sub pedibusque uidet nubes et sidera Daphnis* 57). Finally, and in immediate response to this apotheosis, 'the unshorn mountains toss their voices to the stars' (*ipsi laetitia uoces ad sidera iactant / intonsi montes* 62-3).

Because of the fundamental role Theocritus' First *Idyll* and its song of the dying Daphnis played in the evolution of bucolic poetry, any story that

subsequently involved Daphnis became at the same time a story about
that kind of poetry. In the case of *Eclogue* 5, the account of the ascent of
Daphnis to the stars is also an account of the elevation of bucolic verse into
cosmological verse. Menalcas emphasises this aspect of Daphnis' role here
in a number of ways. In the first place, when he undertakes to raise this
Daphnis to the stars, Menalcas makes it clear that it will not just be the
figure of Daphnis per se he is raising but specifically the Daphnis of
Mopsus' song. As he tells his companion, 'We shall raise *your* Daphnis to
the stars' (*Daphninque tuum tollemus ad astra* 51). A further resonance
between the two songs similarly confirms that this has been first and
foremost a journey of 'voices' towards the stars. For when in response to
Daphnis' arrival at Olympus the mountains toss their 'voices to the stars'
(*uoces ad sidera* 62), this completes the process that began with Daphnis'
mother casting her own voice towards the stars (*astra uocat crudelia* 23).

Above all, though, the ascent of Daphnis towards the heavens also tells
a story about the elevation of bucolic poetry, since it simultaneously
follows an analogous ascent through a number of literary forms, several of
which are themselves mapped out in relation to the stars. The opening
scene of Daphnis dead and seemingly abandoned by the stars, for example,
constitutes an obvious sequel to Thyrsis' song of the dying Daphnis in *Idyll*
1. As such, it presents one version of the legacy left at the end of bucolic
poetry's inaugural performance. In that poem, moreover, Daphnis had
promised to torment Aphrodite even from Hades, asking ironically if she
really thought every sun had now set for him (ἤδη γὰρ φράσδη πάνθ' ἄλιον
ἄμμι δεδύκειν; *Id.* 1.102). If the 'cruel stars' his mother calls upon in *Eclogue*
5 are anything to go by, it would seem that those suns really had aban-
doned him. Yet by the end of Mopsus' song these lowly beginnings have
been left behind and Daphnis has not only reasserted his relationship to
the stars but, in so doing, he has also stepped up to an epic paradigm. His
claim to be 'known from here all the way to the stars' (*hinc usque ad sidera
notus* 43), after all, is a close relative of Odysseus' famous boast towards
the beginning of *Odyssey* 9: 'I am Odysseus, son of Laertes, who am known
to all men for my tricks, and my fame reaches heaven' (εἴμ' Ὀδυσεὺς
Λαερτιάδης, ὃς πᾶσι δόλοισιν / ἀνθρώποισι μέλω, καί μευ κλέος οὐρανὸν ἵκει
Od. 9.19-20).[33]

When it comes to his turn to continue this bucolic ascent, Menalcas
wastes no time in making it complete. He places Daphnis at the threshold
of Olympus, from where he 'sees the clouds and the stars beneath his feet'
(*sub pedibusque uidet nubes et sidera Daphnis* 57). The Latin word *pedes*,
like its English counterpart, has the capacity to signify metrical as well as
physical feet and a passage from the proem to Book 3 of Lucretius' *De
Rerum Natura* provides an important precedent for its use in this context
here.[34] In that passage, and alongside a number of other close parallels
with Menalcas' song in *Eclogue* 5,[35] Lucretius claims that the whole

universe has been revealed to him as a result of Epicurus' teaching, wherein nothing escapes the view 'under my feet' (*sub pedibus*) (*DRN* 3.26-7):

> nec tellus obstat quin omnia dispiciantur,
> sub pedibus quaecumque infra per inane geruntur.

> Nor does the earth stand in my way, but instead all things are clearly discerned whatsoever goes on under my feet throughout the void below.

The specific allusion to Lucretius' 'feet' at this point should remind us that Virgil's bucolic poetry, like its Theocritean predecessor, shares its metre not only with Homeric and other epics but with much philosophical, didactic and cosmological verse as well. Indeed, Homer himself, whose account of Olympus Lucretius adapts in the lines that precede the citation above, was often thought of as a cosmological poet,[36] while the likes of Empedocles, Parmenides, Xenophanes and even, supposedly, Orpheus all utilised dactylic hexameters in their scientific and cosmological writings.[37] Menalcas' depiction of the exemplary figure of bucolic poetry gazing at the clouds and stars beneath his feet is therefore a representation of that poetry's capacity also to take the measure of the cosmos. The detailed echoes of Lucretius that resound throughout Menalcas' song at this point, moreover, recast Daphnis as a kind of bucolic Epicurus,[38] and similarities to Orpheus have been identified here as well.[39]

This reconstruction of the journey Daphnis (and therefore bucolic poetry) makes towards the stars both engages and depends upon the notion of a hierarchy of literary forms: from Theocritus in *Idyll* 1, to Homer in *Odyssey* 9 and, finally, to scientific and cosmological writing of the Lucretian kind. In practice, though, the literary universe of *Eclogue* 5 is much more complicated than this, not least because it re-organises the structure of these literary relations into a distinctly bucolic form. On the one hand, Daphnis' ascension to heaven breaks new ground: he 'marvels' at the 'unaccustomed threshold' (*insuetum miratur limen* 56) of Olympus, while the novelty of his deification – and of the song that relates and celebrates that deification – is reflected in both the 'fresh' milk (*nouo ... lacte* 67) that foams in the cups and the 'fresh' nectar (*nouum ... nectar* 71) that Menalcas proposes to pour in his honour. At the same time, the Theocritean bucolic tradition is by no means left behind as a result of this ascent: after all, 'marvelling' is already a feature of the goatherd's response to his cup in *Idyll* 1 (αἰπολικὸν θάημα *Id.* 1.56) and reminiscences of the *Idylls*, especially *Idyll* 7, in any case become increasingly prominent again in the scenes of celebration that follow on from Daphnis' deification. Indeed, one might even be able to see *Idyll* 1 hitching a lift on the back of *Odyssey* 9 as Daphnis makes his way from the lifeless figure at the start of Mopsus' song to the one who claims celestial fame in the epitaph at its end. For while the first line of the epitaph recalls Odysseus' boast from *Odyssey* 9, the couplet as a whole (5.43-4) –

> Daphnis ego in siluis, hinc usque ad sidera notus,
> formosi pecoris custos, formosior ipse.

> I am Daphnis in the woods, known from here all the way to the stars, the guardian of a beautiful flock, myself more beautiful.

– is structurally akin to Daphnis' self-description at *Idyll* 1.120-1:[40]

> Δάφνις ἐγὼν ὅδε τῆνος ὁ τὰς βόας ὧδε νομεύων,
> Δάφνις ὁ τὼς ταύρως καὶ πόρτιας ὧδε ποτίσδων.

> I am Daphnis, the one who used to pasture his cows here,
> Daphnis, the one who used to bring his bulls and calves here.

Despite the novelty of Daphnis' aspiration towards the stars in *Eclogue* 5, in other words, its mode of transportation remains recognisably Theocritean, since just about every idyll too thumbs a ride from its Homeric relatives.

Through the continued participation of bucolic poetry in this literary ascent to heaven, its practices, modes and procedures also help determine the temporal construction of this ascension. Above all, a number of features of this eclogue actively disrupt the stable and linear temporal progression from Daphnis dead to Daphnis at the threshold of Olympus traced above. In the first place, this progression depends entirely upon the temporality instantiated through the order in which these two songs are sung, with Mopsus going first and Menalcas coming second. Mopsus, however, would seem to suggest that this by no means reflects the order in which these songs were actually composed.[41] For while his own verses are new ('rather, I shall try out these songs, which recently I described on the green bark of a beech tree' *Immo haec, in uiridi nuper quae cortice fagi / carmina descripsi ... / experiar* 13-15), Menalcas' are seemingly less so, since Stimichon had praised his song about Daphnis to Mopsus long ago (*iam pridem Stimichon laudauit carmina nobis* 55). Mopsus, moreover, replicates this inverted temporality in his own song: the epitaph that brings this song to a close and that marks the second stage of Daphnis' ascent to the stars must evidently have been composed before the first stage, when he is lying dead.

Even as it invokes the notion of a clear temporal and generic progression through the order in which these two songs are performed, then, *Eclogue* 5 undermines this same progression through its use of a number of conflicting temporal and generic markers. In so doing, it resists the, endlessly popular, notion that bucolic is an irredeemably low-lying form that constitutes but a step along the road to greater things and replaces it with the prospect that bucolic can itself constitute the path that leads all the way to the stars. As we shall see, singers in the *Eclogues* tend to grow into, rather than out of, this kind of poetry. In *Eclogue* 5, as in *Eclogue* 3, the journey towards and realisation of the cosmological paradigm continues to be configured in distinctly bucolic terms. In *Eclogue* 3, it is the agonistic exchanges between the two herdsmen that provide the prerequisite conditions for the catasterism of the form; in *Eclogue* 5, it is through a comparable, if somewhat more amicable, mode of responsion that bucolic poetry's ascent to the stars is both enacted and acknowledged. When, for example, the landscape affirms Daphnis' deification with the words 'a god, he is a god, Menalcas!' (*deus, deus ille, Menalca!* 64), it echoes Lucretius' similar affirmation of the divinity of Epicurus in the *De Rerum Natura*: 'he was a god, a god, illustrious Memmius' (*deus ille fuit, deus, inclute Memmi DRN* 5.8). At the same time, because the cliffs and the bushes address themselves here to Menalcas in particular, this moment of Lucretian elevation duly takes on the form of a perfectly modulated bucolic response: just as Menalcas undertakes to raise Mopsus' Daphnis to the stars, so does the landscape affirm Menalcas' Daphnis once he arrives there. It is then precisely in response to this Lucretian moment of affirmation that the bucolic festivities get under way, wherein one of bucolic poetry's primary temporalities (repetition) and one of its equally prevalent modalities (responsion) are brought vividly into play, through the institution of an annual litany and the insistent iteration of the number two (5.64-8):

> 'deus, deus ille, Menalca!'
> sis bonus o felixque tuis! en quattuor aras:
> ecce duas tibi, Daphni, duas altaria Phoebo.
> pocula bina nouo spumantia lacte quotannis
> craterasque duo statuam tibi pinguis oliui.

'A god, he is a god, Menalcas!' May you be good and blessed to your people! Look, four altars: look, two for you, Daphnis, two fit for burnt offerings for Phoebus. Each year I shall set up two cups foaming with fresh milk and two mixing bowls of rich olive-oil for you.

To some degree, these rituals recall the sacrifices Tityrus says he will often perform in honour of the unnamed god who had helped him in Rome in *Eclogue* 1.[42] Above all, though, the repetition of the number two in Menalcas' festive vignette – the two altars each for Daphnis and Apollo – confirms that the two cups Menalcas also includes in this scene are at the very least related to those he and Damoetas had described in *Eclogue* 3. For in that poem too these cups had been introduced to an environment in which bucolic transactions take place primarily in denominations of two: they are presented as alternatives to a cow that comes to milking twice a day and suckles two young (*bis uenit ad mulctram, binos alit ubere fetus*

3.30); Menalcas opts for them because he dare not wager anything from a flock that both parents count twice each day (*bisque die numerant ambo pecus* 3.34); they have two symbols on them (*in medio duo signa* 3.40); and Damoetas explicitly states that he owns two of them (*Et nobis idem Alcimedon duo pocula fecit* 3.44). In the immediate context of *Eclogue* 3, this chain of dualities incorporates the cups within the reckoning of amoebaean exchange, although their reappearance in a similar chain in *Eclogue* 5 (which is not an amoebaean work in the same strict sense) suggests that the primary process being enacted here is the more general one of responsion. In this way, both the cups and the cosmos are rendered responsible to recognisably bucolic structures. For just as bucolic ritual is able to respond to the achievement of the cosmological paradigm, so too is that paradigm itself enacted through a number of bucolic figures (most notably Daphnis) and a number of bucolic practices (most notably responsion).

Once one has spotted the reference to the cups of *Eclogue* 3 in the cups that form part of the celebrations of the achievement of the cosmological paradigm in *Eclogue* 5, it becomes possible to spot other allusions to these vessels elsewhere in the poem as well. When, for instance, Daphnis enjoins the shepherds to add a poem to his tomb (an inscription which, as we have seen, charts part of bucolic poetry's passage to the stars) – *tumulo superaddite carmen* (42) – this is only the second of two occasions on which the verb *superaddere* is used in the *Eclogues* (and, indeed, in the whole of Virgil's works). The first occasion involves the addition of a vine to Menalcas' cups in *Eclogue* 3: *lenta quibus torno facili superaddita uitis* ('upon which, with an easy lathe, a pliant vine has been superimposed' 3.38). Through instances such as this, as well as other parallels elsewhere in these poems, the work of Alcimedon's lathe begins to look all the more representative of the inscribings of the *Eclogues* more generally.

I suggested in the previous section of this chapter that the descriptions of the cups of *Eclogue* 3 base part of their bid to make these vessels central to the representations of that eclogue on the emphasis they place on what is depicted at their centres. I then illustrated how the middle of these cups were described at the middle point of these descriptions and tried to follow this trajectory through to the central line of that eclogue, which likewise draws upon the cosmological paradigm. If there is anything in this, it is perhaps not irrelevant that the mid-point of the *Eclogues* as a whole – *Eclogue* 5, line 85 – comes just after the achievement of this paradigm and introduces a passage which, in bringing *Eclogue* 5 to a close, looks back not only to *Eclogue* 2, but also to the poem which had first intimated bucolic's journey to the stars, *Eclogue* 3 (5.85-90):

MENALCAS:
Hac te nos fragili donabimus ante cicuta;
haec nos 'formosum Corydon ardebat Alexin',

haec eadem docuit 'cuium pecus? an Meliboei?'
MOPSUS:
At tu sume pedum, quod, me cum saepe rogaret,
non tulit Antigenes (et erat tum dignus amari),
formosum paribus nodis atque aere, Menalca.

MENALCAS: We shall endow you with this fragile hemlock reed; this taught us 'Corydon was burning for beautiful Alexis', this same reed taught us 'whose flock? Is it Meliboeus'?'
MOPSUS: But you take this crook, which, when he often asked me for it, Antigenes did not receive (and he was then worthy to be loved), it's a beautiful staff with equal knots and bronze, Menalcas.

Like the cups which are now foaming with milk, this exchange of gifts reflects the merging of bucolic and cosmological poetry enacted in this eclogue. The hemlock reed (*cicuta*) which Menalcas presents to Damoetas at the mid-point of the *Eclogues* makes its only other appearance in this sense in Latin poetry (alongside *Eclogue* 2.36) in a passage from Book 5 of the *De Rerum Natura*, in which Lucretius illustrates the origins of this kind of rustic poetry (*DRN* 5.1382-3):[43]

et zephyri, caua per calamorum, sibila primum
agrestis docuere cauas inflare cicutas.

And the whistling of the zephyr through the hollows of reeds first taught rustics to blow into hollow hemlock.

Menalcas' gift to Mopsus of an instrument found outside the *Eclogues* only in the *De Rerum Natura* therefore identifies a history for bucolic poetry that has its place within discourses on the nature of things. Mopsus' return gift of a crook (*pedum*), meanwhile, which recalls the staff (λαγωβόλον) Lycidas gives to Simichidas in *Idyll* 7, replays the important interchange between Lucretius and Theocritus we have traced throughout this eclogue.[44] In this way, both these intertexts inscribe a principle of growth and development into Virgilian bucolic. The passage from Lucretius, for instance, is first and foremost a passage about the origins of this kind of poetry and therefore figures the development of this literary form as a mode of evolution. Lycidas' gift of a staff to the ambitious poet Simichidas in *Idyll* 7, on the other hand, a gesture which in turn recalls the laurel rod the Muses gave to Hesiod in the *Theogony* (30-1), is very much a marker of the poet's coming of age, a sign that he has successfully served his apprenticeship. It therefore characterises the development of the bucolic form in terms of inter-generational transmission and personal biography. Of the two poets in *Eclogue* 5, Mopsus is characterised as the junior partner and so Menalcas' gift of Lucretius' hemlock reed would seem to involve precisely this kind of investiture. Yet Mopsus endows Menalcas as well and this in turn acts as an acknowledgement of how he too has 'grown up' since his first appearance in *Eclogue* 3.[45]

A number of details that appear in the very first exchanges of *Eclogue* 5 signal Menalcas' growth as a poet in the time that has lapsed since *Eclogue* 3 (5.1-4):

> MENALCAS:
> Cur non, Mopse, boni quoniam conuenimus ambo,
> tu calamos inflare leuis, ego dicere uersus,
> hic corylis mixtas inter consedimus ulmos?
>
> MOPSUS:
> Tu maior; tibi me est aequum parere, Menalca.

> MENALCAS: Why not, Mopsus, since we two experts have both come together, you at blowing into light reeds, I at singing verses, why don't we sit down here among the elms mixed with hazels?
> MOPSUS: You are older; it is right that I obey you, Menalcas.

Menalcas' opening lines are reminiscent of the opening of *Idyll* 8, a poem which replays Menalcas' defeat by Daphnis in a song competition and which, as we have seen, is also alluded to in *Eclogue* 3.[46] Menalcas then recalls the song contest of *Eclogue* 3 itself through his suggestion to Mopsus that they sit down together, *consedimus*, before they sing, since this is also the verb Palaemon uses in *Eclogue* 3 when he enjoins the two herdsmen to begin their contest: 'Sing, now that we have sat down together on the soft grass' (*Dicite, quandoquidem in molli consedimus herba* 3.55). By these means, Menalcas creates a biography for himself that reaches back to *Idyll* 8 and includes *Eclogue* 3. When Mopsus begins his response to Menalcas with the words *tu maior*, then, it is unlikely that his words serve only to acknowledge that Menalcas is older than he is. Quite apart from anything else, the opening line of *Eclogue* 4 – the poem that intervenes between Menalcas' two appearances in the *Eclogues* so far – indicates how the comparative form of *magnus* has the capacity to denote the relative magnitude of bucolic song as well: 'Sicilian Muses, let us sing slightly greater things' (*Sicelides Musae, paulo maiora canamus* 4.1). An intertextual reading therefore suggests that Menalcas is not just older than Mopsus and older than he was before, but that he is 'greater' than the Menalcas of *Idyll* 8 and *Eclogue* 3 too, which is something he then proceeds to prove by lifting the figure of Daphnis (who is also the figure of his earlier defeat) all the way to the stars. The interchange between *Eclogues* 3 and 5, in other words, helps fashion the biography of a singer who has grown up into, rather than away from, bucolic song.

That bucolic poetry is able to sustain and not be destroyed by such moments of growth and ascent results from the fact that, in *Eclogues* 3 and 5 at least, two different constructions of time run simultaneously. On the one hand, there is linear time, in which Daphnis ascends to the stars, bucolic poetry rises to new heights and Menalcas grows up as a poet. This semblance of linearity, however, is here largely an effect of the temporality of performance: Daphnis rises to the stars and bucolic poetry rises to new heights in *Eclogue* 5 because the order of the composition of the two songs is reversed. Menalcas' development as a poet, meanwhile, is similarly due to the order of performance in the *Eclogue* book, in which *Eclogue* 3 is to be read before *Eclogue* 5. Above all, though, it is its unwavering commitment to a regular hexametric beat and its continual recourse to a set of recurring figures, words, rituals and motifs that sets the measure of bucolic time. This by no means places the form outside of time, but rather – through the vivid re-enactment of these rhythms in terms of ritual (such as the ritual of amoebaean competition in *Eclogue* 3) and liturgy (such as those of *Eclogues* 1 and 5 alike) – it enables it to instigate, continue and also to respond to and incorporate new events.

Questions of temporality will return in later chapters as well, but for now it is worth noting the degree to which, in *Eclogues* 3 and 5 at least, bucolic time strives to equate itself with cosmological time. In *Eclogue* 3, for instance, the relationship between the *Eclogues* and the *Idylls* is mediated in part through cosmological works such as Aratus' *Phaenomena* and Callimachus' (and Catullus') *Coma Berenices*. As such, literary history takes on the form of cosmological history. In *Eclogue* 5, moreover, the temporality of bucolic liturgy is likewise a response to the new cosmological environment that bucolic responsion (which is itself a manifestation of this temporality) has achieved.

All of this suggests that *Eclogues* 3 and 5 introduce and develop a distinctly bucolic conception of the relationship between poetry and the universe, grounded as it is in such recognisable principles as those of responsion and exchange. We shall return to this theme towards the end of the next chapter, where we shall look in more detail at the workings of this 'bucolic cosmology'. First, however, we should consider another feature of the *Eclogues'* engagement with the cosmological paradigm, which has so far remained largely unmentioned but which nonetheless deserves some attention: the idea that Virgilian bucolic discerns in the cosmos a kind of celestial map of the literary tradition. It is, after all, in relation to this map that the *Eclogues* set the co-ordinates for their own stellar ambitions.

2

Cosmology

Eclogues 3 and 5 both characterise bucolic poetry's attempts to elevate itself to the status of cosmological poetry as a form of catasterism. This characterisation is significant not only for its presence in those two poems in particular, but for what it represents in the *Eclogues* more generally: a belief in some kind of analogy between the literary universe on the one hand and the physical universe on the other. This chapter will therefore illustrate just how pervasive in, and determinative for, the *Eclogues* this analogy can be. It begins with *Eclogue* 9, a poem that illustrates how literary activity is often written in the stars and how the act of reading it might duly come to resemble an act of astronomy.

Eclogue 9: introducing astronomy

Eclogue 9 is another poem that indicates the nature of bucolic poetry by way of its relationship towards the stars. In it, two herdsmen, Lycidas and Moeris, meet on a road that leads to the city and discuss the recent land confiscations.[1] It emerges from their conversation that Menalcas, whom both evidently regard as one of their leading local poets, has been unable to save any of the surrounding area with his songs. The conclusion Moeris draws from this is that 'our songs have as much power among the weapons of Mars, Lycidas, as they say Chaonian doves do when the eagle comes' (*sed carmina tantum / nostra ualent, Lycida, tela inter Martia quantum / Chaonias dicunt aquila ueniente columbas* 11-13).

Perhaps unsurprisingly, *Eclogue* 9 is sometimes assumed to be an entirely negative poem, in which the power of bucolic poetry, so joyously celebrated in *Eclogue* 5, is shown to have very obvious limitations.[2] In particular, its journey towards the city, its fragmented snatches of verse, and Moeris' refusal to engage in a more formal exchange of songs with Lycidas all point to its status as a reversal of *Idyll* 7, a poem which by contrast records a journey from the town to the country, relates a successful and self-avowedly bucolic exchange of song between two herdsmen (Simichidas and another character called Lycidas) and ends with a description of nature's bounty. Yet *Eclogue* 9 also projects its relationship towards *Idyll* 7 upon the stars, and this form of celestial cartography promises to provide not only a slightly different way of construing this poem and its literary relations but of reading the *Eclogues* in general.

In the course of *Eclogue* 9, Lycidas and Moeris manage between them

31

to recall four fragments of song, some if not all of which are by Menalcas. Of these fragments, two are modelled closely on Theocritus (23-5 and 39-43),[3] while the other two concern themselves with contemporary Roman themes (27-9 and 46-50). Explicit references to the cosmos and cosmological poetry appear in the Roman songs alone. In the first of these, which Moeris reveals Menalcas had 'not yet perfected' (*necdum perfecta* 26), the land surveyor Publius Alfenus Varus is assured that swans will carry his name to the stars so long as he spares Mantua from the confiscations (9.27-9):

> Vare, tuum nomen, superet modo Mantua nobis,
> Mantua uae miserae nimium uicina Cremonae,
> cantantes sublime ferent ad sidera cycni.

> Varus, your name, if only Mantua remains to us – Mantua, alas!, too near to pitiable Cremona – singing swans will carry it aloft to the stars.

This promise is based upon the clear understanding that bucolic poetry has the capacity to ascend all the way to heaven, in the manner Menalcas had previously wagered in *Eclogue* 3 and subsequently enacted in *Eclogue* 5. His choice of swans as the preferred mode of transportation reflects, as Clausen suggests, their reputation as 'proverbially the most musical of birds',[4] but it is their Lucretian heritage in particular that shapes the trajectory of their flight here. For in the proem to Book 3 of the *De Rerum Natura*, Lucretius makes the claim that, were he to try to match and even outdo Epicurus in his journey through the cosmos, he would be like a swallow contending in song with a swan (*quid enim contendat hirundo / cycnis DRN* 3.6-7). In the next book, moreover, these birds come to be attributed with an aesthetics of concision as well (*DRN* 4.180-2 and 909-11):

> suauidicis potius quam multis uersibus edam;
> paruus ut est cycni melior canor, ille gruum quam
> clamor in aetheriis dispersus nubibus austri.

> I shall speak in pleasant rather than in many verses; how much better is the brief song of the swan than that clamour of cranes scattered among the lofty clouds by the south wind.

It is precisely this conjunction of brevity and elevation that promises to make swans fit emblems of the *Eclogues'* literary ambitions as well. In the case of the song to Varus in *Eclogue* 9, however, the envisaged flight of these swans towards the stars remains incomplete. As such, it seems to constitute one more example of how this kind of poetry can sometimes fall short and, to this degree, it recalls the hopeless mismatch between the doves of song and the eagle of war evoked just a few lines before (11-13).

And yet the ability of these swans to convey their songs to the stars is not necessarily negated by the breaking off of their journey here. Indeed, through the thrice-repeated '-ae' sounds in line 28 (*uae miserae ... Cremonae*), one might even be able to hear their cries as they begin to make their way there. Varus may not have kept his side of the bargain, but this does not in itself mean that bucolic poetry could not have kept its. Lycidas, for one, does not assume as much when, in response to these lines, he identifies a poetic career for himself that keeps the idea of an elevated trajectory for bucolic poetry very much alive (9.30-6):

> Sic tua Cyrneas fugiant examina taxos,
> sic cytiso pastae distendant ubera uaccae,
> incipe, si quid habes. et me fecere poetam
> Pierides, sunt et mihi carmina, me quoque dicunt
> uatem pastores; sed non ego credulus illis.
> nam neque adhuc Vario uideor nec dicere Cinna
> digna, sed argutos inter strepere anser olores.

May your swarms flee Cyrnean yews and your cows, fed on cytisus, swell their udders – begin, if you have anything. The Pierian Muses have made me a poet too; I too have songs, and the shepherds also call me a bard; but I do not believe them. For I do not yet seem to sing songs worthy of Varius or Cinna, but am like a goose screeching between melodious swans.

The particular stages of the bucolic career Virgil's Lycidas identifies here become all the clearer when they are compared with a similar passage in *Idyll* 7, in which Simichidas tries to persuade Theocritus' Lycidas to participate in an exchange of songs (*Id.* 7.36-41):

> βουκολιασδώμεσθα· τάχ᾽ ὥτερος ἄλλον ὀνασεῖ.
> καὶ γὰρ ἐγὼ Μοισᾶν καπυρὸν στόμα, κἠμὲ λέγοντι
> πάντες ἀοιδὸν ἄριστον· ἐγὼ δέ τις οὐ ταχυπειθής,
> οὐ Δᾶν· οὐ γάρ πω κατ᾽ ἐμὸν νόον οὔτε τὸν ἐσθλὸν
> Σικελίδαν νίκημι τὸν ἐκ Σάμω οὔτε Φιλίταν
> ἀείδων, βάτραχος δὲ ποτ᾽ ἀκρίδας ὥς τις ἐρίσδω.

Let us sing bucolic songs; and perhaps each will profit the other. For I too am a clear-voiced mouthpiece of the Muses, and everyone says that I am the best of bards; but I am not easily persuaded, no, by Zeus; for I do not think I would yet beat in song either the excellent Sicelidas, the one from Samos, or Philetas, but I would compete with them like a frog among grasshoppers.

Simichidas here makes it clear from the outset that the songs he wishes them to sing are specifically bucolic songs: βουκολιασδώμεσθα ('Let us sing bucolic songs'). *Eclogue* 9 more or less translates this verb into more concrete terms when Lycidas expresses the hope that Moeris' cows will eat well and swell their udders in return for the song he encourages Moeris now to sing (9.30-2). Both these passages therefore introduce themselves

33

as accounts of bucolic poetry and, as such, reflect through their own specific differences some of the more thoroughgoing divergences between Theocritus' and Virgil's respective renditions of the form. One of the most crucial of these involves their differing representations of the structures and hierarchies of a poetic career. For while Simichidas says he has been called 'the best of bards' (ἀοιδὸν ἄριστον), a designation which implies a single category of singers differentiated only by ability, Virgil's Lycidas draws a more pronounced distinction between a *uates* ('bard') on the one hand and a *poeta* ('poet') on the other. There has been some disagreement about the precise meaning of *uates* in Latin, although it would seem in general to signify a divinely inspired prophet conversant in the ways of the universe.[5] At any rate, it is clear that Lycidas' understanding of poetic hierarchies invests more in the notion of elevation, and in particular in the bucolic's relationship towards the cosmos, than Simichidas' account of a poetic career in *Idyll* 7. Simichidas, that is, is content to turn to the insect world in order to describe his own ranking relative to acknowledged poets such as Sicelidas and Philetas: next to them, he says, he is like a frog among grasshoppers. Virgil's Lycidas, by contrast, looks up to the sky for the analogy he requires and finds there a goose to convey the kind of song he can already produce and swans for those to which he aspires – the very birds, in other words, that in the fragment of song Moeris had recited just a few lines before, were to carry Varus' name all the way to the stars.[6]

After a further contribution by Moeris, in which he sings the second of the Theocritean vignettes, Lycidas runs through as much as he can remember of the other Roman fragment. Even more than the song to Varus, this piece connects bucolic poetry explicitly with the cosmos (9.43-52):

[MOERIS:
huc ades; insani feriant sine litora fluctus.]

LYCIDAS:
Quid, quae te pura solum sub nocte canentem
audieram? numeros memini, si uerba tenerem:
'Daphni, quid antiquos signorum suspicis ortus?
ecce Dionaei processit Caesaris astrum,
astrum quo segetes gauderent frugibus et quo
duceret apricis in collibus uua colorem.
insere, Daphni, piros: carpent tua poma nepotes'.

MOERIS:
Omnia fert aetas, animum quoque. saepe ego longos
cantando puerum memini me condere soles.

LYCIDAS: What about those things I heard you singing alone under a clear night? I remember the numbers, if only I could manage the words: 'Daphnis, why are you looking up at the ancient risings of the stars? Look! the star of Dionean Caesar has come into view, the star at which cornfields might

rejoice in crops and at which the grape might introduce colour to the sun-drenched hills. Sow pear trees, Daphnis; your descendants will pluck your fruit'.
MOERIS: Time takes everything away; I remember that I often as a boy used to hide long suns with my singing.

This short fragment of song offers yet another illustration of how Virgilian bucolic sets its ambitions and defines its place in the literary tradition in relation to the stars. Yet on this occasion the idea that astronomy might therefore constitute an appropriate reading strategy for the *Eclogues* is brought especially prominently to the fore. After all, the invitation to the exemplary figure of bucolic poetry to look away from the old constellations and towards the new represents on a cosmic scale an evident call to reorientate the form. Indeed, even in the fragment itself, this reorientation is subtly enacted and charted in relation to the stars and in particular to two constellations that are invoked in *Idyll* 7, but hidden in *Eclogue* 9: the Kids and Orion. In the idyll, at the beginning of his performance of a bucolic song, Lycidas expresses the hope that these two harbingers of wet and stormy weather will grant a safe passage to Ageanax, the subject of that song (*Id.* 7.52-6):[7]

ἔσσεται Ἀγεάνακτι καλὸς πλόος ἐς Μιτυλήναν,
χὤταν ἐφ᾽ ἑσπερίοις Ἐρίφοις νότος ὑγρὰ διώκῃ
κύματα, χὠρίων ὅτ᾽ ἐπ᾽ ὠκεανῷ πόδας ἴσχει,
αἴ κα τὸν Λυκίδαν ὀπτεύμενον ἐξ Ἀφροδίτας
ῥύσηται·

There will be a fine sailing for Ageanax to Mytilene, when the Kids appear in the evening and the south wind pursues the watery waves, and Orion sets foot on the ocean, if he will protect Lycidas from being scorched by Aphrodite.

In the Daphnis fragment in *Eclogue* 9, these two constellations are kept hidden away, but Moeris, who is quite possibly the author of this song,[8] signals afterwards that he can still spot them and even, perhaps, that he can still remember putting them there when he recalls how 'often as a boy I used to hide long suns with my singing' (*saepe ego longos / cantando puerum memini me condere soles* 51-2). This remark is usually understood to mean little more than that the younger Moeris had once spent whole days in song (and that he had read his Callimachus),[9] but the return from *Eclogue* 3 of the verb *condere* ('to hide') in such an overtly cosmological context, conjoined with the presence of actual constellations concealed in these lines, suggests that he really did hide stars in his songs as well. In any case, the clues necessary for finding and identifying these hidden constellations have by this point already been supplied. The more transparent of these comes in the fragment's very first line: 'Daphnis, why are you looking up at the ancient risings of the stars?' (*Daphni, quid antiquos*

signorum suspicis ortus?). As was also the case with the figures on Menal-
cas' cups in *Eclogue* 3 (the only other occasion in the *Eclogues* in which this
word appears), this question plays upon the two connotations of the term
signa, which can mean 'symbols' as well as 'stars'. For by following the
trajectory of Daphnis' gaze and by paying attention to the rising of symbols
through these lines, we might note that they spell out in the form of an
acrostic (starting with the first letter of 43 and continuing by way of
alternate lines) one of the ancient stars of *Idyll* 7: h-a-e-d-o ('the Kid'. I
have highlighted this acrostic in my transcription of this passage above
(p. 34) by putting the letters in bold).[10]

The clue to the discovery of the second of these two constellations, Orion,
meanwhile, lies in Lycidas' surprising observation that he had heard this
song being sung at night (44). This is not, of course, a surprising hour to
be gazing at the stars, but it is an unusual time at which to be singing
about it in bucolic song. Here, then, lies one explanation for why the
relationship between bucolic poetry and the cosmos, though pervasive, is
so often hidden: while the former tends to be performed largely by day, the
latter comes into view mostly at night. At any rate, at the time Lycidas
claims to have heard this particular song, the constellations contained
within it should have been especially visible, since the performance took
place 'under a clear night' (44). The clarity of vision promised by such
conditions, moreover, is reduplicated at an intertextual level too. For, as
Clausen remarks, the words Lycidas uses to describe this cloudless night,
pura ... sub nocte, bear comparison with a phrase Aratus deploys in his
Phaenomena: καθαρῇ ἐνὶ νυκτί. What Clausen does not say, however, is
that Aratus places this phrase in a passage about the other constellation
from Lycidas' song in *Idyll* 7: Orion (*Phaen.* 322-5):

Λοξὸς μὲν Ταύροιο τομῇ ὑποκέκλιται αὐτὸς
ΩΡΙΩΝ. μὴ κεῖνον ὅτις καθαρῇ ἐνὶ νυκτὶ
ὑψοῦ πεπτηῶτα παρέρχεται ἄλλα πεποίθοι
οὐρανὸν εἰσανιδὼν προφερέστερα θηήσασθαι.

> Aslant beneath the front-parts of Taurus lies Orion himself. Let no one who
> on a clear night passes him crouching on high believe, as he looks towards
> heaven, that he will see other stars more radiant.

This allusion therefore inscribes the second of *Idyll* 7's two constellations,
like the first, into the sky at which Daphnis is gazing in *Eclogue* 9. In so
doing, it identifies the 'clear night' under which Orion is both concealed (in
the eclogue) and revealed (in Aratus) as the venue for a comparison
between the respective cosmologies of the idyll and the eclogue. The
passage from Aratus even names the bar Orion has set for others to try to
overleap. 'Let no one', it proclaims, 'who on a clear night passes him
crouching on high believe, as he looks towards heaven, that he will see
other stars more radiant'. On the clear night recalled by Lycidas, however,

there was indeed a star more radiant – one so bright, in fact, that Orion is all but eclipsed by it in the cosmos and the text alike. This star, of course, is the Star of Julius Caesar, the comet that had appeared during the games held in his honour in July 44 BC.[11] Its arrival here presages the eclipse of the old bucolic by the new.

In this instance too, then, the *Eclogues* figure their intervention in a recurring bucolic tradition (represented here by the ancient and perennial stars that constitute the Kids and Orion) in terms of an historically specific catasterism. Unlike the Coma Berenices, however, which was the primary model for this process in *Eclogue* 3, or even the apotheosis of Daphnis recounted in *Eclogue* 5 (which, although not strictly speaking an historical event, nonetheless engages this same dynamic of instantiation and repetition), the star of Caesar is not on this occasion confirmed as a permanent feature of the new heaven. Instead, its influence is projected only in the subjunctive: it is 'the star at which cornfields *might rejoice* in crops and at which the grape *might introduce* colour to the sun-drenched hills' (*astrum quo segetes gauderent frugibus et quo / duceret apricis in collibus uua colorem* 47-9).[12] Indeed, the line that enjoins a response from the bucolic world to make the influence of this star continuous, 'Sow pear trees, Daphnis; your descendants will pluck your fruit' (*insere, Daphni, piros: carpent tua poma nepotes* 50), calls the very prospect of such a continuity into question. It does so, moreover, through a parallel act of response and repetition. For by evoking the similar, though more obviously ironic, injunction that Meliboeus issues to himself in *Eclogue* 1, 'sow pear trees, Meliboeus, place your vines in order' (*insere nunc, Meliboee, piros, pone ordine uitis* 1.73), it grafts onto this endeavour the prospect of failure.

This sense of failure is further enhanced by the fragmentary nature of this song, which neither Lycidas nor Moeris are able to continue, and this in turn highlights once again the apparent inability of *Eclogue* 9 to achieve so ready a correlation between instantiation and repetition as had been the case in *Eclogue* 5. Indeed, the numerous points of contact between these two eclogues ensure that the progress of the former is consistently charted in relation to the latter.[13] In particular, the depiction in both eclogues of the figure of Daphnis looking at the stars elevates this act of cartography to the celestial sphere. In this regard, it is not insignificant that the two stars hidden in the Daphnis fragment, the Kid and Orion, lead us directly to Lycidas' sending-away song (or propempticon) for Ageanax in *Idyll* 7, since *Eclogues* 9 and 5 could each be said to engage with the first and second halves of this song respectively. After all, this song, like the idyll as a whole, tells first of a journey and then of bucolic festivities. It requests that two of the signs traditionally associated with stormy weather, the Kids and Orion, grant a safe passage to the subject of its song, Ageanax, and then imagines the scenes of celebration that will attend its achievement. In this, it constitutes a microcosm for *Idyll* 7, which likewise depicts a journey that ends in scenes of festivity. *Eclogue* 5, as we have seen, draws upon both these successful conclusions for its scenes of feasting and singing in commemoration of Daphnis' deification. *Eclogue* 9, by contrast, represents only the journey and at no point does it enact its conclusion, either in the Daphnis fragment (where the effects of the star of Caesar exist only in the subjunctive) or in the closing lines of the poem as a whole. This is highlighted once again when Lycidas tries to characterise their current surroundings as an appropriate place to stop and sing (9.57-60):

> et nunc omne tibi stratum silet aequor, et omnes,
> aspice, uentosi ceciderunt murmuris aurae.
> hinc adeo media est nobis uia; namque sepulcrum
> incipit apparere Bianoris.

> And now the whole plain is settled and silent for you, and all – look! – the breezes of windy murmuring have receded. From here is the middle of our way; for the tomb of Bianor is beginning to appear.

This description recalls not only the tomb of Brasilas in *Idyll* 7, which had not yet appeared when Simichidas and his companions fall in with Lycidas and agree to an exchange of songs (*Id.* 7.10-11), but also the calm conditions for sailing envisaged for Ageanax in the first of these songs (*Id.* 7.57-60):[14]

> χἀλκυόνες στορεσεῦντι τὰ κύματα τάν τε θάλασσαν
> τόν τε νότον τόν τ᾽ εὖρον, ὃς ἔσχατα φυκία κινεῖ,
> ἀλκυόνες, γλαυκαῖς Νηρηίσι ταί τε μάλιστα
> ὀρνίχων ἐφίληθεν, ὅσοις τέ περ ἐξ ἁλὸς ἄγρα.

> Halcyons will smooth the waves and the sea and the south wind and the east, which moves the seaweed at the edges, halcyons, the most beloved of birds to the green-grey daughters of Nereus and to those for whom there is a hunting in the sea.

One might suggest that the fact that *Eclogue* 9 does not follow in the wake of this song and come to rest in scenes of bucolic celebration is here reflected by the contrasting topographies of the two passages. For whereas the Lycidas of the idyll tells of a voyage that progresses from the uncertainties of the sea to the safety and ease of dry land, the setting through which Moeris and Lycidas pass in the eclogue continues to combine qualities of sea and land alike. There is, after all, an evident maritime dimension to Lycidas' description of this 'settled plain' (*stratum ... aequor*), which is perhaps more accurately translated – especially by analogy with the passage from *Idyll* 7 – as a 'calmed sea', and yet Mantua, which seems to provide the setting for this song, lies very much inland.[15] Thus, unlike their counterparts in the idyll, the herdsmen of *Eclogue* 9 are not yet in a position to take their rest, but they continue to travel under the prospect of stormy weather even after the Daphnis fragment, with its evocation of the gloomy star signs of *Idyll* 7, has drawn to a close. Lycidas signals as much when he refers to the animals his companion is carrying and, in the very next sentence, mentions the rain the constellation whose name those animals share often portends (9.62-5):

> hic haedos depone, tamen ueniemus in urbem.
> aut si nox pluuiam ne colligat ante ueremur,
> cantantes licet usque (minus uia laedet) eamus;
> cantantes ut eamus, ego hoc te fasce leuabo.

> Here put down your kids, we shall come all the same to the city. Or, if we fear lest the night gathers rain before then, it is permitted for us to go singing all the way (the road will hurt less); so that we might go along singing, I shall lighten you of this bundle.

Lycidas' first gambit is to suggest to Moeris once again that they settle down and engage in a formal exchange of song of the kind enacted in *Eclogues* 3 and 5. Indeed, the verb he uses to enjoin Moeris to put down his kids, *deponere*, intimates the kind of exchange he has in mind: one in which Moeris is to 'place down' these animals – like the young cow and cups of *Eclogue* 3 – as a stake.[16] For as long as they continue to be held aloft, however, these animals retain the significance of the star sign to which they have given their name and duly threaten rain (the approach of night likewise looks back to the setting of the Daphnis fragment). If this is what Moeris fears, Lycidas continues, they should carry on walking as they sing. This is, after all, the option they would appear to have been following all along[17] and Lycidas goes on to indicate just how adequate a response this mode of singing can be to cosmological conditions such as these. For by repeating the word *cantantes*, each time at the beginning of a line (64-5), as he lays out the prospect of them singing as they go, Lycidas likens himself and Moeris to the singing swans, the *cantantes ... cycni*, that were also to be in motion as they sang the name of Varus to the stars.

Given that *Eclogue* 9 does not in the end settle down to a formal exchange of song of the kind Lycidas repeatedly requests, it is not difficult to see how some commentators have argued that this poem rehearses the defeat and decline of bucolic verse. At no point, in other words, does it adopt the poetic conventions of poems such as *Eclogues* 3 and 5 or of the end of Lycidas' song for Ageanax in *Idyll* 7 or even of *Idyll* 7 itself. It is surely better, however, to see this poem as an exploration of a different kind of bucolic poem, grounded in a poetics of the road, instead: an illustration of bucolic poetry in motion.[18] The subtle analogy Lycidas draws towards the end between the singing herdsmen and the singing swans suggests for a start that the destination of this journey lies not only the city, but also in the stars. After all, the exchanges of *Eclogue* 9 are not entirely without success: there is a genuine responsion between the two herdsmen throughout the poem – in which, for instance, each of them recounts one Theocritean fragment and one Roman song in turn[19] – and it is as a result of this responsion that in this eclogue too bucolic poetry both charts its progress by and sets its course for the stars.

The rising of the constellation of the Kid in particular provides a clear illustration of how the astronomical reading strategy enacted in the Daphnis fragment promotes a way of reading *Eclogue* 9 as a whole. The question that contains the clue to the discovery of this constellation – 'Daphnis, why are you looking up at the ancient risings of the stars?' (*Daphni, quid antiquos signorum suspicis ortus?* 46) – lies within the song itself and yet the symbols Daphnis is there said to be looking at not only extend beyond the actual boundaries of that song, but also encompass lines spoken by both herdsmen alike. In this way, the fragment comes to be a part of, rather than apart from, its immediate environment. Indeed, like the cups of *Eclogue* 3, this evidently cosmological composition would seem to aspire to a greater representative status within the book of *Eclogues* as a whole. Lines 48-9, for instance, which describe the potential effect of the star of Caesar upon the countryside, look back to the discoveries of the connection between the cosmos and the countryside described by the second astronomer on the cups of *Eclogue* 3 (3.42). Likewise, the injunction to Daphnis to sow his pears recalls Meliboeus' injunction to himself to do the same in *Eclogue* 1 (1.73), while the very image of the figure of Daphnis looking at the stars recalls his ascent to the cosmos in *Eclogue* 5.

When, therefore, at the close of the eclogue Moeris declines to participate any further in either of the forms of exchange Lycidas proposes, it is notable that his words are rather more equivocal than they might at first appear (9.66-7):

> Desine plura, puer, et quod nunc instat agamus;
> carmina tum melius, cum uenerit ipse, canemus.

> Cease from more things, boy, and let us do what now stands upon us; then we shall sing our songs better, when he himself comes.

The phrase 'cease from more things, boy' (*desine plura, puer*) is also used by Menalcas in *Eclogue* 5, when he tries to encourage Mopsus to bring their preliminaries to a close and start a proper exchange of song ('but you, cease from more things, boy: we have reached the cave' *sed tu desine plura, puer: successimus antro* 5.19). Its reappearance here, then, holds out the promise of more singing to come even as it brings the conversation between these two herdsmen, along with *Eclogue* 9 itself, to a close. Indeed, looking back from this vantage point, it is remarkable how much of *Eclogue* 9 is provisional and awaits realisation: Menalcas had 'not yet' (*necdum* 26) perfected his song for Varus; Lycidas admits he is still 'not yet' (*neque adhuc* 35) as good as Varius or Cinna; the recitations of these songs are, of course, incomplete; and, by the time the eclogue is already drawing to a close, the two herdsmen are only at the midway point of their journey (*media est nobis uia* 59), where the tomb of Bianor 'is beginning to appear' (*incipit apparere* 60). To this extent, then, while the journey Moeris and Lycidas discuss and enact in the course of *Eclogue* 9 does indeed record examples of absence and loss, its configuration *as* a journey is precisely what makes it, quite literally, a work *in progress*. And this, of course, is what provides it with its trajectory towards the future as well as with its retrospective glances towards the past. In the words with which the eclogue draws to a close: 'Then we shall sing our songs better, when he himself comes' (*carmina tum melius, cum uenerit ipse, canemus* 67).

A further figure for this within the poem is Menalcas himself. An apprentice in *Eclogue* 3, who aspires to sing a cosmological song, and a master poet in *Eclogue* 5, who there achieves that goal, in *Eclogue* 9 he comes to represent for both Lycidas and Moeris the achievements (and failures) of the past and the promise of the future alike. When, for instance, Moeris assures Lycidas that 'Menalcas will nonetheless sing those things to you often enough' (*sed tamen ista satis referet tibi saepe Menalcas* 55), his repetition of the word *saepe* in the same metrical position it had occupied a few lines above intimates that 'those things' Menalcas will *often* sing might well be the 'long suns' Moeris himself *often* used to hide in his singing (51). One is tempted to say that, like the stars, singers such as Menalcas ascend, decline and ascend again.[20] In any case, as a representation of the workings of the literary tradition within the *Eclogues* as a whole, this cosmological model neatly captures its recurrent temporality.

Whether or not *Eclogue* 9 traces a promising future or an irrecoverable past for bucolic poetry, what should have become clear from the above is that in either case it persists in defining itself in relation to the stars. Through the figure of Daphnis, moreover, this poem posits astronomy as a particularly productive way of reading this kind of bucolic poetry. The next section will therefore illustrate more broadly how the astronomy of the *Eclogues* is a helpful guide to their literary and generic identity.

Astronomy

As we saw in the previous section, the Daphnis fragment in *Eclogue* 9 introduces astronomy as a potentially revealing way of reading this kind of poetry. To a certain degree, this approach was already signalled, if somewhat less explicitly, by the two astronomers situated in the middle of Menalcas' cups in *Eclogue* 3. For just as the Daphnis fragment relies upon an equivocation between the two connotations of the word *signa* in order to align the rising of symbols (in this case, letters) with the rising of a star, so too do these astronomers conjoin literature and cosmology through their own designation under this same term ('in the middle are two symbols /

stars' *in medio duo signa* 3.40). Their very presence, that is, invites a reading of the cups, and by extension of the eclogue, that is analogous to their own readings of the celestial spheres. Conon at least had fulfilled this role before. For the very first line of the *Coma Berenices*, πάντα τὸν ἐν γραμμαῖσιν ἰδὼν ὅρον, structures his gaze in such a way that it is unclear whether he here surveys 'the whole of the charted sky' or 'the whole of the sky in charts'.

So what kind of picture of the *Eclogues* do we get if we figure our reading of them as a form of astronomy? In order to answer this question, one needs first to observe the extent to which the night sky in the *Eclogues* relates to and resembles the account of the heavens provided by Aratus in his *Phaenomena*. This relationship is important not least because it enables the *Phaenomena* to act as a kind of guidebook to Virgil's bucolic cosmos and a way of charting its literary and astronomical co-ordinates alike. One can see this, for instance, in the *Eclogues'* single reference to the moon. In the *Phaenomena*, this heavenly body comes to act almost as a literary signature for Aratus and as a sign of his poem's aesthetic identity. For his description of its various phases includes an acrostic that spells out λεπτή, a word which, through its meanings 'slender' and 'refined', acted as a buzzword for the concise, erudite form of poetry produced by the likes of Callimachus and his circle.[21] When Virgil subsequently came to rework this passage in Book 1 of the *Georgics* (lines 427-37), he showed that he too was aware of this acrostic by including one of his own;[22] but while his use of this device highlights his equal commitment to a refined and slender aesthetic, the acrostic itself spells out a part of his own name, P̲ublius V̲ergilius M̲aro. In so doing, it supplements Aratus' use of the moon as a symbol of his poetic allegiances with a claim to ownership of that aesthetic as well. What is less widely recognised is that Virgil had already begun to co-opt Aratus' moon, and to much the same effect, in the *Eclogues*. We have already seen how Lycidas' reference to a 'pure sky' (*pura ... nocte*) in *Eclogue* 9 trumps and eclipses Aratus' description of Orion with the Star of Caesar even as it evokes that description[23] and one might suggest that something similar is in process when Alphesiboeus asserts in *Eclogue* 8 that 'songs can draw down the moon from the sky' (*carmina uel caelo possunt deducere lunam* 8.69).[24] For the verb *deducere* ('to draw down') is used elsewhere in the *Eclogues* to connote the production of a fine-spun song and, as such, it here configures the moon as an emblem of the same kind of slender and refined aesthetic Aratus' acrostic had already ascribed to it in the *Phaenomena*. At the same time, *deducere* can also connote an act of colonisation through military means.[25] Thus, through its drawing down of the moon, an object that is not simply described in the *Phaenomena*, but that comes to act as an emblem of that poem's literary affiliations as well, this line intimates the *Eclogues'* approach to Aratus' literary and cosmological universe alike. That is to say, it illustrates both how the *Eclogues* share a number of the properties and procedures of

Aratus' cosmos and how they nonetheless continue to reorder and reshape it, with a view, not least, to making it their own.

Other examples of how the *Eclogues* invoke Aratus' configuration of the cosmos as a way of charting and identifying their own literary allegiances, aspirations and co-ordinates are provided by the three stars that are named explicitly in these poems: Cancer, Virgo and Vesper.[26] Cancer in particular offers a concise illustration of how individual stars act more or less as literary signposts, which signal the place any given song might occupy in relation to other stellar works from the literary tradition. For when Gallus acknowledges his inability to escape from or assuage the god of Love in *Eclogue* 10 (64-9) –

> non illum nostri possunt mutare labores,
> nec si frigoribus mediis Hebrumque bibamus
> Sithoniasque niues hiemis subeamus aquosae,
> nec si, cum moriens alta liber aret in ulmo,
> Aethiopum uersemus ouis sub sidere Cancri.
> omnia uincit Amor: et nos cedamus Amori.

Our labours are not able to change him, not if we were to drink the Hebrus in the middle frosts of watery winter and endure Sithonian snows, nor if, when the dying bark dries on the high elm, we were to drive to and fro the sheep of the Ethiopians under the star of Cancer. Love conquers everything: we too should yield to Love.

– his mention of Cancer points back to, yet also redirects, an analogous passage in *Idyll* 7, in which, in the second of the two songs there exchanged, Lycidas expresses the hope that Pan will be dispatched to the ends of the earth if he does not bring Aratus (who in this case is probably not the author of the *Phaenomena*)[27] together with his beloved (*Id.* 7.111-14):

> εἴης δ' Ἠδωνῶν μὲν ἐν ὤρεσι χείματι μέσσῳ
> Ἕβρον πὰρ ποταμὸν τετραμμένος ἐγγύθεν Ἄρκτῳ,
> ἐν δὲ θέρει πυμάτοισι παρ' Αἰθιόπεσσι νομεύοις
> πέτρᾳ ὕπο Βλεμύων, ὅθεν οὐκέτι Νεῖλος ὁρατός.

May you be in the mountains of the Edonoi in the middle of winter as you make your way to the river Hebrus, near the Bear, but in summer may you pasture alongside the distant Ethiopians under the rock of the Blemyes, where the Nile is no longer visible.

It is fitting that Gallus should refer to Simichidas' song in *Idyll* 7, since this song anticipates two of the themes of *Eclogue* 10: it begins with the hope that its subject will be reunited with his beloved (as Virgil hopes Gallus will be reunited with Lycoris) and it ends with the suggestion that he might consider abandoning the ways of love and living a life of tranquillity instead (as Gallus imagines transferring himself and his poetry to

Arcadia). The star of Cancer in particular points up this allusion because it participates in the practice of using constellations as literary signposts which Simichidas had also deployed in his song in *Idyll* 7. For when Simichidas places Arctos, the Bear, in the sky in these lines, he is utilising the belief that this constellation points, quite literally, to Orion in order to indicate how his own song points to Lycidas' song (which had mentioned Orion) earlier in the idyll.[28] Gallus' verses in turn position themselves in relation to Simichidas' in much the same way that the Crab positions itself in relation to the Bear. For Aratus for one specifically locates the Crab through reference to the Bear: 'Beneath the head of Helice [the Great Bear] are the Twins; beneath her waist is the Crab' (Κρατὶ δέ οἱ ΔΙΔΥΜΟΙ, μέσσῃ δ᾽ ὕπο ΚΑΡΚΙΝΟΣ ἐστίν *Phaen.* 147). The similarity between Gallus' and Simichidas' lines is therefore reflected in the physical proximity of these two stars in the night sky. At the same time, the Crab and the Bear symbolise very different things and, as such, they point towards the different connotations of these two, otherwise very similar, passages. The switch from a star that presides over winter to one that emblematises summer, in other words, signals the extent to which Gallus has reversed the terms of Simichidas' song and has given up all hope of achieving the tranquillity that both he here and Simichidas by the end of his song had previously professed.

Cancer, then, is a fitting star to shine in the bucolic heavens, since it demonstrates its ability to participate in such bucolic modalities as responsion and inversion. Virgo, which rises in *Eclogue* 4 and there marks the return of a golden age ('now the maiden [Virgo] returns, and the reign of Saturn returns' *iam redit et Virgo, redeunt Saturnia regna* 4.6), serves a similar function, since, even more than Cancer in *Eclogue* 10, it locates the poem within which it appears upon the historical, literary and cosmological map alike. As far as the historical context is concerned, it is generally agreed that *Eclogue* 4 refers to the Pact of Brundisium in 40 BC at which, in a spirit of reconciliation, it was decided that Antony would marry Octavian's sister as a statement of their newfound accord.[29] Given that Virgo usually becomes visible between September and November, it is likely to have been the zodiacal sign that presided over the negotiations which led up to the signing of this treaty in the September or October of that year.[30] But even if this historical event does not provide the impetus for this poem, Virgo constitutes a fitting star to mark the gradual return of the golden age which *Eclogue* 4 then proceeds to describe. For her return reverses Aratus' story of the departure of Justice (Δίκη) from the earth during the Bronze Age, when she had left in disgust at humankind's behaviour and had taken her place in the heavens as Virgo, 'The Maiden' (Παρθένος), instead.[31] What is more, the presence of Virgo also helps establish *Eclogue* 4 as one of the destinations for the cosmological aspirations of *Eclogue* 3. But in order to see this more clearly, we shall have to turn first to the star that recurs most often in the *Eclogues*: Vesper.

44

2. Cosmology

In its role as the evening star, Vesper (or Hesperus) brings *Eclogue* 6, *Eclogue* 10 and, with this last, the book as a whole to a close. It also, however, doubles up as the morning star and it is in this form that the herdsman Damon calls upon it at the beginning of his song in *Eclogue* 8: 'Be born, Light-Bringer, and, coming in advance, lead in the nurturing day' (*Nascere praeque diem ueniens age, Lucifer, almum* 8.17). The notion of recursion inherent in this star is therefore one of the attributes that makes it such an appropriate witness for the opening and closing of songs which themselves look consistently from their beginnings to their ends and from their ends to their beginnings. The line with which *Eclogue* 10 concludes, for instance – 'go home, replete she-goats, go, Hesperus comes' (*ite domum saturae, uenit Hesperus, ite capellae* 10.77) – leads straight back to Meliboeus' address to his flock in *Eclogue* 1, a line which is itself an intimation of an end: 'go, my she-goats, go, my once happy flock' (*ite meae, felix quondam pecus, ite capellae* 1.74). The image of Vesper emerging from Olympus in the final line of *Eclogue* 6, moreover, engages in an even more intricate cosmological mapping of beginnings and ends than this. For the song of Silenus which Vesper's rising draws to a close itself begins with the first shining of the sun ('and now the lands are astounded by the new sun shining' *iamque nouum terrae stupeant lucescere solem* 6.37) and, even as it is brought to an end by the rising of a star, it sets its final destination among the heavens: '[all these things] he sings and the struck valleys refer them to the stars' (*ille canit, pulsae referunt ad sidera ualles* 6.84).

The appearance of this star in both its Greek (Hesperus) and Roman forms (Vesper, Lucifer)[32] is another attribute that makes it such a suitable usher for the songs of the *Eclogues*, since these too consistently marry elements from the two cultures. Marriage is not an inopportune metaphor here, because this star is also none other than the planet Venus, an identification Virgil gestures towards by associating it twice with the verb *uenire*, from which Cicero at least proposed the name Venus was derived: *Venus, quia uenit ad omnia* ('Venus, because she comes to everything' *DND* 3.24.62).[33] One of the other verbs Vesper attracts in the *Eclogues*, moreover, *procedere* ('to come into view') – *et inuito processit Vesper Olympo* ('and Vesper *came into view* from unwilling Olympus' 6.86) – is also used of the star of Caesar in the Daphnis fragment of *Eclogue* 9: *ecce Dionaei processit Caesaris astrum* ('Look! the star of Dionean Caesar has come into view' 9.47). Together with the epithet 'Dionean', which refers to Dione, the mother of Aphrodite,[34] this verb duly points in addition towards the supposed connection between Venus and the line of Julius Caesar.

Above all, though, Venus is the goddess of love and therefore of love poetry and it has been noted that the two eclogues which the rising of her star brings to a close, *Eclogues* 6 and 10, both involve the elegiac poet Gallus.[35] Her appearance as the evening star in particular in both these instances, moreover, signals that the relevant mode of love poetry invoked at these moments is that of the wedding song, or epithalamium. The final two words of *Eclogue* 6, for instance, which depict Vesper leaving Olympus at the end of the day – *Vesper Olympo* – come from the very first line of one of Catullus' wedding songs, poem 62 (Cat. 62.1-4):

> Vesper adest, iuuenes, consurgite: Vesper Olympo
> exspectata diu uix tandem lumina tollit.
> surgere iam tempus, iam pinguis linquere mensas,
> iam ueniet uirgo, iam dicetur hymenaeus.

> Vesper is present, young men, get up! Vesper has now at long last raised her long awaited lights from Olympus. Now is the time to rise, now is the time to leave the rich tables; now the maiden will come, now the wedding song will be sung.

Catullus' poem takes the form of an amoebaean exchange, a kind of song contest between the male and female wedding guests to determine whether the newly-wed wife should enter the bridal chamber. To this extent, it shares an obvious structural affinity with several of Virgil's eclogues. But the rising of Vesper, which, as the figure of allusion here, brings this affinity to light, also marks the moment when these two forms of poetry diverge and move apart. In both cases, that is, the arrival of the evening star brings the feasting to a close[36] and causes both sets of singers to rise,[37] but in so doing it thereby aligns the time the wedding song begins with the time Virgil's bucolic poetry frequently ends.[38]

This, in many respects antithetical, relationship between these two literary forms is also in evidence in *Eclogue* 8, in which one of the herdsmen, Damon, mentions both the morning and the evening star in the course of what proves to be a failed wedding song (we shall return to this song in the next section). In the interchange between *Eclogues* 3 and 4, by contrast, it is precisely by way of such references to Catullus' wedding songs that these two poems identify their cosmological aspirations and mark their progress towards achieving them.

As we have seen, *Eclogue* 4 may well have been written in response to an actual marriage that took place around this time, but its status as a marriage song is in any case reinforced by the numerous gestures it makes towards Catullus 64, a poem which tells of the marriage of Peleus and Thetis and which anticipates the birth of their own miraculous child, Achilles.[39] Strictly speaking, this poem celebrates the child it hopes will be born as a result of this marriage rather than the wedding itself, but one might suggest that the nuptials leading up to this event have already been hinted at in *Eclogue* 3.[40] The final line of that poem, for instance, – 'close now the streams, boys; the meadows have drunk enough' (*claudite iam riuos, pueri; sat prata biberunt* 3.111) – comes to a halt, as it were, right at the bridal chamber door, since it recalls the line that brings another of Catullus' epithalamia, poem 61, towards its close at precisely this point: 'close the doors, maidens: we have played enough' (*claudite ostia, uirgines:*

/ *lusimus satis* Cat. 61.224-5).[41] That Catullus 61 is here being used to recast *Eclogue* 3 as a prelude to *Eclogue* 4 is also suggested by a further allusion to this poem towards the end of the second of these two eclogues. For when Virgil encourages the child in *Eclogue* 4 to recognise his mother with a smile (4.60-2), he recalls Catullus' hope that the child he anticipates will issue from this marriage will likewise smile at his father (*dulce rideat ad patrem* Cat. 61.212).

Above all, though, the carrying over of the wedding theme from *Eclogue* 3 into *Eclogue* 4 adheres primarily to the itinerary established by the lock of Berenice, which was itself an emblem of the strength of her marriage with Ptolemy.[42] The beginning of the lock's catasterism, for instance – the moment it is cut from Berenice's head – is, as we have seen, alluded to in *Eclogue* 3, while its final resting place, near Virgo, is similarly gestured towards in *Eclogue* 4. Indeed, the *Coma Berenices* acts as a kind of literary 'road map' for the journey these two eclogues make between these two points as well, since its stopping-off places prefigure sites from the literary tradition which *Eclogues* 3 and 4 also take in along the way.

In the *Coma Berenices*, the lock is first taken by winged horse to the temple of Arsinoe II in Zephyrium, where it is placed in the lap of Venus (Cat. 66.51-8). Arsinoe II was the sister and second wife of Ptolemy II Philadelphus and had been deified as Arsinoe-Aphrodite. By bringing the lock here, therefore, Callimachus elevates the royal marriage between Berenice and Ptolemy III to the same status as that enjoyed by their predecessors. When Virgil re-enacts the lock's catasterism in *Eclogues* 3 and 4, he repeats this equation between these two Ptolemaic generations on an intertextual level. Instead of referring to Ptolemy Philadelphus and Arsinoe themselves, that is, both these eclogues refer to a poem that praises Ptolemy Philadelphus and, towards its close, his marriage with Arsinoe as well: Theocritus' *Idyll* 17. Like the *Coma Berenices*, moreover, whose beginnings are recalled in *Eclogue* 3 but whose final destination lies in *Eclogue* 4, the first line of *Idyll* 17 is reworked in *Eclogue* 3,[43] while the poem as a whole comes to form one of the most important intertexts for *Eclogue* 4.[44] Indeed, the final lines of this eclogue, which anticipate the child's future marriage with a goddess and thereby constitute a mini-epithalamium in their own right – 'he who has not begun to smile at his parent, neither will a god deem him worthy of his table nor a goddess of her bed' (*qui non risere parenti, / nec deus hunc mensa, dea nec dignata cubili est* 4.62-3) – recall Theocritus' comparison of Ptolemy II's marriage to his sister with those of the heavenly gods.[45]

Once the lock has been received in Zephyrium, Venus elevates it to the heavens so that it can achieve parity with the garland of Ariadne (Cat. 66.59-62). *Eclogue* 4 in turn replicates this act by conjoining references to the *Coma Berenices* with references to a poem which relates the story of Ariadne: Catullus 64. The goddess' intentions for this lock, moreover, that it should be 'a new star among the ancient constellations' (*sidus in antiquis*

diua nouum posuit Cat. 66.64), likewise reflect the *Eclogues'* own cosmo-
logical ambitions – as illustrated, for instance, by the attempted staking
of the cups in *Eclogue* 3, by the celebration of the new god Daphnis in
Eclogue 5 and by the fragment of song to Daphnis in *Eclogue* 9.

The lock's final resting-place is close to Virgo (Cat. 66.65), the very star
that presides over *Eclogue* 4 and its various concordances: of Antony and
Octavia, of lions and flocks (4.22), of the cosmos and human history
(4.46-52), of these events and the singer's future songs (4.53-9) and of this
miraculous child with the feasts of the gods and the bed of a goddess
(4.60-3). In this way, *Eclogue* 4 comes to envisage the culmination both of
a cosmological ascent and of epithalamic verse, and to this extent it
participates in a literary tradition that has celebrated, among others, the
'celestial' marriages of Ariadne and Dionysus (Catullus 64), Ptolemy
Philadelphus and Arsinoe (*Idyll* 17) and Ptolemy III and Berenice II
(Callimachus' *Coma Berenices* and Catullus 66). Even if *Eclogue* 4 was not
composed in order to celebrate an actual marriage, the form of the epitha-
lamium is nonetheless obviously of some importance to Virgilian bucolic's
conception of itself, not least as a way of configuring its attempts to
compose cosmological verse. It has long been observed that bucolic poetry
reworks and defines itself in relation to several of the motifs and stock
situations of elegiac poetry more generally (including, for instance, the
conceit of the locked-out lover or paraclausithyron),[46] but less often has its
relationship towards wedding songs been systematically explored. This,
however, is a feature of the *Eclogues* that can hardly be ignored if one
figures one's reading of these poems as a form of astronomy.

In several respects, the practice of reading the *Eclogues* for their stars
reaffirms a number of their primary modalities. All of them engage, for
instance, in a degree of responsion: Vesper towards Catullus' wedding
songs; Cancer towards the Bear and therefore *Idyll* 7; and Virgo towards
both the *Coma Berenices* and, perhaps, the contemporary political situ-
ation. Likewise Vesper, as both the morning and the evening star, presides
over the recurrent bucolic process of recursion. The practice of inversion,
moreover, characterises all three of these stars and, in the case of Vesper
at least, helps structure the relationship between these poems and epitha-
lamia. Cancer, for instance, as a midsummer star, inverts the Bear, the
star that shines over the frozen landscape in an otherwise analogous
passage in *Idyll* 7. Virgo too, through the very act of returning reverses her
abandonment of the earth in Aratus and Hesiod. Vesper, meanwhile,
marks the time when bucolic poetry ends but wedding songs begin. Indeed,
this technique of inversion is a consistent feature of the *Eclogues'* engage-
ment with Catullus' epithalamia: they change, for instance, Catullus' girls
('close the doors, maidens' *claudite ostia, uirgines* Cat. 61.224) into boys
('close now the streams, boys' *claudite iam riuos, pueri Ecl.* 3.111) and his
father figure ('may he smile sweetly at his father' *dulce rideat ad patrem*

Cat. 61.212) into a mother ('begin, small child, to recognise your mother with a smile' *incipe, parue puer, risu cognoscere matrem Ecl.* 4.60).

This, often contrastive, relationship between bucolic poetry and wedding songs would seem to be a reasonably appropriate one for the two poems that are brought to a close by the rising of the evening star: *Eclogue* 10, which describes Gallus abandoned by his beloved, Lycoris, and *Eclogue* 6, which lists a number of failed or illicit love affairs. When it comes to the interchange between *Eclogues* 3 and 4, however, it is clear that the form of the epithalamium serves to prefigure the achievement of cosmological verse. Modelled as it is on the ascent of the lock of Berenice to the heavens, with all the epithalamic connotations that particular catasterism bears, the aspiration of Virgilian bucolic to achieve this status reaches its culmination in a vision of the future presented towards the end of *Eclogue* 4. Here, the birth and development of the child meet with cosmological assent and promise to usher in a period of even greater poetic achievement (*Ecl.* 4.46-59):

> 'Talia saecla' suis dixerunt 'currite' fusis
> concordes stabili fatorum numine Parcae.
> adgredere o magnos (aderit iam tempus) honores,
> cara deum suboles, magnum Iouis incrementum!
> aspice conuexo nutantem pondere mundum,   50
> terrasque tractusque maris caelumque profundum;
> aspice, uenturo laetentur ut omnia saeclo!
> o mihi tum longae maneat pars ultima uitae,
> spiritus et quantum sat erit tua dicere facta!
> non me carminibus uincet nec Thracius Orpheus   55
> nec Linus, huic mater quamuis atque huic pater adsit,
> Orphei Calliopea, Lino formosus Apollo.
> Pan etiam, Arcadia mecum si iudice certet,
> Pan etiam Arcadia dicat se iudice uictum.

'Hasten such generations' the Parcae said to their spindles, concordant with the stable power of the fates. O set out upon those great honours (the time will soon be present), dear offspring of the gods, great increase of Jove! Look! the firmament is nodding with its convex weight, the lands and the tracts of the sea and the deep heaven! Look! how all things rejoice in the coming generation! Neither will Thracian Orpheus conquer me with songs nor will Linus, even if the one has his mother beside him and the other his father, Calliope with Orpheus and beautiful Apollo with Linus. Even Pan, if he were to compete with me with Arcadia as judge, even Pan, with Arcadia as judge, will say that he has been conquered.

The aspiration to produce songs that are, in bucolic terms at least, even better than those of the archetypal cosmological poet Orpheus is evidently here reserved for the future. But it nonetheless engages with a question that is at issue throughout these poems: of how poetry such as this is both influenced by and might in turn be able to influence the workings of the cosmos. This is the question we shall address for the remainder of this chapter.

Eclogue 8: cosmology and poetry

The relationship between poetry and cosmology we have traced so far has largely been one of analogy, but their interaction is in practice much more involved than this. In these poems, songs occasionally aspire to shape the cosmos even as the cosmos sometimes appears to shape those songs.

There is at the very least a correspondence between the movements of the heavenly bodies and the singing of bucolic verse. The setting sun which doubles the growing shadows in *Eclogue* 2, for instance, parallels the way Corydon there reduplicates the role of Theocritus' Polyphemus.[47] Likewise, the ending of the day accords with the ending of song in *Eclogues* 1, 2, 6 and 10. At times, however, the cosmos would seem to be the dominant force in this relationship, setting the conditions for bucolic poetry, determining its topics and prescribing its stylistic rules. The casting of shadows that results from the movement of the sun is but one example of how the cosmos can determine both the when and the where of that song. As for its 'what', the most obvious example of the cosmos supplying a topic for bucolic comes in *Eclogue* 4, where the central figure of the piece, the miraculous child, is quite literally sent down from the sky (*iam noua progenies caelo demittitur alto* 4.7). This event influences the literary style of this poem as well, since such an occurrence requires an elevated mode of composition in response, as the very first line openly acknowledges: 'Sicilian Muses, let us sing slightly greater things' (*Sicelides Musae, paulo maiora canamus* 4.1).

By contrast with this, there are also moments when bucolic poetry in turn attempts to assert its authority over the cosmos. The song of Silenus in *Eclogue* 6, for instance, more or less sings the universe into existence, while, as we have seen, Alphesiboeus' song in *Eclogue* 8 boasts of the capacity of song to reshape the literary and cosmological universe alike by drawing down the moon from the sky (*carmina uel caelo possunt deducere lunam* 8.69). Above all, though, it is through their competitive relationship with Orpheus, the archetypal cosmological poet, that the *Eclogues* chart their ability to hold sway over the universe. Orpheus first appears as the figure in the middle of Damoetas' set of cups in *Eclogue* 3 and, as such, emblematises the prospect of composing cosmological verse (3.46), a prospect that Damoetas would seem to mock and dismiss on this occasion. In *Eclogue* 4, on the other hand, Virgil similarly defers to the future his hopes of celebrating in verse events that are sanctioned by the whole of the cosmos, but he nonetheless still entertains the hope that, when that time comes, he might be able to defeat even Orpheus in song (4.46-59). *Eclogue* 6 then completes this trajectory from aspiration to achievement by re-hearsing a song that pleases the natural world even more than Orpheus is able to delight Rhodope or Ismarus (*nec tantum Rhodope miratur et*

50

Ismarus Orphea 6.30). Damon's song in *Eclogue* 8, by contrast, once again undermines this growing sense of confidence by bringing into question the idea that a poet such as Tityrus might be able to match Orpheus in his ability to influence the natural world: 'and may owls compete with swans, may Tityrus be Orpheus, Orpheus in the woods, Arion among the dolphins' (*certent et cycnis ululae, sit Tityrus Orpheus, / Orpheus in siluis, inter delphinas Arion* 8.55-6).[48]

Eclogue 8 is an appropriate poem to mention in this regard, since it offers two contrasting visions of the capacity of bucolic poetry to influence the natural world, both of which illustrate this capacity in relation to the cosmos. It begins with a representation of the effect that the song contest between Damon and Alphesiboeus has upon their surroundings (8.1-5):

> Pastorum musam Damonis et Alphesiboei,
> immemor herbarum quos est mirata iuuenca
> certantis, quorum stupefactae carmine lynces,
> et mutata suos requierunt flumina cursus,
> Damonis musam dicemus et Alphesiboei.

> The muse of the shepherds Damon and Alphesiboeus, at whom, competing, the heifer, forgetful of the grass, marvelled, by whose song lynxes were stupefied, and streams, changed, rested their courses, we shall tell of the muse of Damon and Alphesiboeus.

Commentators often point out how such a scene bears comparison with representations of the effect singers such as Orpheus had upon the natural world[49] and certainly the language of wondering (*mirari*) and 'being stupefied' (*stupefeci*) relates to other cosmological moments in the *Eclogues*.[50] In particular, the frozen nature of this scene, enhanced as it is by the image of animals distracted from their activities and of streams stilling their courses, recalls to some degree the, presumably static, picture of 'Orpheus ... and the woods following' (*Orpheaque ... siluasque sequentis* 3.46) on Damoetas' cups in *Eclogue* 3. On that occasion, we are left to imagine the music that draws the trees along in Orpheus' wake,[51] whereas here the poem proceeds to recount the very songs that have produced such a miraculous effect. But between this frozen image of the response of the natural world to the two herdsmen's songs and the retelling of those songs themselves, a further eight lines intervene which serve both to balance and to contrast with this opening scene. They address an unnamed reader who, unlike the animals and streams that are there held spellbound by these songs, is very much on the move (8.6-13):

> tu mihi, seu magni superas iam saxa Timaui
> siue oram Illyrici legis aequoris, – en erit umquam
> ille dies, mihi cum liceat tua dicere facta?
> en erit ut liceat totum mihi ferre per orbem
> sola Sophocleo tua carmina digna coturno?

a te principium, tibi desinam: accipe iussis
carmina coepta tuis, atque hanc sine tempora circum
inter uictricis hederam tibi serpere lauros.

You, for me, whether you are now overcoming the rocks of great Timavus or
are hugging the shore of the Illyrian sea, – will it ever be that day, when it
might be permitted for me to tell of your deeds? Will it ever be that it might
be permitted for me to carry through the whole world your poems, which
alone are worthy of the buskin of Sophocles? From you is my beginning, with
you shall I cease: receive songs begun at your orders, and allow this ivy to
entwine around your temples among your conquering laurels.

With its allusion to the opening of Aratus' *Phaenomena* at line 11 – 'From
you is my beginning, with you shall I cease' (*a te principium, tibi desinam*)[52]
– this (as it were) second proem to *Eclogue* 8 also aligns itself with a form
of cosmological verse, although in this case it is a verse that participates
in a sense of procession rather than one that freezes everything in motion.
Thus, we are introduced to two different versions of cosmological poetry
from the very start. This conjunction of, and to some extent tension
between, the still and the moving which the juxtaposition of these two
passages introduces at the outset of the eclogue carries over into the songs
themselves. There, an analogous effect is created, for instance, by the
refrains that are a feature of both these songs.[53] On the one hand, these
refrains instil a sense of rhythm and progression into these recitals
through the very acts of repetition they perform, as well as through the
slight modification in their wording that takes place when they are recited
for the last time: in Damon's case, from 'Begin with me Maenalian verses,
my pipe' (*incipe Maenalios mecum, mea tibia, uersus*) to 'Cease from
Maenalian verses, now cease, pipe' (*desine Maenalios, iam desine, tibia,
uersus*); and in Alphesiboeus' from 'Draw home from the city, my songs,
draw Daphnis' (*ducite ab urbe domum, mea carmina, ducite Daphnin*)
to 'Cease, Daphnis has come from the city, now cease, songs' (*parcite, ab
urbe uenit, iam parcite carmina, Daphnis*). On the other hand, this
same repetition and the fact that these refrains consistently interrupt
the telling of the story also work to hold back the linear development of
that story.[54]

As is fitting for two songs that have been introduced by way of two
different versions of cosmological verse and that are in any case suppos-
edly in competition with one another, Damon's and Alphesiboeus'
performances tell antithetical stories about the efficacy of bucolic poetry.
Indeed, rather than present a song contest in which one singer is success-
ful and one unsuccessful, this particular eclogue transposes these notions
of success and failure into the content of the songs themselves: Damon,
that is, takes on the role of the unsuccessful singer and lover, while
Alphesiboeus plays his opposite. The roles each of them adopts, moreover,
are to some degree already predetermined by their names: Damon is the

unsuccessful herdsman whom Damoetas claims to have defeated in a song contest in *Eclogue* 3 and who is there notably unwilling to relinquish his rights to something he regards as his own (namely, a goat which may not even have been his in the first place, 3.17-24), while Alphesiboeus is one of the figures who participates in the celebrations that attend Daphnis' ascent to heaven in *Eclogue* 5 (5.73). More than this, though, Alphesiboeus also takes his name from a Greek adjective which, in Homer's *Iliad* at least, is used to denote virgins who gain cattle for their parents as wedding gifts.[55] It is therefore a fitting name for one who in *Eclogue* 8 assumes a female role in his song, who strives to win a bucolic contest (the literary equivalent of 'gaining cattle') and who does so by attempting to draw back the exemplary figure of bucolic poetry, Daphnis – a figure, it should be added, who is here characterised as the singer's 'husband' (*coniunx* 8.66). The reason both these performances close with cliff-hanger endings, then, leaving us to wonder whether Damon's character really does jump to his death and if Alphesiboeus' really has succeeded in drawing Daphnis back from the city, could well be because both now await external ratification from whoever was supposed to have been judging their competition. Damon would indeed have taken a dive if he is to be declared the loser, while Alphesiboeus could equally be said actually to have drawn Daphnis back from the city if he walks off as the winner in this bucolic battle.

In both of these songs, the absent lover is described as the singer's spouse, or *coniunx* (18, 66). As a result, they both draw upon the form of a wedding song. When Alphesiboeus, for example, who by taking on the role of a female character introduces a series of gender reversals from the very start of his song,[56] uses as 'her' refrain, 'Draw home from the city, my songs, draw Daphnis' (*ducite ab urbe domum, mea carmina, ducite Daphnin*), 'she' evokes the practice of the *deductio in domum*, the part of the wedding ceremony in which the bride was led to the house of her husband (this evocation is reinforced by the fact that Alphesiboeus' song comes to a close, like the *deductio in domum*, at the threshold).[57] Damon, by contrast, who equates the rejection of his ability as a bucolic singer with the marriage of his wife to another (32-3), likewise uses this verb *ducere* ('to lead') to characterise his loss. Once, he himself had been Nysa's 'leader' (*dux ego uester eram* 38), but now, addressing his victor Mopsus, he acknowledges that 'a wife is being led to you' (*tibi ducitur uxor* 29). As with other instances in the *Eclogues*, the time for weddings and for wedding songs is associated with the rising of the evening star: 'sprinkle nuts, husband: Hesperus is deserting Oeta for you' (*sparge, marite, nuces: tibi deserit Hesperus Oetam* 30). What distinguishes its appearance here is that, while in those other cases Hesperus and the beginning of the wedding song bring bucolic poetry to a close, in this instance it is the singer himself who will now meet his end.

Indeed, the risings of the planet Venus in the form of both the morning star (Lucifer) and the evening star (Hesperus) participate in a number of the inversions that inform Damon's song. Lucifer, for instance, is instructed to 'be born' and to 'lead in the blessed day' (*Nascere praeque diem ueniens age, Lucifer, almum* 17). Yet what it also heralds is the singer's own 'final hour' (*extrema ... hora* 20) as he threatens to throw himself off a mountain into the sea as his 'final gift' (*extremum ... munus* 60) to the happy couple (58-60). Likewise, the wedding ceremonies signalled by the rising of Hesperus in the evening also promise to introduce a number of inversions of the kind witnessed in *Eclogue* 4. Here too they presage a return to something akin to a golden age (8.27-8):

> iungentur iam grypes equis, aeuoque sequenti
> cum canibus timidi uenient ad pocula dammae.

> now griffins will be joined with horses, and in the following age timid deer will come to drink with dogs.

As a consequence of his perception that the marriage of his erstwhile wife Nysa to his rival Mopsus indicates a reversal of the natural order, Damon (or at least the character he here plays) orders yet more inversions to take place (8.52-4):

> nunc et ouis ultro fugiat lupus, aurea durae
> mala ferant quercus, narcisso floreat alnus,
> pinguia corticibus sudent electra myricae.

> Now may the wolf flee the sheep, and may hard oaks bear golden apples, may the alder flower with narcissus, may tamarisks sweat rich amber from their bark.

On this occasion, however, these inversions are extended to the singer himself (8.55-6):[58]

> certent et cycnis ululae, sit Tityrus Orpheus,
> Orpheus in siluis, inter delphinas Arion.

> and may owls contend with swans, may Tityrus be Orpheus,
> Orpheus in the woods, Arion among the dolphins.

These edicts demanding a reversal of nature are drawn largely from Daphnis' final words in *Idyll* 1, in which he sees an alteration in the natural order as a fitting way to commemorate his death (*Id.* 1.132-6). The conflation of Tityrus with Orpheus, though, is Damon's own invention and therefore both highlights yet also brings into question one of the *Eclogues'* most distinctive features: their oft repeated ambition to align bucolic poetry with cosmological poetry. To some degree, Damon's song rehearses the failure of bucolic poetry to achieve this kind of status, while Alphesiboeus' promises to live up to its belief that 'songs can draw down the moon from the sky' (8.69). At the same time, there is at least one respect in which the retelling of Damon's song demonstrates a greater capacity on the part of the singer than that of Alphesiboeus' response. For while the narrator of *Eclogue* 8 admits that he is unable to recall all of Alphesiboeus' song without the help of the Muses (8.62-3) –

> Haec Damon; uos, quae responderit Alphesiboeus,
> dicite, Pierides: non omnia possumus omnes.

> This is what Damon was singing; you, Pierians, tell me what Alphesiboeus responded: we are not all capable of all things.

– Damon aligns the beginning of his song with the time at which he himself begins to sing (at dawn) and in that very gesture displays his power over nature by commanding the morning star to rise and lead in the day (8.14-17):

> Frigida uix caelo noctis decesserat umbra,
> cum ros in tenera pecori gratissimus herba:
> incumbens tereti Damon sic coepit oliuae.
> 'Nascere praeque diem ueniens age, Lucifer, almum ...'

> Scarcely had the cold shade of night withdrawn from the sky at the time when the dew, most pleasing to flocks, was on the soft grass: Damon, leaning on a smooth olive, begins as follows. 'Be born, Light-Bringer, and, coming in advance, lead in the blessed day ...'

There is therefore a tension in both these songs between the power of poetry as celebrated or denigrated in the songs themselves and in the capacity displayed in their retelling. Indeed, the whole eclogue could be said to be structured around a sequence of such contrasts: between, for instance, success and failure, and the moving and the still. This includes, of course, the opening scene of this eclogue and is highlighted, for instance, by the fact that the Orphic powers there displayed do not reside in either one of these two songs in particular, but rather in the exchange between them: what the heifer marvels at, in other words, are not the singers themselves, but their competition (*quos est mirata iuuenca / certantis* 2-3).[59] Which of them is successful in this competition, moreover, depends not just on these animals and the nearby streams, but on the response of the unnamed addressee who likewise listens to them within the parameters set by the cosmological paradigm.[60] If the opening five lines are anything to go by, this decision hangs very much in the balance.

Eclogue 8 therefore upholds what we observed earlier in relation to *Eclogues* 3 and 5: the notion that the ascent to the stars and the achievement of the cosmological paradigm are both structured and realised in terms of certain distinctive bucolic modalities, most notably those of responsion and exchange. As we shall see in the final section of this chapter, it is these modalities that help enable the cosmos to chart the place, configuration and potential of bucolic poetry at any given instance. For the time being, one might simply note that these same modalities render the cosmos and bucolic poetry not only analogous with one another, but actively interrelated as well. In this way, neither is cosmological poetry excluded from bucolic poetry, nor is bucolic poetry cut off from the rest of the cosmos, but both cohere in this distinctly responsive structure. As for what all of this amounts to, that will be the subject of the final section of this chapter.

The bucolic cosmos

In his *Institutio Oratoria*, composed in the first century AD, the rhetorician Quintilian makes the observation that 'whoever is ignorant of the workings of the stars cannot understand the poets' (*nec si rationem siderum ignoret poetas intellegat* Quint. *Instit.* 1.4.4). In as far as this is true of any selection of poems, it is certainly true of the *Eclogues*. And yet this aspect of these poems has generally been overlooked in recent times. Whatever the reasons are for this oversight, it rather neatly reiterates the fact that the influence of the cosmos remains largely hidden in the *Eclogues* – in much the same way, that is, that the night sky remains hidden during the day, the usual time for bucolic song. Despite this, the Daphnis fragment in *Eclogue* 9 and the descriptions of the two sets of cosmological cups in *Eclogue* 3 – which quite possibly allude to Varro's derivation of *caelum* ('heaven') first from *caelare* ('to rise') and thereby from its antithesis *celare* ('to hide') and which are in any case both categorised as *condita* ('hidden' or 'stored away') – nonetheless dim the lights for just a moment and offer us a glimpse of the influence the physical universe has upon these poems.

Once this influence has been discerned, it becomes evident that the cosmos acts as a kind of map for the *Eclogues*, upon which they mark out the principal co-ordinates of their poetic programme. The guide books one needs to find one's way around this map, moreover, have already been provided by such pre-existing cosmological surveys as Aratus' *Phaenomena* and Callimachus' *Coma Berenices* (in close proximity with Catullus' translation): the first of these indicates how Gallus' reference to Cancer in *Eclogue* 10, for instance, relates to Lycidas' reference to the Bear in *Idyll* 7; while the *Coma Berenices* not only helps structure the *Eclogues*' own cosmological aspirations more generally, but it also provides a much more detailed itinerary for the journey from *Eclogue* 3 to *Eclogue* 4. Indeed, and as this last example suggests, the workings of the cosmos can accordingly give shape to the book of *Eclogues* as a whole, a capacity that is most obviously in evidence when the ascent of Hesperus into the evening sky brings the final line of the final poem to a close.

Above all, though, the celestial map constituted by the physical universe enables the *Eclogues* to set their ambitions and establish their bearings by way of other stellar works from the literary tradition. Instances of this are legion, but include the ascent of the exemplary figure of bucolic poetry, Daphnis, to Olympus in *Eclogue* 5, an ascent that takes the form of a catasterism and that charts its progress in relation to such literary luminaries as Homer, Theocritus and Lucretius. As far as more general genre definitions are concerned, it is the distinction between the nocturnal setting of much Roman elegy on the one hand and the daytime setting of much Virgilian bucolic on the other that, along with other customary differences between them such as those which centre on contrasts between the country and the city (for more on which, see Chapters 3 and 4 below), contributes to the impression that the one often represents the inverse image of the other. The primary relationship illuminated by an astronomical reading of these poems, however, lies with the epithalamium or wedding song. This literary form provides a kind of 'end point' for the *Eclogues* in two senses: in the first place, Roman wedding songs commonly begin at the very moment (the rising of Hesperus) at which bucolic poetry tends to come to a close; and, more importantly, it draws the bucolic's own impulse towards 'convenings' – in which singers, songs and so on all strive to 'come together' – into the additional conceptual framework of marriage.[61] The prospect of achieving the cosmological paradigm, that is, whereby bucolic song accords entirely with the workings of the cosmos, is repeatedly figured in the *Eclogues* in terms of a wedding.

In the end, the *Eclogues*' use of the cosmos as an arena within which to express and pursue their literary ambitions emphasises both the height and breadth of those ambitions. As we saw at the close of the previous section, the interrelationship between poetry and cosmology in these poems is such that neither is cosmological poetry excluded from bucolic poetry nor is bucolic activity cut off from the rest of the cosmos, but both cohere in a distinctly responsive structure. The principle of reciprocity operative in this relationship, moreover, entails that it is never fixed or stable but is instead always evolving. Indeed, it is worth noting that the full achievement of cosmological song is consistently deferred to the future in these poems, even in *Eclogue* 4, in which the contest with Orpheus is still to come, even in *Eclogue* 5, in which the festivities are envisaged as taking place at some undefined later date, and even in *Eclogue* 8, in which the scene of nature wondering at Damon's and Alphesiboeus' songs is set against the presentation of these songs to another kind of reader, where they are characterised primarily as 'beginnings' (*principium* 8.11; *coepta* 8.12).

Like the wedding songs with which they are often aligned, that is, the cosmological ambitions of the *Eclogues* repeatedly await further issue. Their engagement with the cosmos illustrates the extent of these ambitions, but their chosen modes of transportation – which include such vehicles as repetition, responsion, reciprocity and exchange – nonetheless ensure that the relationship between poetry and the cosmos is one that is continually evolving. As such, it prevents these restless, nomadic works from ever finally arriving or settling.

3

Geography

It is time to return to earth. But as we do so, we might note in passing that the very concept of the earth taken as a whole is one that plays an important part in the *Eclogues*' processes of self-definition. Indeed, of the five occasions on which the word *orbis* appears in the book – and its distribution is such that it thereby recurs in exactly half of these ten poems[1] – on three of them it is accompanied by the adjective *totus* ('whole'). At first sight, a number of these occurrences would seem to intimate that the earth is introduced into the conceptual world of the *Eclogues* as a way of articulating the limitations of their own reach and compass by comparison. In the proem to *Eclogue* 8, for example, the narrator draws a contrast between the songs he is about to sing in the present moment and those he anticipates singing in the future, in which he intends to tell of his addressee's deeds and to carry his poems 'through the whole world' (*totum ... ferre per orbem* 8.9). The ambition to encompass the whole earth with his songs, in other words, is here deferred for another day, rather than explicitly enacted in the bucolic present. Much the same could also be said of the global ambitions expressed in *Eclogue* 4, in which the prospect of the promised child ruling over 'the pacified earth with his ancestral virtues' (*pacatumque reget patriis uirtutibus orbem* 4.17) would seem to have to wait – like the vision of a song that will accord with the concrete agreement of land, sea and sky (4.50-9) – for the future.[2]

Two other occasions on which the notion of the globe is invoked, however, suggest that the relationship between the *Eclogues* and the 'whole earth' is in practice rather more nuanced than this. To start with the example from *Eclogue* 1, one of the reasons Meliboeus imagines he will no longer be able to sing any more songs is that he now has the prospect of finding himself among a people, the Britons, who are 'deeply divided from the whole earth' (*et penitus toto diuisos orbe Britannos* 1.66). The conclusion one might draw from this is that, in Meliboeus' eyes at least, bucolic poetry is not itself so cut off from the rest of the world and could not survive if it were. Indeed, the other far-flung places Meliboeus mentions here – Africa to the south, Scythia to the north and Oaxes (possibly)[3] to the east – align this eclogue with the boundaries of a world which, like the poem itself, has Rome at its centre.[4] One effect of this view beyond the Roman world may well be to make the *Eclogues*, like the *Idylls*, begin with an anticipation of their own cessation, but by outlining the contours of such a geopolity at their very beginning rather than their end, such a move also introduces the existential and epistemological parameters within which all ten of these poems are to be both performed and heard.

It is the example from *Eclogue* 6, though, that best introduces the concerns of the three chapters to follow. For when Silenus there sings towards the beginning of his song how 'the tender orb of the earth coalesced' (*ipse tener mundi concreuerit orbis* 6.34), he is reflecting the activity of the *Eclogues* upon the soft and malleable world of literary tradition. At the very least, this moment offers an instance of how bucolic poetry can on occasion encompass the whole of the earth in its song. But more than this, the epithet afforded to the earth here, 'tender' (*tener*), is also a common attribute of the flora and fauna of the eclogue world more generally[5] and, as such, it indicates that the earth is susceptible to being fashioned by that song, as well as referenced and inhabited by it. The next three chapters will pursue this suggestion further. By looking in turn at the geography, topography and landscape of these poems, they will illustrate how the *Eclogues* conceive of the literary tradition as a world they not only inherit and inhabit, but also redefine and reorder.

Terra noua

From the geographical references contained in these poems alone, two things are immediately apparent about the world they inhabit: it is innovative and it is extensive. In as far as the extant literary record can be relied upon, it would seem that, prior to the advent of the *Eclogues*, Latin poetry had not previously been stalked by Phoenician lions or Armenian tigers,[6] for instance, let alone by the Garamantes, a tribe from the eastern Sahara who do not appear in any extant Greek poetry either.[7] Nor indeed had it previously produced Hyblaean honey (Hybla was a town in Sicily) or hosted anything Sicanian (the Sicani were a people residing in Sicily), Actaean (designating Attica), Caucasian, Cyrnean (for Corsica), Cydonian (from Cydonia in the north of Crete), Libethrian (denoting either a town east of Mount Olympus in the Pierian district or a peak in the Helicon range),[8] Sithonian (denoting one of the peninsulas of Chalcidice) or even Cynthian (an epithet derived from Mount Cynthus on Delos, Apollo's birthplace).[9]

Several of these epithets do have a history in Greek poetry, but not all. *Sicelides*, for instance, which means 'Sicilian', here assumes a Greek form but has no Greek precedent,[10] while the word *Sicani*, which denotes one of the peoples resident on Sicily, appears on only two previous occasions in the Greek tradition, with both instances coming from the Hellenistic period.[11] Other place names and epithets employed in the *Eclogues* also occur in earlier Latin poetry, but not in the exact same form: Lucretius, for instance, mentions Ismarus too, which is either a town (where Homer's Cicones are to be found) or a mountain in Thrace, but whereas he and all subsequent Latin poets deploy the neuter plural form, *Ismara*, Virgil alone uses the masculine singular *Ismarus*.[12] Epithets such as 'Cumaean' and 'Syracusan' are likewise attested elsewhere, but on no other occasion in previous Latin poetry do they take on the distinctively Greek forms they demonstrate here: *Cumaeus* (4.4) and *Syracosius* (6.1) respectively.[13]

One of the more obvious effects of this deployment of largely unprecedented geographical epithets is that the *Eclogues* come to present a world that is in several respects unlike any other, either in literature or reality. Most of the individual reference points may well have been familiar to Virgil's early readers, but the way in which these have been reconstituted and reordered contributes to a sense of a domain that is variously innovative, bold, exhilarating and unsettling. The continuing difficulties scholars have experienced in trying to reconcile the apparent settings of these poems with certain geographical realities suggests that this is in many respects still the experience of readers today.[14] It is also testimony to the fact that the geography of these poems has remained remarkably distinctive, despite their considerable influence on the subsequent western, and especially pastoral, tradition. This is so not only because some of the geographical epithets these poems introduce have enjoyed less of an afterlife than others ('Cyrnean', for instance, was to prove far less popular than 'Hyblaean'),[15] but also because they remain unique within Virgil's corpus as well. Never again, in other words, does his poetry look out towards the Oaxes or imagine anything Actaean, Cyrnean, Hyblaean, Sicelidian, Syracosian or Sithonian.

Another striking feature of the geography of these poems is its considerable reach. This in itself does not distinguish it from the cartographic make-up of the *Idylls*, which refer not only to Greece, the Greek Islands and Sicily, but also to places in Italy, Africa (especially around the Hellenistic literary centres in Egypt), and several countries, regions and cities further east, such as Arabia, Scythia, Lydia, Phrygia, the Caucasus, Pontus, Colchis and Troy. Indeed, these two sets of poems by and large cover very similar ground, geographically as well as poetically. Rather, the differences between them can be ascribed partly to the personal biography of each poet (so Virgil puts on the bucolic map places from his native region in the north of Italy: Mantua, Cremona and the river Mincius) and partly to the geopolitical changes that had occurred between the lifetimes of the two poets. Not the least of the contributions the *Eclogues* make to bucolic cartography, after all, is the introduction of Rome in *Eclogue* 1.

Geography and poetry

In addition to denoting the innovative nature and ambitious range of Virgilian bucolic, the geography of the *Eclogues* also helps define the type of song these poems set out to sing. The association between poetry and place is rendered especially explicit by the number of occasions on which a geographical epithet is attached to a noun for a song, verse, muse or nymph. Here one finds, for instance, Sicilian muses, Libethrian nymphs and Syracusan, Maenalian and Chalcidic verses.[16] In each of these cases, the epithet points to a specific poet, poem or type of song: Sicilian muses and Syracusan verses evoke Theocritus, for instance, who was a native of Syracuse; Chalcidic verses suggest Euphorion of Chalcis;[17] as do the Libethrian nymphs;[18] while Damon in *Eclogue* 8 provides an explanation for what he means by Maenalian verses the very first time he mentions them (8.21-4):

> incipe Maenalios mecum, mea tibia, uersus.
> Maenalus argutumque nemus pinusque loquentis
> semper habet, semper pastorum ille audit amores
> Panaque, qui primus calamos non passus inertis.

> Begin Maenalian verses with me, my pipe. Maenalus always hosts a clear-sounding grove and talking pines, he always hears the loves of shepherds and of Pan, who first did not allow the reeds to remain inert.

Through this brief explication, we learn that the kind of song Damon here intends to sing reflects the sounds of nature, addresses the theme of love, and is associated with Pan, the god of Arcadia and originator of music played on the reed.

These geographical epithets also convey literary connotations even when they are not attached to nouns explicitly denoting music or song. The 'Sicilian shepherd' of *Eclogue* 10 (*pastoris Siculi* 10.51), for example, is either Theocritus himself or one of his Sicilian singers and it is a way of pointing up his affiliation with one of these singers, Polyphemus, that Corydon declares he has a thousand lambs wandering in the 'Sicilian mountains' (*Siculis ... in montibus* 2.21) in *Eclogue* 2. In much the same way, the 'Chaonian doves' of *Eclogue* 9 (*Chaonias ... columbas* 9.13) evoke the birds of the famous oracle of Zeus of Dodona and in so doing gesture towards the prophetic element in the *Eclogues*, while the 'Parthenian passes' (*Parthenios ... saltus* 10.57) Gallus mentions in *Eclogue* 10 are just as likely to allude to Callimachus and the Greek poet Parthenius, who may have taught Virgil and who composed his *Erotica Pathemata* ('On the Sorrows of Love') for Gallus, as they do to Mount Parthenius in Arcadia.[19]

We shall return shortly to a number of these examples again to see in more detail how the *Eclogues* use geographical references as a way of plotting their own place within the literary tradition. But it is worth considering first an example of how such references can also help structure these poems and indicate their nature on something like their own terms. Within this context, the word *Pierides*, which serves to designate the Pierian Muses, constitutes one of the most important toponyms in the *Eclogues*. The fact that Virgil does not call upon these particular muses again either in the *Georgics* or the *Aeneid* indicates that the use of this name is more than just a poetic convention here, but that it has a specific resonance for these poems in particular.[20] Indeed, in *Eclogue* 3, the Pierians are explicitly associated with the kind of song the two herdsmen are there engaged in singing when Damoetas calls upon them to reward 'their reader', Pollio, for liking his muse, 'even though she is rustic' (3.84-5):

> Pollio amat nostram, quamuis est rustica, musam:
> Pierides, uitulam lectori pascite uestro.

> Pollio loves our muse, even though she is rustic: Pierians, feed a young cow for your reader.

The request that they should feed a 'young cow' (or *uitula*) for their reader provides one explanation for why the Pierian Muses should find their place in the *Eclogues* rather than, say, the *Georgics* or *Aeneid*, since such an offering emblematises a number of qualities that are central to the Virgilian conception of bucolic poetry: namely, their investment in beginnings and their recurrent desire for growth and elevation.[21] After all, just as the 'young cow' is a fitting prize for the contest of *Eclogue* 3 on the grounds that it reflects the status of the two singers as literary apprentices, so too are the Pierians often associated with beginnings and with the achievement of an analogous literary ascent. As Hesiod recounts in his *Theogony*, the nine Muses were born and resided initially in Pieria, 'a little way from the topmost peak of Olympus' (*Theog.* 62), but subsequently 'they went to Olympus, glorying in their beautiful voices, with ambrosial song, and the dark earth resounded about them as they chanted, and the thud of their feet as they went to their father was lovely' (*Theog.* 68-71). In this, one might suggest, lies a pretty good description of the songs of the *Eclogues* as well. Indeed, the recounting of the song of Silenus in *Eclogue* 6, which begins (after the poem's prologue) with the injunction 'Hasten, Pierians' (*Pergite, Pierides* 6.13) and ends with Olympus (*Olympo* 6.86) notably follows the same itinerary as the Muses themselves.

The Pierian Muses also fulfil a structural function within the book of *Eclogues* as a whole. Of their five appearances in five different eclogues, four occur in the second half of the volume.[22] The only exception to this comes in the example cited above, when Damoetas calls upon them to feed a young cow for Pollio in *Eclogue* 3, and it is surely no coincidence that *Eclogue* 3 is the counterpart to the only poem in the second half of the book, *Eclogue* 7, in which they do not appear. One can only speculate why the Pierians are shepherded almost exclusively into four of the last five poems in this way, but it is perhaps significant that they make their first appearance in the eclogue which first expresses a desire to ascend to the heavens, *Eclogue* 3, while all the other examples come after the ascent of the bucolic figure of Daphnis to the *limen Olympi*, the 'threshold of Olympus' (the Virgilian equivalent to Hesiod's 'little way from the topmost peak of Olympus', perhaps) in *Eclogue* 5.

To return, however, to the notion that the *Eclogues* employ geographical references as a way of plotting their own place within the literary tradition, two passages in *Eclogue* 6 offer especially vivid examples of this practice. The first of these comes at the very moment Silenus begins his song, whereupon the narrator remarks that 'neither does the rock of Parnasus rejoice as much in Apollo / nor do Rhodope and Ismarus marvel so much at Orpheus' (*nec tantum Phoebo gaudet Parnasia rupes, / nec tantum Rhodope miratur et Ismarus Orphea* 6.29-30). Quite clearly, these lines make the claim that the song of Silenus is better than those of Apollo and Orpheus. Through the geographical references they employ, moreover, they also imply that this song is better than Theocritus' *Idyll* 7 and Apollonius' *Argonautica* as well,[23] since the *Parnasia rupes* ('rock of Parnasus') recalls the 'Castalian nymphs, inhabitants of the steep of Parnassus' (Νύμφαι Κασταλίδες Παρνάσιον αἶπος ἔχοισαι *Id.* 7.148) whom Theocritus addresses towards the end of that idyll, while the mention of Orpheus and his traditional stamping grounds recalls his song of the creation of the world in the first book of the *Argonautica*.[24]

A second and more elaborate example from this eclogue comes within Silenus' song itself. In the course of this song, Gallus is first found wandering by the streams of Permessus (*errantem Permessi ad flumina* 6.64), is led by one of the Muses into 'the Aonian mountains' (namely, Helicon: *Aonas in montis* 6.65), where he is given the reeds of 'the Ascraean old man' (that is, Hesiod: *Ascraeo ... seni* 6.70) and is instructed to sing the origin of the Grynean grove (*his tibi Grynei nemoris dicatur origo* 6.72). The preponderance of geographical epithets in these lines helps co-ordinate the literary journey Gallus here undertakes.[25] The Permessus, for a start, is a river that flows through the valley beneath Helicon. It is named by Hesiod as one of the streams in which the Muses would bathe before returning to the highest slope of Helicon to perform their dances;[26] its setting further down the mountain therefore aligns it with one of the lower-lying genres: in this instance, probably love poetry.[27] The Aones, who here serve to characterise Helicon, are a barbarian people not certainly attested before Callimachus and so this initiation scene relates back not purely to Hesiod's initiation on Helicon as described in his *Theogony*, but also to Callimachus' reworking of Hesiod more generally.[28] Ascra, meanwhile, is a town in the region of Helicon and supposedly the place where Hesiod was born. Finally, the *Gryneus nemus* was a grove in Aeolis in Asia Minor, sacred to Apollo, and may well have been the subject of works by Euphorion, Parthenius and possibly Gallus himself.[29] 'The only interpretation which Virgil's lines (64-73) will bear' Wendell Clausen argues, 'is the obvious one: Gallus quits the valley (Permessus-Aganippe) for the mountain; he rises, so to speak, from a lower to a higher level of poetry (Hippocrene), from love-elegy and Lycoris to aetiology and the Grynean Grove'.[30] In this case, then, we have a fairly concise, if carefully gradated, example of how geographical markers can be used to map a journey between a number of literary traditions and paradigms. In the next section, by contrast, we shall turn instead to a rather more extensive manifestation of this practice and to another poem that from its very first line charts its relationship to the literary tradition and to other contiguous genres in primarily geographical terms: *Eclogue* 10.

Eclogue 10: Poems and places

Eclogue 10 is a prime example of a poem that uses geographical markers as a way of defining its own nature and place within literary history.[31] It begins with an invocation to Arethusa in which its relationship towards epic and elegiac, as well as earlier examples of bucolic poetry, are all brought suggestively into play (10.1-7):

> Extremum hunc, Arethusa, mihi concede laborem:
> pauca meo Gallo, sed quae legat ipsa Lycoris,
> carmina sunt dicenda; neget quis carmina Gallo?
> sic tibi, cum fluctus subterlabere Sicanos,
> Doris amara suam non intermisceat undam,
> incipe: sollicitos Galli dicamus amores,
> dum tenera attondent simae uirgulta capellae.

> Arethusa, yield to me this final labour: a few poems are to be sung for my Gallus, but ones which Lycoris herself might read; who would deny songs for Gallus? So, when you flow under the Sicanian waters, may bitter Doris not intermingle her wave with you, begin: let us sing the anxious loves of Gallus, while the snub-nosed she-goats graze the tender undergrowth.

This appeal to Arethusa sets the poem within a distinctly bucolic tradition. The spring, which emerges on the island of Ortygia in Syracuse, is mentioned both by Daphnis in *Idyll* 1 and by the anonymous author (once thought to have been Moschus of Syracuse) of the *Lament for Bion*, which was probably composed in the first century BC. In both cases, moreover, it helps figure the relationship between bucolic poetry on the one hand and elegiac and epic poetry respectively on the other. In the *Lament*, the bucolic poet Bion is set alongside Homer as a fellow native of Smyrna, but what sets them apart again is that, while the epic poet drank from Hippocrene on Helicon, Bion took his refreshment from Arethusa.[32] The relationship between bucolic poetry and elegiac poetry, meanwhile, is very much the theme of Thyrsis' song in *Idyll* 1. Here, the archetypal bucolic singer, Daphnis, chooses to die rather than yield to love and Arethusa is one of the features of the local landscape to which he bids farewell just before he descends to Hades and Thyrsis' song draws to a close (*Id.* 1.117).

By aligning its song for Gallus with the journey Arethusa is to make beneath the waves, then, *Eclogue* 10 displays a similar interest in charting bucolic poetry's place within the generic order. Indeed, its stipulation that this song and this journey are to involve the telling of 'the anxious loves of Gallus' (*sollicitos Galli dicamus amores* 6) – where the term *amores* points to Gallus' love poetry as well as to his love life – gives this interest a particular focus and direction. We shall return to this theme more explicitly in a moment, but first we shall approach it more indirectly by considering how the passage of Arethusa and the use of other geographical markers in the poem help co-ordinate its relationship towards its primary extant model and the poem that, as mentioned above, initiated the bucolic form with a rejection of love and, with it, of love poetry: *Idyll* 1.[33]

In addition to importing *Idyll* 1's question of the relationship between a bucolic singer and an elegiac poet, the invocation to Arethusa at the very outset of *Eclogue* 10 also re-activates that idyll's intricate confounding of beginnings and ends. Just as *Idyll* 1 inaugurates the bucolic tradition with a depiction of its own demise, that is, so too do the *Eclogues* commence their 'final labour' (*extremum ... laborem*) with a retrospective glance at those beginnings. Or rather, they go one stage further by appearing to recast this glance back to *Idyll* 1 as in some senses also a glance forward to that poem. In order to see this, one needs to be aware of the story of Arethusa to which this invocation alludes. It was widely believed that the source of this spring was actually in Arcadia in the Peloponnese and, as a corollary of this, that Arethusa was a nymph who, in an attempt to escape the amorous advances of the river god Alpheus, had been transformed by Diana into liquid form, whereupon she had fled through the sea to Sicily.[34] By pitching its wish that Arethusa enjoy an uncontaminated passage to her destination in the future tense, therefore, *subterlabere* ('when you will flow' 10.4), this eclogue duly characterises Arethusa's journey beneath the waves as one that has still to take place. To this extent, then, it could be said to address her at an earlier stage in that journey than the idyll and consequently at an earlier point in time: before she has reached Sicily and before Daphnis has lain down to die and bidden her farewell.[35]

It would not quite be right, however, to deduce from this that *Eclogue* 10 therefore tries to retroject itself to a place and a time prior to *Idyll* 1 in anything like a straightforward manner. Quite apart from anything else, the central figure of Gallus himself subsequently draws attention to his own post-Daphnic and post-Theocritean status by explicitly evoking an earlier Sicilian bucolic tradition to which he aspires to belong: 'I shall go and modulate to the oat of the Sicilian shepherd songs which I have stored up in Chalcidic verse' (*ibo et Chalcidico quae sunt mihi condita uersu / carmina pastoris Siculi modulabor auena* 10.50-1). Indeed, it is noteworthy that when Gallus appears for the first time in the narrative proper he does so in the imperfect tense: 'What groves or which passes held you, Naiad girls, when Gallus <u>was perishing</u> of an unworthy love?' (*Quae nemora aut qui uos saltus habuere, puellae / Naides, indigno cum Gallus amore <u>peribat</u>?* 10.9-10). The use of the imperfect tense here places Gallus in a past that is ongoing and continuous and, as such, it inscribes repetition as a key feature of his current situation. His sufferings, in other words, are characterised from the very start as repetitious and, as the poem proceeds, we come increasingly to recognise what they are repetitions of: his own previous love pangs; his own previous love poetry; and the sufferings and songs of those others – such as Daphnis – who have shared or will share his present predicament. All of this, moreover, is intimated in the opening address to Arethusa, which aligns the poem to come not solely with her point of departure nor even with her destination (which are in any case to a certain degree simultaneous), but with the journey itself, a journey she presumably makes not once but again and again.

Here, as elsewhere in the poem, the complex temporal relations between *Eclogue* 10 and *Idyll* 1 are introduced and expressed by way of its spatial, and largely geographical, markers. Because the fountain that brings the curtain down on the first act of Theocritean bucolic here brings the curtain up on the final act of its Virgilian counterpart, one might suggest that the appearance of Arethusa in the very opening line of the eclogue sets the poem's compass towards *Idyll* 1 whilst also marking its distance from it. This is a dynamic, moreover, that is repeated throughout the eclogue, both in terms of the individual characters (Gallus, for instance, moves in and out of his role as the dying Daphnis) and on those other occasions when geographical markers are used to co-ordinate the relationship between these two poems. One such occasion occurs the moment the invocation to Arethusa is over, at the very start of the song for Gallus (10.9-12):

> Quae nemora aut qui uos saltus habuere, puellae
> Naides, indigno cum Gallus amore peribat?
> nam neque Parnasi uobis iuga, nam neque Pindi
> ulla moram fecere, neque Aonie Aganippe.

What groves or which passes held you, Naiad girls, when Gallus was perishing of an unworthy love? For neither the ridges of Parnasus, nor those of Pindus made any delay for you, nor Aonian Aganippe.

This brief survey of some of poetry's more familiar domains both complements and contrasts with the review Thyrsis offers at the start of his song about Daphnis in the idyll (*Id.* 1. 66-9):

> πῆ ποκ᾿ ἄρ᾿ ἦσθ᾿, ὅκα Δάφνις ἐτάκετο, πῆ ποκα, Νύμφαι;
> ἦ κατὰ Πηνειῶ καλὰ τέμπεα, ἦ κατὰ Πίνδω;
> οὐ γὰρ δὴ ποταμοῖο μέγαν ῥόον εἴχετ᾿ Ἀνάπω,
> οὐδ᾿ Αἴτνας σκοπιάν, οὐδ᾿ Ἄκιδος ἱερὸν ὕδωρ.

Where were you then, when Daphnis was wasting away, where were you, Nymphs? Were you among the beautiful valleys of Peneus, or of Pindus? For certainly you were not occupying the great stream of the river Anapus, nor the top of Etna, nor the holy water of Akis.

To a certain degree, Virgil's 'reply' seeks to invert and cap Theocritus' 'original' (if one might use such terms within such a convoluted chronology). Bound together by a similar argumentative structure and through their shared reference to Pindus (which in both instances appears at the end of its line), the eclogue nonetheless reverses the trajectory of the idyll and implies that its own location, Arcadia, boasts a certain advantage over its rival's setting in Sicily. For while the idyll acknowledges that the nymphs were not with Daphnis in Sicily and speculates where they might otherwise have been, the eclogue lists a number of places they categorically were not and leaves it open whether they were with Gallus in Arcadia instead. This, of course, is all part of the contest between Sicily and Arcadia which their connection through Arethusa brings into being and which figures the competition between *Idyll* 1 and *Eclogue* 10 more broadly. For while Thyrsis in the idyll asserts his identity as a Sicilian at the beginning of his song and then proceeds to sing of Daphnis dying in a demonstrably Sicilian setting, the narrator of the eclogue places Gallus in Arcadia and appears to locate himself there as well (*Ecl.* 10.26-7):[36]

> Pan deus Arcadiae uenit, quem uidimus ipsi
> sanguineis ebuli bacis minioque rubentem.

> Pan the god of Arcadia came, whom we ourselves have seen red with the blood-red berries of danewort and minium.

By allowing Pan to be glimpsed by its main protagonist and its narrator alike, moreover, *Eclogue* 10 claims yet another advantage over its opponent. For while in *Idyll* 1 the dying Daphnis begs Pan to abandon the two Arcadian mountains of Lycaeus and Maenalus and to come to him in Sicily (*Id.* 1.123-5), the implication of *Eclogue* 10 (which also depicts those same two mountains weeping over Gallus at lines 14-15) is that Pan has chosen to attend Gallus rather than Daphnis, to stay in Arcadia rather than travel to Sicily, and therefore to give his support to the eclogue rather than to the idyll.

In so far as any kind of victory is declared openly in this eclogue, however, it is in favour of love: 'Love conquers everything', Gallus asserts in the very last line of his soliloquy, 'we too should yield to Love' (*omnia uincit Amor: et nos cedamus Amori* 69). This assertion, which would seem to be upheld both by the narrator's opening wish to sing 'the loves of Gallus' (6) and by his closing expression of love for his fellow poet (72-4), could be taken to pass judgement upon the exchange between the song for Gallus on the one hand, in which the protagonist eventually accepts this conclusion, and Thyrsis' song about Daphnis on the other, in which the bucolic singer persists in resisting love right up the very end; but this does not of itself thereby mean that it adjudicates between Sicily and Arcadia as such. Indeed, just before his capitulation to Love, Gallus dismisses his Arcadian surroundings in much the same way that Daphnis in Theocritus has to forego his native Sicily as he is dragged off into Hades by that same god: 'now once again neither do Hamadryades nor do our songs themselves please us; now once again yield, woods' (*iam neque Hamadryades rursus nec carmina nobis / ipsa placent; ipsae rursus concedite siluae* 10.62-3).[37] Rather, just as the temporal relationship between *Eclogue* 10 and *Idyll* 1 is neither one of absolute anteriority or posteriority, so too is it difficult to assign any kind of cartographic precedence to Virgil's Arcadia over and against Theocritus' Sicily. This again is a feature of the eclogue's grounding in the course pursued by Arethusa, in which the point of contact the spring establishes between the eclogue and the idyll is also a point of departure. One of the consequences of this ever-shifting and hybrid cartography, moreover, is that so far from being comfortably settled in his new surroundings, the figure who combines the role of Daphnis and 'himself' – namely, Gallus – is instead thoroughly displaced. Indeed, two of the locations listed earlier as sites where the nymphs were definitely not to be found, Parnassus and Aonian Aganippe, are reminiscent of *Eclogue* 6, the poem in which Gallus was imagined climbing the Aonian mountains and receiving sanction to sing of the Grynean grove. The evocation of a similar topography in *Eclogue* 10, now abandoned even by the nymphs, suggests that Gallus has here been interrupted and disturbed from that particular project as well.

The fluid geography of *Eclogue* 10 is therefore in many respects a reflection of its grounding in the journey of Arethusa between Arcadia and Sicily. Both that geography and that grounding, moreover, are in turn expressive of bucolic poetry's dialectical impulses, especially when these are enacted, as is the case here with the contest between those two localities, in distinctly agonistic terms. The militaristic potential of such exchanges, along with their likely impact upon the bucolic world and its poetry, is given its most obvious concrete expression in *Eclogues* 1 and 9, in which the primary agents of the current inhabitants' displacement, and as often as not the inheritors of their lands, are identified as soldiers. A similar rhetoric infiltrates *Eclogue* 10, when Gallus takes on the role of a soldier in order to describe, and to a certain degree account for, his sufferings as a lover (10.44-9):[38]

> nunc insanus amor duri me Martis in armis
> tela inter media atque aduersos detinet hostis.
> tu procul a patria (nec sit mihi credere tantum)
> Alpinas, a! dura niues et frigora Rheni
> me sine sola uides. a, te ne frigora laedant!
> a, tibi ne teneras glacies secet aspera plantas!

69

Now insane love of hard Mars detains me in battles in the middle of arms and hostile enemies. You far away from the fatherland (may I not believe such a thing!), hard one, see Alpine snows, ah! and the cold streams of the Rhine alone without me. Ah, may the frosts not harm you! Ah, may the rough ice not cut your tender feet!

Taken by themselves, these lines conjoin elegiac and epic poetry and articulate the dislocations that result when a lover adopts the vocabulary of a soldier.[39] After all, when Gallus speaks of his 'insane love of Mars' (*insanus amor ... Martis*),[40] he is reanimating the common characterisation of the elegiac hero as a 'soldier of love' (*militia amoris*) by reversing the terms of this metaphor. The immediate consequence of this elision of the two generic codes, moreover, is to offer an explanation for the distance between himself the soldier and Lycoris his beloved: while he is detained in battle, Lycoris is far away, looking out upon Alpine snows and the cold streams of the Rhine. At the same time, the embedding of this passage in a poem that itself tries to transform this soldier-lover into a herdsman ensures that it has consequences for the bucolic genre as well. Indeed, if Servius is to be believed, it is in these lines that *Eclogue* 10 most immediately achieves its goal of singing the *Amores* of Gallus and that Virgilian bucolic and Gallan elegiac thereby come to be most closely aligned. For in his note to line 46 of this poem, Servius makes his much-cited remark that 'all these verses are by Gallus, transferred from his poems' (*hi autem omnes uersus Galli sunt, de ipsius translati carminibus*).[41] At the very least, the intermingling of martial and elegiac terminology that takes place throughout this passage both mirrors the effects of, and therefore bears repercussions for, the exchanges between bucolic and elegiac poetry that infuse the eclogue as a whole. Even as Gallus' investiture as a soldier serves to offer at least one explanation for his separation from Lycoris, it also detaches him from his current bucolic surroundings. He is not, after all, obviously detained 'among the middle of arms and hostile enemies' in the lines immediately prior to these, where he imagines Phyllis gathering garlands for him, Amyntas singing to him and where he lists the cold fountains, soft meadows and groves he invites Lycoris to come and share with him (10.41-3).

To this extent, one might suggest that the herdsman, the lover and the soldier all inhabit different settings, just as the generic codes they embody presuppose the countryside, the city and the battlefield (as well as great expanses of land and sea) respectively. Yet as this particular passage proceeds, it becomes increasingly evident that the sequence of displacements enacted here is also expressive of the intermingling of these same roles and their codes. It is by no means true, for instance, that Gallus in these lines is solely playing the part of the soldier and Lycoris that of the beloved, since she too is living a military life in pursuit of love. She shares, for a start, her epithet 'hard' (*dura*) with the god of war (*duri ... Martis*) and the reason she is 'far from the fatherland' (*procul a patria*) at the

70

boundaries of the empire is, as Apollo has already pointed out, that she 'has followed another through the snows and the grim camps' (*tua cura Lycoris / perque niues alium perque horrida castra secuta est* 22-3). The moment Gallus characterises his love life as a series of battles, in other words, he at once transports himself into a world of adversaries, campaigns and expansive vistas. A comparable disorientation therefore also occurs when he, like *Eclogue* 10 more broadly, attempts to displace his *amores* onto the bucolic landscape as well (just as Lycoris herself is transported in the one instance to the edges of the empire and in the other to the cold fountains, soft meadows and groves of Arcadia). Indeed, the paradigmatic quality of this passage for the *Eclogues* as a whole extends much further than this, since Lycoris' displacement to the Alps and the Rhine is reminiscent above all of Meliboeus' envisaged exile to one or other of the four corners of the known world in *Eclogue* 1. Both Lycoris and Meliboeus, moreover, are caused to leave the fatherland through the appearance of soldiers,[42] one of whom Lycoris follows through the snows and military camps, while another is to replace Meliboeus on his land[43] (it has even been conjectured that he himself would have to become a soldier were he really to see Africa, Britain, Scythia or the Oaxes).[44]

Given this sequence of equations between literary codes and character roles, and between those codes and roles on the one hand and certain specific places and settings on the other, it is hardly surprising that poems in which lovers become soldiers and herdsmen, herdsmen become lovers and soldiers, and soldiers become herdsmen should be characterised by such a complex, fluid and often confusing geography. Indeed, viewed in either its Theocritean or Virgilian form, it is impossible to extract a purist notion of bucolic poetry that is either untainted by, or in any way unrelated to, its epic or elegiac counterparts. To some degree, *Eclogue* 10's invocation to Arethusa at the moment she is about to leave Arcadia for Sicily does mark an attempt to experience bucolic poetry at its very source, and the hope that she remains untouched by the bitter waters of the sea as she makes her way there likewise constitutes a desire for purity. But her involvement here in a song for Gallus, which is intended to tell of the 'loves' of Gallus and in so doing to bring him and Lycoris back together again, would seem to work against this. After all, the waters with which she is encouraged not to mix are those of Doris, the sea, and not those of her would-be lover Alpheus, while the terms in which she is encouraged to yield this song to the narrator of *Eclogue* 10, *mihi concede*, are likewise suggestive of that river's hopes that she might 'yield' to him as well. And to pursue the connotations of this injunction a little further, just as here the verb *concedere* may well therefore point to bucolic poetry's inability to escape love poetry even at its very source, so too does this same verb indicate on the next occasion it appears in this eclogue that elegiac is not so easily disentangled from bucolic either. For the very injunction with which Gallus later enjoins the bucolic scenery to disappear – 'yield once more you woods' (*ipsae rursus concedite siluae* 10.63) – itself reignites the imperative with which this particular bucolic song was instructed to begin.

There has been a tendency in recent times to read *Eclogue* 10's exploration of its various literary and generic relationships in largely serious tones.[45] There is nonetheless something to be said for seeing this poem as one big tease, a literary 'will they? won't they?' that applies to lovers, texts and genres alike. More than anything else, the opening invocation to Arethusa sets both the tone and the context for the game of chase that is to ensue, a 'catch me – or elude me – if you can'. Even at the poem's very end, when the narrator calls upon the Pierian Muses, declares his love for Gallus and rises to leave, we cannot be sure whether he has actually crossed the finishing line or, through the reference he makes in the very last line back to *Eclogue* 1,[46] is instead continuing to chase his tail.

This last observation points us to some degree towards the recursive and therefore 'ecological' structure of bucolic nature that will increasingly emerge as we proceed. For the time being, however, we should also keep in mind the sheer adventure involved in the *Eclogues'* use of geographical markers. For even as these markers serve to inscribe the literary tradition upon the physical world, to chart the *Eclogues'* own place within that tradition and, as often as not, thereby to enact and observe the unsettling and displacing of poetry and people from their customary habitats, they do so persistently in a spirit of audacity, ambition, innovation and even fun.

4

Topography

The distribution and representation of topographical features in the *Eclogues* fulfils a similar function to that of the geographical markers we have just explored. More than anything else, it offers a further set of insights into how these poems characterise their own nature and their relationship towards the literary tradition. This chapter will therefore illustrate how these poems align the literary world with the physical world and will highlight how the specific demarcation and delineation of the one accordingly relates to the demarcation and delineation of the other. In particular, we shall see how this interrelationship between poetry and topography renders the acts of land confiscation recorded in the *Eclogues* paradigmatic of, rather than antithetical to, the conventions of bucolic competition.

Types of topography and types of song

Regardless of how far and wide they might subsequently proceed to range, almost every song in the *Eclogues* issues forth from a specific location. Indeed, every one of these poems takes place within a particular setting, whether that setting is introduced at the very outset of the poem (as it is, for instance, in *Eclogue* 7) or whether it emerges as the poem proceeds (as it does, for instance, in *Eclogue* 3). The only eclogue of which this is perhaps not entirely true is *Eclogue* 4, although even here the poem projects itself as a landscape that is to be traversed by the reader as if it were a place in nature.[1] At the very least, this practice of associating songs with specific settings – regardless of how realistic (or otherwise) or coherent (or otherwise) those settings might be – suggests a more thoroughgoing correlation between the contours of any given song and the contours of the environment within which it is sung. We shall therefore begin our survey of the topography of the *Eclogues* with an overview of what that correlation might entail.

The topography of the *Eclogues* is almost entirely rustic, combining as it does both wild and cultivated regions. It consists of mountains, hills, cliffs, rocks, seas, rivers, streams, plains, fields, meadows, pastures, woods, groves, passes and various delineations thereof. In a very general sense, every one of these topographical features helps categorise the individual song in question by indicating such things as the scale of its ambition – whether it is 'high' or 'humble', for example – and its relationship to other texts in the same area. Gallus' ascent from the valley to the top of Mount Helicon in *Eclogue* 6, which we looked at in the previous chapter, provides perhaps the most obvious enactment of this kind of equation between literary and topographical altitude, although examples can be found throughout the book. The opening lines of *Eclogue* 4, for instance, offer another case in point (4.1-3):

> Sicelides Musae, paulo maiora canamus!
> non omnis arbusta iuuant humilesque myricae;
> si canimus siluas, siluae sint consule dignae.

Sicilian Muses, let us sing slightly greater things! Copses and humble tamarisks do not please everyone; if we sing of woods, let woods be worthy of a consul.

This opening invocation to the Sicilian Muses brings the idea of a Sicilian bucolic tradition immediately into play. Through the specific mention of tamarisks, moreover, a plant that is a recurring feature of the landscape of the *Idylls*, and copses, which appear only in the first half of the *Eclogues*, the topography of this passage serves to identify exactly which examples of this tradition the present song aims to transcend.[2] What is more, it identifies its own and its predecessors' respective places on the literary scale through the carefully ordered sequence of gradations it maintains from copses and tamarisks at one end to woods at the other. At the same time, the introduction of this decidedly sylvan scale at this point in the book does not so much denote a departure from previous bucolic practice or point solely to a 'higher' verse to come as it provides a means of measuring both the examples that have come before and those which are to follow after. After all, the Sicilian Muses *Eclogue* 4 addresses here are still potentially those of the *Idylls*, just as the copses and tamarisks are not different in kind from the woods of which the poem aspires to sing. On the contrary, these woods are but larger and more variegated manifestations of the same phenomenon and, as such, are capable of incorporating these copses and tamarisks within their compass.[3] Indeed, the tamarisks themselves, which look back to Homer (among others) as well as to Theocritus, and which thereby already engage the relationship between epic and bucolic poetry,[4] continue to appear from this point on at regular intervals in the *Eclogues*,[5] even as these woods are already present from the opening lines of *Eclogue* 1, wherein Meliboeus encounters Tityrus teaching them to re-echo beautiful Amaryllis (1.1-5).

Such questions of scale often lead on to questions of genre and it is certainly the case that the *Eclogues* structure their relationship towards other literary genres topographically as well as thematically. We saw in the last chapter, for instance, how the flight of the spring Arethusa beneath the Sicilian waves at the outset of *Eclogue* 10 helps figure bucolic poetry's relationship towards both epic and elegy, and one might suggest that the sea fulfils a similar function in other eclogues as well.[6] Perhaps above all, though, it is through references to the city, the supposed antithesis to the country, that the nexus of relations between bucolic poetry on the one hand and both epic and elegiac on the other are most obviously engaged.[7] Poems such as *Eclogues* 2 and 10, for instance, make considerable capital out of the transfer of elegiac themes, tropes and – in the likely case that Gallus in *Eclogue* 10 is citing from his own works – verses from their usual settings in the city to the countryside.[8] Meliboeus' recourse to such potentially epic terms as 'fatherland' (*patria*) and 'kingdom' (*regnum*) in *Eclogue* 1, meanwhile, similarly reflects the potentially epic journeys and vistas that await him in exile.

But what does this interchange between the city and the countryside in the *Eclogues* tell us about the way in which these poems conceptualise and configure the relationship between these three literary codes? The remarkable reversal that takes place between the final line of *Eclogue* 8, in which the city serves as a point of departure, and the first line of *Eclogue* 9, in which it becomes a destination, is indicative of the pull that the one location and its attendant set of generic codes exerts upon the other. The herdsman Alphesiboeus brings the first of these two poems to a close with a song in which an abandoned lover attempts to bring back Daphnis from the city with the power of her songs. This goal is kept constantly before us through the use of the refrain: 'Draw home from the city, my songs, draw Daphnis' (*ducite ab urbe domum, mea carmina, ducite Daphnin*). Reconstituted in generic terms, the singer's ambition is clear: to rescue the archetypal figure of the bucolic, Daphnis, from the attractions of the city and in so doing to rescue him from such things as heroic battles and the attentions of an (urbane) elegiac lover. The fear that Daphnis might be susceptible to the allure of either one of these two lifestyles is not entirely without basis, given that he is associated with both epic and elegiac modes in *Eclogue* 5, where he lays claim to a fame equal to that of Odysseus and where we are told that he 'loved' leisure and his fellow herdsman Menalcas alike.[9] Indeed, by no means does the tug-of-war between the countryside and the city that Alphesiboeus' song instigates in *Eclogue* 8 represent a straightforward contest between a clearly demarcated rustic form of poetry (namely, bucolic) on the one hand and equally delimited urban forms (namely, epic and elegiac) on the other. Rather, it too is a love song that takes on a clearly epic dimension when the singer likens herself to Circe, casts Daphnis (again) as Odysseus[10] and in so doing aligns those songs with Circe's spells, with the account of those spells in the *Odyssey*, with their reworking in *Idyll* 2 and with her own songs recorded here.[11] To this extent, then, the deployment of the two poles of 'city' and 'home' in this song serves to engage and acknowledge the relationship between bucolic poetry and its epic and elegiac counterparts even as it tries to reconfigure the structure of that relationship. It is, after all, the recognition that the

75

'home' of Daphnis and this kind of song is in the countryside that makes this first and foremost a bucolic piece; but the fact that the very conceit of a journey home is the primary plotline of the *Odyssey* means that other generic modes such as the epic are by no means left behind by this apparent 'return' of the bucolic figure of Daphnis from the city to the country.

While *Eclogue* 8 ends with the singer apparently satisfied that Daphnis has been successfully reclaimed from the city – 'Cease, Daphnis has come from the city, now cease, songs' (*parcite, ab urbe uenit, iam parcite carmina, Daphnis* 8.109) – *Eclogue* 9 begins with two herdsmen travelling in the opposite direction: 'Where are your feet taking you, Moeris?' Lycidas asks, 'Is it where the road leads, to the city?' (*Quo te, Moeri, pedes? an, quo uia ducit, in urbem?* 9.1). It has long been recognised that *Eclogue* 9 reverses the journey ἐκ πόλιος ('from the city') recorded in *Idyll* 7, as well as of the trip Socrates takes into the countryside with Phaedrus in Plato's dialogue of that name, which is itself sometimes cited as a key text in the pre-history of bucolic poetry.[12] But one might also suggest that both the trajectory and the nature of the bucolic genre as a whole are being demarcated here as well. For the precise terms in which Lycidas frames his opening question to Moeris – 'Where are your *feet* taking you, Moeris?' – draws attention to the metrical feet, the dactylic hexameter, which all of Virgil's and Theocritus' herdsmen share with martial epic. By asking 'where is your metre taking you?', that is, and by setting 'the city' as the likely answer at the end of the road and the line alike, the opening of *Eclogue* 9 casts that city, along with the epic itself, as the ultimate destination for this kind of poetry, as well as the place from which it sets out.[13]

The characterisation of bucolic poetry which this particular configuration of the city-country dynamic gestures towards is one that seems especially appropriate for such an overtly nomadic form. For it suggests that, in as far as it 'wanders away from' its origins in the city and martial epic, the bucolic is an aberrant form of epic poetry composed in dactylic hexameters. By constituting itself at one and the same time as a reversal of *Idyll* 7 and a journey towards the city, therefore, *Eclogue* 9 both re-engages and redirects the relationship between bucolic poetry and the *Odyssey* that is such a prominent feature of the *Idylls*. In particular, it takes the *Odyssey*'s primary plotline of a return home and renders it paradigmatic of individual eclogues, in which herdsmen order their flocks home,[14] and of the bucolic genre as a whole. The irony, of course, is that the city and the generic codes that go with it no longer look like home to the herdsmen of the *Eclogues* and it is notable that *Eclogue* 9 itself only follows Lycidas and Moeris as far as the midway point of their journey. There thus remains a fair degree of tension between these two branches of what is ostensibly the same family and it is in this tension that the distinctions between them are largely grounded.

One might recognise this configuration again, for instance, in the simile Moeris draws a few lines later when he remarks that 'our songs have as much power among the weapons of Mars, Lycidas, as they say Chaonian doves do when the eagle comes' (*sed carmina tantum / nostra ualent, Lycida, tela inter Martia quantum / Chaonias dicunt aquila ueniente columbas* 9.11-13).[15] The specific reference to 'our' songs (*carmina ... nostra*) indicates that the battle here is not simply between poetry on the one hand and armies on the other, but between two different types of poetry: the poetry of herdsmen (namely, the bucolic) and the poetry of war (namely, martial epic). The choice of two kinds of birds as the point of comparison, moreover, hovers between bucolic and martial epic modes of speech and in so doing sustains the analogy between them;[16] it identifies each of them, that is, as two species of the same kind. At the same time, the terms of this simile also differentiate between the single but powerful epic on the one hand and the more numerous but less overtly bellicose bucolics and, in the process, indicate that they are not yet able to share the same space.[17]

A similar story could also be told about the interchange between bucolic and that other urban mode we have been considering, the elegy. Moeris' characterisation of himself and his fellow herdsmen as *tristes* ('sad' 9.5) deploys a key term from elegy and as such casts those herdsmen, to some degree at least, as disappointed lovers.[18] This theme is then continued when, of the four fragments of song Lycidas and Moeris proceed to recite, the two that derive from Theocritus both constitute reconfigurations of stock elegiac situations: namely, the herdsman's failed attempts to entice Amaryllis out of her cave in *Idyll* 3 (*Ecl.* 9.23-5); and Polyphemus' equally futile pursuit of Galatea in *Idyll* 11 (*Ecl.* 9.39-43). For some readers *Eclogue* 10 resolves the relationship between bucolic and elegy once and for all by demonstrating how neither bucolic poetry nor the kind of settings it inhabits are able to contain the power of love.[19] At the very least, the relationship this poem bears towards *Idyll* 1 extends beyond Gallus' more immediate attempts to play the part of Theocritus' Daphnis and reanimates, partly through reversal, the rejection of the role of the elegiac lover which the archetypal figure of the bucolic there enacts.

All the same, poems such as *Eclogues* 8, 9 and 10 remain recognisably bucolic works, not least because they involve exchanges between herdsmen, because they constantly refer to other bucolic poems (including other eclogues) and because they continue to transfer epic and elegiac topoi to the countryside.[20] Much the same could also be said of *Eclogue* 1, a poem that, with Tityrus' remark exactly midway through the poem that 'here [in Rome] I saw that young man, Meliboeus' (*hic illum uidi iuuenem, Meliboee* 1.42), locates the city at its very centre. For not only does the exchange between the city and the country determine both who is allowed to stay on the land and who is told to depart – it is 'here' in the city, after all, that Tityrus receives his licence to 'feed the oxen as before' (*pascite ut ante boues*

1.45) – but the very configuration of this relationship as an exchange is what enables it to operate in recognisably bucolic terms. Indeed, when Tityrus earlier deployed a simile to describe the relationship between Rome and the town to which he and his fellow herdsmen are accustomed to drive their lambs, the structure of this simile is analogous to that of the doves and eagle conjured up by Moeris in *Eclogue* 9: it identifies a certain continuity between these two settlements, even as it seeks to clarify the differences between them. In this case too, that is – and as was also the case with the careful gradation of copses, tamarisks and woods at the start of *Eclogue* 4 – the simile serves to acknowledge an overarching 'family relationship' even as it asserts a difference of 'species' (1.19-24):[21]

> Vrbem quam dicunt Romam, Meliboee, putaui
> stultus ego huic nostrae similem, quo saepe solemus
> pastores ouium teneros depellere fetus.
> sic canibus catulos similis, sic matribus haedos
> noram, sic paruis componere magna solebam.
> uerum haec tantum alias inter caput extulit urbes
> quantum lenta solent inter uiburna cupressi.

The city which they call Rome, Meliboeus, I thought in my stupidity it was similar to this one of ours, where we shepherds are often accustomed to drive the tender young of sheep. So I knew puppies were similar to dogs, so kids to mothers, so was I accustomed to compare great things with small. But this city raises its head among other cities as much as cypresses are accustomed to do among pliant shrubs.

Shortly after he has produced this simile, Tityrus speaks openly of the transaction that takes place between his folds and the city. Even though he represents the rate of exchange as heavily in favour of the latter, both the terms and the conditions of this exchange mean that it nonetheless remains a recognisably bucolic way of doing business (1.33-5):

> quamuis multa meis exiret uictima saeptis,
> pinguis et ingratae premeretur caseus urbi,
> non umquam grauis aere domum mihi dextra redibat.

Even though many a victim was going out from my folds, and rich cheese was being pressed for the ungrateful city, never did my right hand return home heavy with bronze.

Trading and exchanging are common activities in the bucolic world, whether these take the form of a trade-off between an artefact (such as a cup or a pipe) and a song, an animal and a song, or one song and another. It is therefore still a recognisably bucolic process when this exchange involves bucolic tokens on the one hand and those from other literary codes on the other, even if the bucolic seems to lose out in the process. This, after

all, is the case both here in *Eclogue* 1, in the exchange between Tityrus'
agricultural goods and the city's bronze, and also in *Eclogue* 2, when
Corydon explicitly depicts his contest with Iollas as a contest of value
between urban and rustic goods (2.56-7):

> rusticus es, Corydon; nec munera curat Alexis,
> nec, si muneribus certes, concedat Iollas.

> You are rustic, Corydon; neither does Alexis care for your gifts, nor, if you
> contend with gifts, will Iollas concede.

As all these examples suggest, the exchange in which bucolic poetry
engages with other forms of poetry, like the concomitant exchange be-
tween the country and the city, may not always be a success, but it is
nonetheless a process that is fundamental to it and that consequently
helps define what bucolic poetry actually is.

In addition to this correlation between certain types of topography and
certain types of song, the positions the herdsmen of the *Eclogues* take up
within their surroundings similarly serve to bring into play a range of
generic relationships. When Gallus is first introduced to *Eclogue* 10 'lying
under a lonely cliff' (*sola sub rupe iacentem* 10.14), for example, he adopts
the posture of the archetypal bucolic figure, Daphnis, from *Idyll* 1 and of
disappointed elegiac poets from across the Greco-Roman literary tradition
alike.[22] Likewise, when Tityrus or any other herdsman sits down or re-
clines beneath a tree, his station is one that simultaneously signals the
beginning of song in bucolic poetry and the end of a journey in epic.[23]
Indeed, journeys themselves, such as those recounted in *Eclogue* 9 or, more
obliquely, *Eclogue* 1, recall not just other instances of bucolic sojourns of
the kind recorded in *Idyll* 7 or Plato's *Phaedrus*, but the more extensive
wanderings of epic heroes such as Odysseus.

To this degree, then, both the settings from which the songs of the
Eclogues issue forth and those they bring into being establish, reflect and
gesture towards the nexus of literary relations in which those songs are
constantly engaged and out of which they concurrently evolve. So far, we
have focused almost entirely on the generic relationships this correspon-
dence between poetry and topography sustains; in what follows, we shall
look at how poetry and topography give shape to one another more
generally and in particular at how the one repeatedly adopts a number of
the processes and qualities of the other.

Topography and poetry

The close affiliation between the topography and the poetry of the *Eclogues* is
indicated in the first place by the numerous occasions on which topographical
features participate in the production and transmission of bucolic song. One

might cite in this regard the mountains and cliffs that transmit news of Daphnis' apotheosis in *Eclogue* 5 (5.62-4), or the valleys which project to the stars the song the river Eurotas once heard Apollo sing and then ordered the bay trees to learn in *Eclogue* 6 (6.82-4). In addition, topographical markers sometimes serve the same kind of purpose in helping categorise the nature of a particular song or verse as the geographical epithets we looked at in the previous chapter. In *Eclogue* 5, for instance, Menalcas compares Mopsus' song to sleep to the weary on grass and to the quenching of thirst from a leaping stream of sweet water on a hot day (5.46-7), while Mopsus returns the compliment by suggesting that Menalcas' song has given him more pleasure than the whispering of the south wind, than shores struck by a wave and than streams hastening through rocky valleys (5.82-4). On numerous other occasions, meanwhile, topographical features share the same qualities as song. The epithet *argutus* ('clear-sounding'), for example, is attached both to an ilex tree (7.1) and to Corydon's flute (7.24) in *Eclogue* 7, to a grove at 8.22 and to swans at 9.36. Likewise 'to talk' (*loqui*) is a quality the narrator of *Eclogue* 6 (6.74) shares with the mountains, wild beasts and woods of *Eclogue* 5 (5.28), as well as with both the narrator (8.20) and the pine trees (8.22) of Damon's song in *Eclogue* 8. Another such correlation is brought into play by the programmatic epithet *agrestis* ('of the fields'), which Tityrus attributes to his reed in *Eclogue* 1 (1.10) and to his muse in *Eclogue* 6 (6.8). We shall return to this particular epithet and its companion *siluestris* ('of the woods') shortly, but first we should consider one of the other ways in which the topography of the *Eclogues* contributes to the production of its song: through the instruments that are fashioned out of the reeds and plants which flourish throughout.

In many instances, these instruments come equipped with a specific history and aetiology. In *Eclogue* 2, for example, Corydon first identifies the origins of the reed (the *calamus*) he hopes Alexis will play when he joins him in the woods (2.31-4):

> mecum una in siluis imitabere Pana canendo
> (Pan primum calamos cera coniungere pluris
> instituit, Pan curat ouis ouiumque magistros),
> nec te paeniteat calamo triuisse labellum.

Together with me in the woods you will imitate Pan in singing (Pan first instituted the practice of joining many reeds with wax, Pan cares for sheep and the masters of sheep), neither may it pain you to have rubbed your lip with a reed.

Then he reveals more about the history of his own pipe, or *fistula* (2.36-8):[24]

> est mihi disparibus septem compacta cicutis
> fistula, Damoetas dono mihi quam dedit olim,
> et dixit moriens: 'te nunc habet ista secundum'.

80

4. Topography

I have a pipe, fastened together with seven hemlock reeds of unequal length, which Damoetas once gave me as a gift, and, dying, said: 'now this pipe has you second'.

Since Damoetas is also the name of the herdsman who imitates Polyphemus in *Idyll* 6, the passing on of his pipe to Corydon here (who similarly imitates the Cyclops in this eclogue) signals a certain continuity between Virgilian and Theocritean bucolic. In these two passages, in other words, Corydon endows the instruments of the herdsmen's world with both a mythical origin in the god Pan and a recognisable history in literary tradition. Indeed, in the line that stands at the very centre of the *Eclogues*, the history of this particular pipe is taken further and is also aligned with yet another myth of origins. For at *Eclogue* 5.85, it becomes the pipe that Menalcas gives to Mopsus and which had taught him *Eclogue* 2 itself, as well as *Eclogue* 3: 'We shall endow you with this fragile hemlock reed' (*Hac te nos fragili donabimus ante cicuta*).[25] As we saw in Chapter 1, the specific designation of this instrument as a 'hemlock reed' (*cicuta*) here and in *Eclogue* 2 recalls its only other appearance in this sense in extant Latin poetry, in which Lucretius illustrates the origins of this kind of rustic poetry: 'And the whistling of the zephyr through the hollows of reeds first taught rustics to blow into hollow hemlock' (*et zephyri, caua per calamorum, sibila primum / agrestis docuere cauas inflare cicutas* DRN 5.1382-3). In the *Eclogues* too, that is, bucolic progression is figured in terms of natural history and literary history alike.

Indeed, this interchange of terms, properties and processes between poetry and nature is such that there is often an elision between the representation of space in the text and the space of the text. This manifests itself most obviously through the alignment between the creation of the world and the creation of poetry that takes place in the song of Silenus in *Eclogue* 6, in which Silenus not only sings about the creation of the world but actively sings that world into existence,[26] and in *Eclogue* 9, when Lycidas imagines a world deprived of the singer Menalcas and asks 'Who would sing the Nymphs? Who would sprinkle the ground with flowering herbs or introduce springs with green shade?' (*quis caneret Nymphas? quis humum florentibus herbis / spargeret aut uiridi fontis induceret umbra?* 9.19-20). What is more, it is also in evidence on those occasions when the people of the *Eclogues* carve out their poems upon the bark of trees, as Mopsus has already done in *Eclogue* 5 or as Gallus imagines himself doing in *Eclogue* 10.[27] In the proem to *Eclogue* 6, moreover, an explicit parallel is drawn between tamarisks and groves on the one hand and the page on which this particular poem is written on the other (6.9-12):

> si quis tamen haec quoque, si quis
> captus amore leget, te nostrae, Vare, myricae,
> te nemus omne canet; nec Phoebo gratior ulla est
> quam sibi quae Vari praescripsit pagina nomen.

81

Nonetheless, if anyone will read these things too, if anyone will read them captured with love, of you our tamarisks, Varus, of you the whole grove will sing; neither is there any page more pleasing to Phoebus than one which has written the name of Varus at its top.

The effects of this alignment between the depiction of topography in the text and what might be called the topography of the text will be discussed further in the two chapters to come. What one might highlight in the meantime is the extent to which this alignment of groves and tamarisks on the one hand and a page of text on the other engages both natural and literary space alike in the processes of bucolic competition. Just as herdsmen set their songs against one another, that is, so too does this association establish an antagonistic relationship between the places with which those (and other) songs are associated.[28] What is more, this alignment applies not only to competition between poems, but competition within poems as well. By providing not just the context for bucolic song but some of its content too, in other words, it turns arguments about poetry into arguments about land, and vice versa. In what follows, we shall look at how these competitive topographies are identified and brought into play in relation to *Eclogue* 1 in particular.

Eclogue 1: topographies of poetry

Eclogue 1 begins with one herdsmen, Meliboeus, who is heading off into exile, hailing another, Tityrus, who is somehow staying put (1.1-5):

> Tityre, tu patulae recubans sub tegmine fagi
> siluestrem tenui musam meditaris auena;
> nos patriae finis et dulcia linquimus arua.
> nos patriam fugimus; tu, Tityre, lentus in umbra
> formosam resonare doces Amaryllida siluas.

> Tityrus, you, reclining under the cover of the wide-spreading beech, contemplate the woodland muse on your slender oat; we are leaving the boundaries of the fatherland and the sweet fields. We are fleeing the fatherland; you, Tityrus, at ease in the shade are teaching the woods to re-echo beautiful Amaryllis.

It has been well remarked that this opening scene of a herdsman reclining beneath a tree constitutes the 'archetypal image of the *Idylls*'.[29] Even the very herdsman who here adopts this pose, Tityrus, is a figure from those *Idylls*, as is the woman whose name he teaches the woods to re-echo, Amaryllis.[30] Indeed, in these particular lines at least, the name 'Amaryllis' is constituted more by the sound of its syllables than by an actual person. For apart from anything else, her epithet *formosam* ('beautiful') translates the apostrophe she receives on both her appearances in the *Idylls*, ὦ χαρίεσσ' Ἀμαρυλλί (*Id.* 3.6 and 4.38); as such, it suggests that, even as he sings her name to them, Tityrus also teaches the woods some version of *Idyll* 4 and, more likely, *Idyll* 3.[31] What we therefore find at the outset of the *Eclogues* is a character from Theocritus (Tityrus), who still adopts a Theocritean pose (that of reclining beneath a tree) and who continues to sing a Theocritean song (in this case, the *Amaryllis*).

The numerous reminiscences of Theocritus in these lines, moreover, are figured precisely as echoes. The echoic nature of the environment within which Meliboeus encounters Tityrus is signalled most overtly by the verb *resonare*, which has the woods 're-echo' Tityrus' song even as that song itself re-echoes the *Idylls*. The very sound of the words in this passage likewise participates in this play of echoes. As Richard Hunter remarks, 'Virgil alludes to the opening of *Idyll* 1 in the sound of v. 1, which "mimics" both the sound of the panpipes and the sound of *Idyll* 1.1'.[32] To this one might add that, just as Thyrsis there equates the sound of the goatherd's pipe with the sound of the pine tree's whisper, so here is the sound of Tityrus' song, *Amaryllida*, quite literally reflected and repeated in the sound of the woods, the *siluas* (an effect that is heightened still further by the emphasis placed on these two syllables by the rhythm of the line).

The ability of the woods to act in this way – and, in fact, the fundamental role this ability plays in the evolution of the bucolic genre itself – is signalled by yet another echo that is grounded in both poetry and nature alike: the characterisation of this whole aesthetic effect as the work of the *siluestris musa*, or 'woodland muse'. This phrase derives directly from a passage in the *De Rerum Natura*, in which Lucretius explains how the echoing of voices in a landscape gives rise to a belief in the music of Pan (4.577-89):

> sex etiam aut septem loca uidi reddere uoces,
> unam cum iaceres: ita colles collibus ipsi
> uerba repulsantes iterabant docta referri.
> haec loca capripedes satyros nymphasque tenere   580
> finitimi fingunt et faunos esse loquuntur
> quorum noctiuago strepitu ludoque iocanti
> adfirmant uulgo taciturna silentia rumpi
> chordarumque sonos fieri dulcisque querelas,
> tibia quas fundit digitis pulsata canentum,   585
> et genus agricolum late sentiscere, cum Pan
> pinea semiferi capitis uelamina quassans
> unco saepe labro calamos percurrit hiantis,
> fistula *siluestrem* ne cesset fundere *musam*.

I have seen places give back six, even, or seven voices, when you threw one: in this way, hills upon hills were driving back and iterating the words they had been taught to reflect. The neighbouring peoples assume that goat-footed satyrs and nymphs occupy these places and they say there are fauns by whose night-roaming clamour and playful games they assert that the quiet silences are openly ruptured and that the sounds of strings and sweet complaints come into being, which the pipe struck by the fingers of singers pours forth, and far and wide the rural race begins to notice them, when Pan shaking the pine-coverings of his half-wild head often passes quickly over the gaping reeds with his lip curved, so that the pipe should not cease to pour forth the *woodland muse.*

This account of the woodland muse includes a number of features that recur throughout the *Eclogues*. In addition to the crucial involvement of echo itself, we also find some of the inhabitants of Virgil's bucolic world, such as satyrs, nymphs and Pan himself, various of their instruments[33] and music that is characterised as a 'witty game' (*ludoque iocanti* 582), involving 'sweet complaints' (*dulcisque querelas* 584). What is more, *Eclogue* 1's remarkable image of Tityrus 'teaching' the woods to re-echo beautiful Amaryllis is to be found here as well, with the notion that the hills throw back the sounds they have been 'taught' to repeat. It is far from insignificant, too, that this process of echo is associated with the woodland muse in particular, since the word for woods in Latin, *silua*, like its Greek counterpart ὕλη, was often employed in Latin literature to denote the literary tradition as a whole.[34]

Through its ability to instigate and sustain this series of echoes, therefore, the topography Tityrus inhabits at the very beginning of *Eclogue* 1 connects him both with the natural origins of the form (as described in Lucretius) and with its origins in literary history (as constituted by the opening lines of *Idyll* 1).[35] At the same time, these echoes are not entirely exact and this fact both signals and reflects a feature of these poems that is already indicated in lines 3-4 and that becomes ever more apparent as the eclogue proceeds: that both the poetic and the geopolitical world has changed and so bucolic poetry cannot be the same in the *Eclogues* as it was in the *Idylls*. The figure of Tityrus, for a start, has risen above his status in Theocritus and has taken on the role of those he either served or sang about in the *Idylls*. Thus, in contrast with *Idyll* 3, in which he is called upon to look after the goats while the narrator goes off to woo Amaryllis, by the start of *Eclogue* 1 he is singing the *Amaryllis* himself.[36] What is more, when it transpires later in the eclogue that Tityrus has actually won the girl for himself (1.30-9), one might suggest that he has thereby capped the singer of *Idyll* 3 (who closes with an apparent admission of failure) and in so doing has effectively defeated him in song.[37] Likewise, whereas in *Idyll* 7 Tityrus offers to tend Comatas' goats as the latter reclines beneath a tree and sings, in *Eclogue* 1 it is Tityrus himself who now sits beneath a tree and sings.[38] In both instances, that is, the masters from whom Tityrus has since won his freedom are as much his literary models as they are any putative farmer or slave owner.

A further example of how echo structures the relationship between the opening scene of *Eclogue* 1 and comparable settings in the literary tradition comes in the form of the tree under which Tityrus reclines: the *fagus* or 'beech'. This is by no means an established or common tree in Greek and Latin poetry prior to this point,[39] but it nonetheless appears in five of the book's ten eclogues and, as such, serves as a distinctive marker of these poems.[40] Beech trees are unknown to the *Idylls* and to this extent they serve as one of the markers of the changes that have taken place between the two collections. At the same time, the name of this tree, *fagus*, still signals a connection with the *Idylls* to the extent that it echoes the Greek name of a different kind of tree that is found in those poems, the φηγός or 'oak'.[41] Indeed, the immediate context of *Eclogue* 1, in which Meliboeus is depicted making his way into exile, brings one such mention of this tree in the *Idylls* in particular to mind. For in *Idyll* 12, the narrator informs his beloved that 'I hasten towards you as a wayfarer hastens to the shady oak when the sun is scorching' (σκιερὴν δ᾽ ὑπὸ φηγὸν / ἠελίου φρύγοντος ὁδοιπόρος ἔδραμον ὥς τις *Id.* 12.8-9). This change from Theocritus' oak tree to Virgil's beech is due not only to the chance coincidence of the sound of the words φηγός and *fagus*, but also to the changing nature of the ground this kind of poetry must now inhabit. For the tree that represents a more literal translation of the Greek φηγός, the Latin *quercus*, also makes an appearance in this eclogue, where its striking by lightning signals this change from an earlier cultural order. Meliboeus recalls this event in the following terms (1.16-17):

> saepe malum hoc nobis, si mens non laeua fuisset,
> de caelo tactas memini praedicere quercus.

I remember that the oaks struck from the sky often predicted this evil to us, if only I had been in my right mind.

This couplet introduces the oak tree to the *Eclogues* in a role it will uphold throughout the book: as a site of prophecy.[42] More immediately, though, it indicates that this tree no longer provides the same kind of shelter as that anticipated by the singer in *Idyll* 12 or even of the kind now offered by the *fagus* in *Eclogue* 1. The first occurrence in the book of the verb *memini* ('I remember') promotes the sense that this lightning bolt strikes right to the heart of bucolic poetry's 'memory' of reclining under oaks. At the same time, the bolt is itself also a product of that memory. For the axiom which this message from above most obviously recalls is Callimachus' programmatic claim that 'it is not for me to thunder, but for Zeus' (βροντᾶν οὐκ ἐμόν, ἀλλὰ Διός *Aetia* fr. 1.20).[43] Since this claim is usually understood to express a desire to compose small, intricate works rather than the greater fury of martial epic, the contrast in the eclogue between the shelter provided by the *fagus* on the one hand and the destruction by lightning of the *quercus* on the other indicates that the oak tree no longer provides any shelter from the incursion upon the bucolic bower of the figures and forms of martial epic. As for the beech, which for the time being at least continues to provide a haven for the recumbent singer, it is noteworthy that the word denoting the protection it provides, *tegmen*, returns in the *Aeneid* to signify the various parts of a soldier's armour, including a cap or helmet (*Aen.* 7.689, 742), a shield (*Aen.* 10.887) or the armour (*Aen.* 9.518) as a whole.[44] The military connotations of this particular haven obviously relate to the sanction to remain in it that it subsequently emerges Tityrus has received from Rome, yet it also relates to the militaristic and politicised engagement with the literary tradition that is first introduced in these lines and that continues throughout the book. By the time we get to *Eclogue* 9, of course, and to Lycidas' reference to 'the old beech trees, their peaks now broken' (*ueteres, iam fracta cacumina, fagos* 9.9), even these trees would seem to have been unable to provide sufficient shelter for the herdsmen, and this in itself is a sign that the natural world in the *Eclogues* continues to change and evolve. But to stay with *Eclogue* 1, its division of Theocritus' Greek φηγός into the Latin *quercus* and *fagus* illustrates how this poem explores different poetic issues and maps itself in relation to various poetic positions in largely topographical terms. It is therefore not surprising that, in his reply to Meliboeus, Tityrus does not entirely accept his companion's description either of his song or of the grounds upon which he reclines and sings, but he instead corrects several aspects of both (1.6-10):

> O Meliboee, deus nobis haec otia fecit.
> namque erit ille mihi semper deus, illius aram
> saepe tener nostris ab ouilibus imbuet agnus.
> ille meas errare boues, ut cernis, et ipsum
> ludere quae uellem calamo permisit agresti.

> O Meliboeus, a god has created this leisure for us. For he will always be a god to me, and a tender lamb from our pens will often drench his altar. He permitted my cows to roam, as you see, and me myself to play what I wish on the reed of the fields.

In the first place, Tityrus drops the rather unusual 'oat' (*auena*) Meliboeus had bestowed upon him, and takes up the more traditional type of 'reed', the *calamus*, instead.[45] There may well be a degree of erudition and wit in Meliboeus' original attribution and Tityrus' response alike, because Tityrus' name would itself seem to constitute a gloss on the bucolic reed (κάλαμος).[46] While Meliboeus gestures towards this 'etymology' by framing the first distich with the words *Tityre* and *auena*, however, Tityrus himself goes one better by returning the Greek κάλαμος to its more familiar (and literal) translation *calamus*. Another 'correction' Tityrus makes to Meliboeus' opening characterisation involves the topographical content and context of his song. For whereas Meliboeus categorises Tityrus' song as the 'muse of the woods', the *siluestris musa*, Tityrus makes no mention of woods at all, but instead calls the instrument upon which he plays 'the reed of the fields', the *calamo ... agresti*. Indeed, when Tityrus returns as the narrator of *Eclogue* 6, he similarly replaces Meliboeus' *siluestris* 'you contemplate the woodland muse on your slender oat' (*siluestrem tenui musam meditaris auena* 1.2) with the epithet *agrestis* 'I shall contemplate the muse of the fields on my slender reed' (*agrestem tenui meditabor harundine musam* 6.8). Meliboeus, though, finds a music grounded in the fields hard to believe (1.11-13):

> Non equidem inuideo, miror magis: undique totis
> usque adeo turbatur agris. en ipse capellas
> protinus aeger ago; hanc etiam uix, Tityre, duco.

> I for my part do not look askance at you, rather I am amazed: from every side and all the way there is disturbance in all the fields. Look! I myself in sickness lead my goats forward; this one, Tityrus, I can scarcely lead.

Following immediately after Tityrus' reference to his 'reed of the fields' (*agrestis calamus*), Meliboeus' amazement expresses his astonishment that anyone can play upon such an instrument when the fields themselves (the *agri*) are everywhere in confusion. Indeed, the manner in which his self-description, *aeger ago* ('I lead in sickness'), picks up upon and re-echoes the very word for fields, *agri*,[47] indicates the close identification he assumes between a herdsman, his songs[48] and his lands. The relationship between these woods and these fields evidently requires a further look.

Woods and fields: the *siluestris musa* and the *agrestis musa*

As we have just seen, Tityrus ignores Meliboeus' characterisation of his song as a woodland piece that is constituted first and foremost by a sequence of echoes. As far as he is concerned, his reed belongs to the fields and a god is to thank for letting him play it.[49] In the course of the eclogue, moreover, it becomes increasingly evident that these two herdsmen look upon the physical world in widely divergent ways. This culminates above all in the contrasting beliefs they hold about the current natural order. For Tityrus, the prospect of a Parthian in exile drinking from the Arar and of Germany moving in the opposite direction to drink from the Tigris is as unlikely as stags taking to the air and fish abandoning the seas for dry land (1.59-63); for Meliboeus, on the other hand, this kind of border crossing promises to become an imminent reality (1.64-6). It would be a mistake, however, to deduce from this that the kinds of poetry these two herdsmen ascribe to the fields and the woods respectively are mutually exclusive. After all, Meliboeus' opening vignette locates Theocritus in the fields as well as the echoing woods. When he remarks of his own situation that 'we are leaving the boundaries of the fatherland and the sweet fields' (*nos patriae finis et dulcia linquimus arua* 1.3), both the noun *patria* ('fatherland') and the adjective *dulcia* ('sweet') characterise the place he is leaving behind as (among other texts) the *Idylls*. There was, after all, a tradition in Latin poetry of characterising literary succession in terms of fathers and sons, and the designation of the *Idylls* as a fatherland simply reconfigures this practice in spatial terms.[50] The description of the fields as 'sweet' similarly recasts the *Idylls* as a distinctive and clearly demarcated feature of the local topography, since 'sweetness' is a familiar attribute of idyllic song and the idyllic landscape alike, not least in the passage with which the *Idylls* begin and to which we have already seen the opening of the *Eclogues* alludes.

It is also by no means the case that the *Eclogues* gradually distance themselves from the *siluestris musa* and adopt the *agrestis musa* in its place.[51] Instead, the woods continue to recur in every eclogue bar the ninth and continue to fulfil an important role in sustaining such key modalities as responsion and echo.[52] Even the passage in *Eclogue* 6 in which the notion of the *agrestis musa* is explicitly introduced is not only preceded by an account of how Tityrus' muse, Thalea, 'first deigned to play with Syracusan verse and neither did she blush to inhabit the woods' (*Prima Syracosio dignata est ludere uersu / nostra neque erubuit siluas habitare Thalea* 6.1-2), but it is also succeeded by the promise that 'if anyone also were to read these things, if anyone were to read them captured with love, of you our tamarisks, Varus, of you the whole grove will sing' (*si quis tamen haec quoque, si quis / captus amore leget, te nostrae, Vare, myricae, / te nemus omne canet* 6.9-11). The 'muse of the fields' Tityrus here undertakes to contemplate, in other words, sets both its beginnings and its ends in the woods.

Indeed, the clear affiliation between the woodland muse and the muse of the fields is already evident in the poem in which these categories make their first appearance in Latin verse, the *De Rerum Natura*. As is also the case in the *Eclogues*, the *siluestris musa* and the *agrestis musa* each appear on only one occasion in Lucretius and the passages in which they do so closely resemble one another.[53] We have already seen how Lucretius describes the woodland muse; here is the account he gives of the muse of the fields (*DRN* 5.1379-98):

> At liquidas auium uoces imitarier ore
> ante fuit multo quam leuia carmina cantu   1380
> concelebrare homines possent aurisque iuuare.
> et zephyri, caua per calamorum, sibila primum
> agrestis docuere cauas inflare cicutas.
> inde minutatim dulcis didicere querelas,
> tibia quas fundit digitis pulsata canentum,   1385
> auia per nemora ac siluas saltusque reperta,
> per loca pastorum deserta atque otia dia.
> haec animos ollis mulcebant atque iuuabant   1390
> cum satiate cibi; nam tum sunt omnia cordi.
> saepe itaque inter se prostrati in gramine molli

propter aquae riuum sub ramis arboris altae
non magnis opibus iucunde corpora habebant,
praesertim cum tempestas ridebat et anni   1395
tempora pingebant uiridantis floribus herbas.
tum ioca, tum sermo, tum dulces esse cachinni
consuerant. *agrestis* enim tum *musa* uigebat.

But imitating the liquid voices of birds with the mouth came long before men
were able to come together to produce smooth songs with singing and to
please the ears. And the whistling of the zephyr through the hollows of reeds
first taught rustics to blow into hollow hemlock. Then, little by little, they
learnt sweet complaints, which the pipe struck by the fingers of singers pours
forth, heard through the pathless groves and the woods and the passes,
through the deserted places of shepherds and the divine tranquillity. These
things used to soothe them and give them pleasure once they were sated with
food; for then everything is enjoyable. Often in this way, stretched out in
company on the soft grass beside a stream of water under the branches of a
tall tree, they refreshed their bodies pleasantly without great expense,
especially when the weather was smiling on them and the seasons of the year
were painting the greening grasses with flowers. Then jokes, then conversa-
tion, then sweet laughter was customary. For then the *muse of the fields* was
full of vigour.

Line 1386 in particular (*auia per nemora ac siluas saltusque reperta*)
makes it abundantly clear that woods, groves and passes participate in the
sounds of the *agrestis musa* and are by no means excluded from it. Indeed,
as this passage proceeds, it becomes increasingly obvious that there are a
number of qualities these two types of song actively share: both are capable
of taking the form of 'sweet complaints';[54] the musical technique that
produces the sylvan and the rustic muse alike is so close that the same line
is used to describe that technique in both instances;[55] and the posture
Lucretius' early musicians assume as they make their agrarian music
beneath the branches of a tall tree is very much the posture Meliboeus has
Tityrus adopt as he depicts him contemplating the sylvan muse.

Given, then, that there are so many parallels between these two types
of song in the *De Rerum Natura* and given that both the woods and the
fields continue to act as important sites for poetry throughout the rest of
the *Eclogues*, why in the opening lines of *Eclogue* 1 should Tityrus appear
to ignore the sylvan label Meliboeus applies to his verse and seek to align
it with the fields instead? The answer lies in part with the different
function Lucretius ascribes to his accounts of these two types of song and
to the different temporal dimensions they each acquire as a result. For
while the *siluestris musa* serves in the *De Rerum Natura* to account for an
ongoing phenomenon of nature, namely echo, and is to this degree a-tem-
poral, the *agrestis musa* is associated with the early development of
human society and culture and is to this extent aligned with the progress
of history. These two differing temporalities are likewise also in evidence

in *Eclogue* 1. For his part, Meliboeus follows up his attribution of the *siluestris musa* to Tityrus by consistently characterising his fellow herdsman and his surroundings in distinctly Theocritean terms and by emphasising the things he will continue to enjoy. In so doing, and through the contrast this forms with his own very present plight, he places Tityrus outside of time and history. Tityrus himself, by contrast, tells of his recent journey to Rome and uses such contemporary, 'prosaic' words as *peculium* ('money or property owned by a slave')[56] to characterise his situation in present-day, Roman terms. Not the least of the indications he gives that his own song is very much grounded in contemporary reality and not, as Meliboeus would have it, in a timeless literary paradigm lies in his assertion that the instrument upon which he plays is not an oat that addresses itself to the woods, but a 'reed of the fields', a *calamus agrestis*, instead.

The terms of this exchange between Tityrus and Meliboeus make it clear that the tension between a poetry that stands outside history and one that is implicated in it is expressed precisely through reference to these two Lucretian categories of woods and fields. We shall return to the phenomenon of echo and to the kind of temporality this instils in literary relations in the final chapter of this book. For what remains of this, we shall continue to take the measure of these fields, since the demarcation and distribution of land constitutes more than just a historical principle in the *Eclogues*: it is also a process that replicates the acts of redefinition and redistribution which these poems enact upon the various elements of the literary tradition.

Land surveys

It has long been recognised that the land confiscations which took place after the Battle of Philippi in 42 BC form an important part of the historical backdrop to *Eclogues* 1 and 9.[57] It has less often been noted, however, how this process of land confiscation also reflects and enacts in more concrete terms the rules of bucolic exchange.[58] Indeed, in the *Eclogues* these two activities operate more or less as mirror images, or extensions, of one another. The relationship between them is grounded in the first place in the equation between land and song we have been observing throughout. In *Eclogue* 1, for instance, Meliboeus' fear that 'I shall sing no songs' (*carmina nulla canam* 1.77) is explicitly connected with his imminent departure from his 'fatherland' (*patria*) and, with it, from the bucolic literary tradition to which he thereby claims to have been heir. There are a number of other correspondences between the process of land confiscation and the rules of bucolic song as well. When Moeris describes the plight of those who have lost their land in *Eclogue* 9, for example, it is notable that the term he uses to characterise them, 'conquered' (*uicti*), serves on every other occasion in which it appears in the *Eclogues* to describe someone who has been 'conquered' in song.[59] Likewise, when Moeris in that same eclogue refers to the legal steps he was taking to have his land restored to him, the language of litigation he employs ('but if a crow on my left hand side had not warned me from a hollow ilex to cut off in some way or other my new <u>lawsuits</u> ...' *quod nisi me quacumque nouas incidere <u>lites</u> / ante sinistra caua monuisset ab ilice cornix* 9.14-15) parallels the language to which Palaemon resorts when he admits he is unable to resolve the contest between the two singers, Menalcas and Damoetas, in *Eclogue* 3: 'We are not able to settle the <u>suits</u> between you' (*Non nostrum inter uos tantas componere <u>lites</u>* 3.108).

To this extent, the equation the *Eclogues* draw between the land confiscations on the one hand and the traditions of bucolic song competitions on the other extends, but by no means breaks away from, one of the most common features of pre-Virgilian bucolic: the convention that, whenever a herdsman loses such a contest, he should hand over a prize to the victor, which as often as not is an animal from his flock. Thus, when Moeris in *Eclogue* 9 tells Lycidas about the new owner of his plot, the *possessor agelli*, and remarks that (9.5-6)

> nunc uicti, tristes, quoniam fors omnia uersat,
> hos illi (quod nec uertat bene) mittimus haedos.

> now, conquered and sad, since chance overturns everything, we are sending these kids to him (and may it not turn out well).

he is acting out in concrete terms his defeat as a herdsman and a singer alike. Indeed, the simile he then uses to liken the dispute between them to a fight between Chaonian doves and the eagle of Mars further characterises his current predicament as analogous to defeat in a song contest: his opponent does not just have the might of Rome on his side, he also has the more powerful metaphors and poetic modes that go with such a display of Roman military force.

Even as the losses Virgil's herdsmen suffer as a result of the land confiscations reflect and re-enact the losses they might suffer as singers, moreover, in *Eclogue* 1 at least the right to remain on the land is conversely characterised as a successful bucolic exchange. When Tityrus there describes the moment he was given sanction to continue to herd his cattle and play his pipe, he relates the story as if it were but another instance of bucolic poetry's favoured mode of call and response (1.44-5):[60]

> hic mihi responsum primus dedit ille petenti:
> 'pascite ut ante boues, pueri; summittite tauros'.

> Here, he first gave a response to my petition: 'feed the oxen as before, boys; rear bulls'.

By configuring the relationship between the herdsman Tityrus and the 'young man' (*iuuenis*) in Rome in this way, the instruction to carry on as before accordingly functions as more than just an edict about land and the herdsman's life. Indeed, precisely through its characterisation as a 're-sponse', this injunction itself participates in – and perpetuates – the very same poetic traditions it here enjoins these herdsmen to continue.

One of the consequences of this close connection between the processes of land confiscation and the conventions of bucolic exchange is that both the struggle for supremacy in bucolic song and the struggle for supremacy over bucolic ground become in effect struggles to achieve ownership of – or, at least, residence in – the bucolic tradition. One sees this, for instance, in the 'small plot of land' (*agellus*) Moeris and others have been ordered to cede to another in *Eclogue* 9; one sees it in the discussion about the ownership of the flock with which *Eclogue* 3 begins and which clearly renders the 'handing over' of livestock analogous to the 'handing down' of a pipe;[61] and one sees it, above all, in *Eclogue* 1, where Meliboeus is to lose his land to someone he considers a 'soldier' and 'barbarian' (*miles ... barbarus* 1.70-1). There has been a tendency to see this process of land confiscation as in some way alien to and therefore disruptive of the bucolic way of life and of bucolic poetry in particular. As we have already seen, however, there are too many parallels between the effects of these confiscations and the conventions of bucolic poetry for the former to be entirely antithetical to the other. What is more, a closer look at the precise delineation of the ground that is being ceded in these poems suggests that many of those who are defeated here, Moeris and Meliboeus among them, have themselves been at one stage or other complicit in this process.

The very first word Meliboeus uses to describe the land he is leaving behind, *patria*, for example, simultaneously creates a bucolic genealogy for that land whilst also distinguishing it from anything that has come before. As was mentioned earlier, the designation of this ground as a 'fatherland' plays upon the familiar Roman construction of literary history as a succes-sion of fathers and sons, and yet at no stage do the *Idylls* themselves, the most obvious constituents of that fatherland, describe the settings they inhabit in anything like this way.[62] Indeed, the sense that Meliboeus is throughout the eclogue realigning and redefining certain pre-existing notions of the parameters of bucolic space even as he characterises that space as something known, familiar and native is encouraged by the fact that when he later uses the adjective *patrius* (connoting 'ancestral' or 'of the fatherland'), it comes attached, as does *patria* here, to the word for boundaries: *fines*.[63] The recognition of boundaries is an important compo-nent of Meliboeus' account of the bucolic locale, as well as a feature of other eclogues too.[64] So when he comes to describe the bliss Tityrus will enjoy as he remains in his familiar environment and continues to listen to Theocritean song, which is signalled here by the presence of Hyblaean bees, Meliboeus is careful to keep Tityrus' flock apart from his neighbour's

4. Topography

and to place that song and those bees within earshot, but on the other side
of the hedge (1.46-58):

Fortunate senex, ergo tua rura manebunt
et tibi magna satis, quamuis lapis omnia nudus
limosoque palus obducat pascua iunco:
non insueta grauis temptabunt pabula fetas,
nec mala uicini pecoris contagia laedent.   50
fortunate senex, hic inter flumina nota
et fontis sacros frigus captabis opacum;
hinc tibi, quae semper, uicino ab limite saepes
Hyblaeis apibus florem depasta salicti
saepe leui somnum suadebit inire susurro;   55
hinc alta sub rupe canet frondator ad auras,
nec tamen interea raucae, tua cura, palumbes
nec gemere aëria cessabit turtur ab ulmo.

Fortunate old man, therefore your fields will remain and they are enough for
you, even though naked stone and swamp blocks all the pastures with muddy
rush: no unaccustomed food will tempt your pregnant ewes nor will an evil
contagion from a neighbouring flock harm them. Fortunate old man, here among
known streams and holy springs you will seek shady cool; from here, as always,
from the neighbouring boundary a hedge of willows, its flower fed upon by
Hyblaean bees, will often persuade you to enter into sleep with its gentle
whispering. From here under a high cliff the leaf stripper will sing to the breezes,
nor, meanwhile, will raucous wood pigeons, your care, nor will the turtle dove
cease to groan from a lofty elm.

The 'gentle whispering' of line 55, with its repeated 's' sounds (especially
in the onomatopoeic *susurro*) recalls first and foremost the whispering, the
ψιθύρισμα, of the very first line of *Idyll* 1. Yet the pervasive sense of
continuity that prevails throughout, in which Tityrus himself is an old
man, reaching back in time (possibly as far back as *Idylls* 3 and 7), in which
the streams are already known, no new contagions are allowed to intrude
and in which the sounds of music and nature are both repetitive (*saepe*
'often') and timeless (*hinc tibi, quae semper* 'from here, as always ...'),
suggests that the *Idylls* as a whole are very much in mind. At the same
time, it is clear that this sense of continuity is itself expressed and enabled
through a careful restructuring and re-demarcation of Tityrus' immediate
locale: he can hear the leaf stripper and the gentle whispering of the
willows with their Hyblaean bees, but these are the sounds of neighbours,
not compatriots. Indeed, to return to the designation of *patria* that Meli-
boeus earlier assigned his notion of bucolic ground, while one might
further argue that the existence of boundaries (*limites* 53) in this passage
evolves directly from the muddy (*limosus* 48) nature of the ground that
remains to Tityrus,[65] it is at the very least the case that the redrawing of
the literary map which the advent of the *Eclogues* here enacts, introduces
and requires is but a manifestation in aesthetic terms of the redrawing of

93

the geopolitical map which their other fatherland, Rome, similarly imposed upon the rest of the world.

In order to retrace the contours of this new cartography more closely, we need to move beyond our initial survey of such natural features as mountains, trees, cliffs, woods and meadows and look more carefully at how the *Eclogues* actively cultivate these inherited localities. There is, after all, much more to this topography than unshorn mountains, thicket-ridden cliffs, cool caves, wild woods, untilled valleys and meadows fit only for pasture. Instead, and as is fitting for a collection of poems that themselves consistently rework sophisticated pieces from the literary tradition, much of the ground of the *Eclogues* has itself already evidently been 'worked' and subjected to some kind of order. Indeed, despite the fact that *Eclogue* 4 offers an evocative vision of a world in which the earth will pour forth wandering ivy, baccar, colocasia and acanthus without any human cultivation (4.18-20) and in which 'the red berry will hang from uncultivated briars' (*incultisque rubens pendebit sentibus uua* 4.29), the influence of agriculture is evident in that poem too, just as it is in every other.[66] Thus, farmers and farm-hands such as leaf strippers, reapers, ploughmen and vineyard workers appear throughout the collection[67] and the presence in the background of such farm buildings as villas, stalls, folds and pens is significant too, since it suggests that the elements of the bucolic tradition enter the *Eclogues* in an orderly fashion, even if those elements then become dispersed and cannot always return home again once eclogue song (which always takes place out of doors) has come to an end.[68] The informing image for this equation between poetic order and the ordering of one's flocks comes from the epigram Artemidorus of Tarsus placed at the start of his anthology of bucolic poetry in the first half of the first century BC, in which he claims that (*Anth. Pal.* 9.205):

Βουκολικαὶ Μοῖσαι σποράδες ποκά, νῦν δ᾽ ἅμα πᾶσαι
ἐντὶ μιᾶς μάνδρας, ἐντὶ μιᾶς ἀγέλας.

The Bucolic Muses were once scattered, but now all are together within one fold, within one flock.

By the simple fact of their existence alone, the *Eclogues* set these muses out to pasture once again and witness them scatter both far and wide. Nonetheless, their repeated use of the home, the fold, the pen or the stable as the place from which their sheep, cows and goats issue and to which they ought to return once the time for herding and singing is over actively adopts Artemidorus' image for the orderly arrangement of the bucolic tradition. For the most part, the focus of the herdsmen of the *Eclogues* is in getting their flocks back home again.[69] This is hardly surprising given that in every one of these poems the herdsmen and their animals are already out to pasture and that the return of these animals to the farm-stead signals both the successful completion of bucolic verse and the restoration of order in the bucolic tradition. A prime example of this comes at the close of *Eclogue* 6, where the appearance of Vesper compels them 'to drive the sheep to the stables and to make a note of their number' (*cogere donec ouis stabulis numerumque referre / iussit* 6.85-6), since this very deed repeats the act of 'recording' the 'numbers' of poetry that the song of Silenus, with its catalogue of poetic themes, has only just performed.[70] But perhaps the most significant instance comes in the very last line of the book, where the narrator, who has only just finished weaving his emblematic basket of hibiscus, orders his flocks home: 'go home, replete she-goats, go, Hesperus comes' (*ite domum saturae, uenit Hesperus, ite capellae* 10.77). This injunction, which, as we have already seen, recalls Meliboeus' ironic instruction to his own flock in *Eclogue* 1, leaves it in the balance whether bucolic order has in practice been restored and, if it has, whether it is quite the same order as that which the *Eclogues* inherited at the very start.

Such things as stalls and folds have their place in the *Idylls* as well, but they do not there serve as emblems of bucolic order or closure to anything like the same degree.[71] Indeed, one might suggest that the recurring presence of these structures in the *Eclogues* points not only to the concern these poems express for a return to bucolic order but to the possibility that they have themselves helped create the initial sense of order from which they then proceed to depart and to which they subsequently aspire to return. This notion that the bucolic tradition has in some way been tidied up at some stage between the end of the *Idylls* and the opening of the *Eclogues* is in any case very much what the current state of the land would seem to imply. For in addition to the marshy and stone-ridden lands Meliboeus says Tityrus enjoys, the topography of these poems also in-cludes crops and harvests, orchards, vineyards, gardens, irrigated meadows and tilled lands.[72] Thus, while the *agellus*, or 'little plot of land', Moeris has lost in *Eclogue* 9 is reminiscent of the first ventures into agriculture made by Lucretius' primitive societies,[73] the lands Meliboeus is to cede are anything but: they produce corn (*aristas* 1.69) and other crops (*segetes* 1.71) and it would appear from his ironic remark at line 73 that he had at one point or other been considering planting pear trees and vines in an orderly manner as well ('graft now your pear trees, Meliboeus, place your vines in order' *insere nunc, Meliboee, piros, pone ordine uitis*). All in all, the fields Meliboeus is to leave behind are by no means indicative of a primitive mode of existence,[74] but are instead reflective of the degree to which he himself has cultivated what might loosely be termed the 'poetic space' of the *Idylls* and to which he himself has thereby contributed to the creation of the bucolic order he now must forego. Quite apart from any-thing else, the term he uses for these 'sweet fields' at line 3 – which, as we saw earlier, point directly to the 'sweet' poetry of the *Idylls* – *arua*, does not so much signify 'fields' in general but 'fields that have been ploughed' in particular.[75] What is more, when he describes these fields again in more detail in his final speech in the eclogue, he identifies his own crucial involvement in their cultivation. For not only did he himself participate in planting the seeds for his crops in this ground (*his nos conseuimus agros* 1.72), but his choice of the term *nouale*, which can mean 'land, or a field, brought under cultivation for the first time',[76] to designate 'these so culti-vated fields' (*haec tam culta noualia* 1.70) implies that he was among the very first to do so.

It is a sign of Meliboeus' investment in the notion of culture and cultivation that he contrasts the soldier who will replace him with his fellow 'citizens' (*ciuis* 71) and calls him a 'barbarian' (*barbarus* 71). It has sometimes been remarked that the very real prospect Meliboeus now faces of becoming a soldier himself renders the distinction he wishes to draw between them more wishful than real, but one might also suggest that his past and present indicate that both he and his successor already have a certain amount in common as it is. For a start, given that this is the first appearance of a character called Meliboeus in extant ancient bucolic, both of them are newcomers to the bucolic tradition and in both cases their arrival there reflects and results in a re-demarcation, re-distribution and re-ordering of bucolic ground. What is more, Meliboeus himself encourages a militaristic view of the land he has been occupying when he refers to his hut and crops as 'my kingdom' (*mea regna* 1.69).

These several parallels between the people and cultural practices of bucolic verse on the one hand and the people and practices of the land confiscations on the other all lead to the same conclusion: namely, that even though the sequence of dispossessions enacted within the *Eclogues* introduce something new to the bucolic literary tradition, they are alien neither to the conventions of the form nor to Virgilian bucolic behaviour in particular. Instead, they are both an essential and even enabling feature of their poetic programme. After all, when Moeris repeats the words of the new owner of his little plot, 'these are mine; old farmers, migrate' (*haec mea sunt; ueteres migrate coloni* 9.4) his specific choice of the word *colonus* casts both him and his companions not only as 'old farmers' but, potentially at least, as 'former colonisers' as well.[77] We have seen on a number of occasions already how recursion is a prominent feature of the *Eclogues*. In the particular case of the sufferings of figures such as Meliboeus and Moeris, it would appear that what goes around, comes around.

Virgil's *deductum carmen*

As a coda to this chapter and an illustration of how extensively the process of land confiscation reflects and relates to the poetic programme of the *Eclogues*, I would like to close with the proposition that a recognition of this relationship can help us unpack Virgil's famous notion of the *deduc-*

tum carmen, or 'drawn-down song'. This concept is introduced in the opening lines of *Eclogue* 6, in the course of what is now occasionally referred to as the book's 'proem in the middle'.[78] Having begun with the statement that 'Our Thalea first deigned to play with Syracusan verse and neither did she blush to inhabit the woods' (*Prima Syracosio dignata est ludere uersu / nostra neque erubuit siluas habitare Thalea* 6.1-2), Tityrus continues with the lines we shall be considering here (6.3-9):

> cum canerem reges et proelia, Cynthius aurem
> uellit et admonuit: 'pastorem, Tityre, pinguis
> pascere oportet ouis, deductum dicere carmen'.
> nunc ego (namque super tibi erunt qui dicere laudes,
> Vare, tuas cupiant et tristia condere bella)
> agrestem tenui meditabor harundine musam:
> non iniussa cano.

When I was singing of kings and battles, the Cynthian tugged my ear and warned me: 'a shepherd, Tityrus, ought to feed his sheep to be fat, to sing a drawn-down song'. Now I (for there will remain for you those who desire to sing your praises, Varus, and to found sad wars) will contemplate the muse of the fields on my slender reed: I do not sing things unordered.

It is now generally agreed that the kind of song Apollo has in mind when he enjoins Tityrus to sing a *deductum carmen* is a 'slender' or 'fine-spun' piece, which is to be distinguished from such 'fat' modes as epic and which adheres to a small-scale Callimachean aesthetic instead. The reasons for thinking this are numerous, but derive almost entirely from the clear affiliation this passage bears towards the famous scene from the *Aetia* in which Callimachus similarly receives some poetic advice from Apollo (fr. 1.21-4 Pf.):

> καὶ γὰρ ὅτε πρώτιστον ἐμοῖς ἐπὶ δέλτον ἔθηκα
> γούνασιν, Ἀπόλλων εἶπεν ὅ μοι Λύκιος·
> '..ἡ... ἀοιδέ, τὸ μὲν θύος ὅττι πάχιστον
> θρέψαι, τὴν Μοῦσαν δ᾽ ὠγαθὲ λεπταλέην.'

For when I first placed a writing tablet on my knees, Lycian Apollo said to me: 'Poet, feed your burnt offering to be as fat as possible, but your muse, my friend, keep her slender.'

Because of the evident parallelism between these two passages and because the Latin verb *deducere* and the Greek epithet λεπταλέος both suggest the production of textiles,[79] it seems reasonable to assume that Virgil's *deductum carmen* ('drawn-down song') does indeed translate Callimachus' concept of a Μοῦσα λεπταλέη ('slender muse') and connote, in part, a 'slender' verse. After all, Tityrus' response to Apollo's intervention includes an undertaking to play on an instrument that promises to produce precisely that: 'I will contemplate the muse of the fields on my <u>slender</u> reed' (*agrestem <u>tenui</u> meditabor harundine musam* 6.8). The exchange between Apollo and Tityrus in *Eclogue* 6, however, includes a number of additions to its Callimachean predecessor, as well as changes of emphasis and detail, and these together suggest that the god had more than just *tenuitas*, or 'slenderness', in mind when he instructed Virgil's shepherd to sing a 'drawn-down' song.[80] In what follows, and by paying more attention to the connotations of the verb *deducere* elsewhere in Virgil, as well as to the specific context in which it is deployed here, we shall try to recover a sense of what some of those other things might have been.

In Chapter 2, I made the suggestion that the part of the wedding ceremony known as the *deductio in domum*, or the leading of the bride to the home of her new husband, serves in these poems to help structure the *Eclogues'* aspirations to reach for and take their place among the stars. The strong cosmological content of *Eclogue* 6, particularly at the start of the song of Silenus, makes it more than likely that this is also one of the meanings of the *deductum carmen* requested by Apollo here. Over and above these specific cosmological connotations, however, on the two other occasions on which the verb *deducere* appears in the *Eclogues*, it signifies the reshaping of nature through the medium of poetry more generally. We have already seen how, in Alphesiboeus' claim that 'songs can <u>draw down</u> the moon from the sky' (*carmina uel caelo possunt <u>deducere</u> lunam* 8.69), the verb *deducere* does not only attribute to the moon a slender and refined (which is to say, λεπταλέος) aesthetic, but in so doing it concurrently lays claim to ownership of that moon and that aesthetic. One might note, moreover, how an equivalent re-ordering of nature is also in evidence when this verb reappears later in *Eclogue* 6 itself, where it describes the pipes with which Hesiod 'was accustomed to <u>draw down</u> the rigid ash trees from the mountain with his singing' (*quibus ille solebat / cantando rigidas <u>deducere</u> montibus ornos* 6.70-1).

These two examples alone make it clear that the verb *deducere* is capable of sustaining the connection between poetry and the redistribution of land for which I have been arguing throughout. A comparable passage at the beginning of Book 3 of the *Georgics*, moreover, explicitly aligns this process of 'drawing down' with acts of colonisation and represents its achievement in the form of a military triumph. There, in terms redolent of the *Eclogues*, and of *Eclogue* 6 in particular, Virgil expresses the hope that 'First I, if only life remains, shall return to my fatherland and shall <u>draw down</u> the Muses with me from the Aonian peak' (*primus ego in patriam mecum, modo uita supersit, / Aonio rediens <u>deducam</u> uertice Musas* Geo. 3.10-11).[81] The ensuing account of how he intends to commemorate this feat throws further light on what this act of 'drawing down' is likely to involve: he will bring Idumaean palms to Mantua; build a temple there with Caesar in its centre; and, as a 'victor' (which, as we have seen, is a key term in the *Eclogues* too), drive one hundred four-horse chariots towards him in triumph (*Geo.* 3.12-18). 'For me,' he boasts, 'the whole of Greece will leave Alpheus and the groves of Molorchus and will compete in races and the crude boxing-glove' (*cuncta mihi Alpheum linquens lucosque Molorchi / cursibus et crudo decernet Graecia caestu Geo.* 3.19-20). To a certain degree, these particular games and the relocation of Greece to Italy they involve reflect the literary practice of the *Eclogues*, in which the contests the herdsmen there engage in often effect an analogous transfer of Greek texts into the Latin language. Indeed, the fact that the river Mincius, which constitutes both the setting for these games in *Georgics* 3 and the destination for their accompanying acts of cultural relocation, is described in terms derived directly from *Eclogue* 7, gives further grounds for recognising this analogy.[82] One of the conclusions one might therefore draw from this analogy is that the overt equations the *Georgics*' 'proem in the middle' enacts between the poetic act of 'drawing down' on the one hand and such military activities as colonisation, conquest and triumph on the other informs the concept of the *deductum carmen* enjoined in the *Eclogues*' 'proem in the middle' as well.[83] Careful attention to the context within which this concept is introduced in the proem to *Eclogue* 6 indicates that this is so.

I suggested above that the subtle, but numerous, differences between the opening of *Eclogue* 6 and the prologue to Callimachus' *Aetia* indicate that Virgil's concept of a *deductum carmen* connotes more than an aesthetics of tenuity. I would like now to add that these distinctions also serve to redirect and redefine the relationship this kind of 'slender song' might be thought to bear towards other literary modes as well. After all, and partly as a result of its evident evocation of the prologue to the *Aetia*, it is commonly supposed that the *deductum carmen* enjoined in *Eclogue* 6 stands in contrast both to the 'kings and battles' Tityrus was singing about when Apollo intervened and to the 'fat' sheep the god instructs him to feed. Yet in both cases, the relationships between these various categories are in practice far more nuanced than such antitheses might initially imply.

In relation to the apparent distinction between a 'slender' song and a 'fat' sheep, for instance, while it is true that Tityrus does indeed proceed to play upon the 'slender' reed, the *tenuis harundo*, in line 8, Apollo does not draw as explicit as contrast between the fat sheep (the *pinguis ouis*) and the *deductum carmen* here as he had between the fat offering and the slender muse in Callimachus. In the passage from the *Aetia*, the opposition between the two is emphasised by the use of the μέν ... δέ ('on the one hand ... on the other') construction. In the eclogue, meanwhile, there is no explicit 'but' or indeed any connective at all. Apollo simply says: 'a shepherd, Tityrus, ought to feed his sheep to be fat, to sing a drawn-down song' (*pastorem, Tityre, pinguis / pascere oportet ouis, deductum dicere carmen* 6.4-5). It is worth making this point because *pinguis* is a reasonably common epithet in the *Eclogues*, describing as it does such familiar bucolic items as cheese, plants, pine wood, fields, olive oil and amber.[84] The nouns to which this epithet attaches itself may not in themselves explicitly signify poetry, but it is by no means as easy to draw a clear distinction between the elements of the eclogue world and the elements of eclogue song as it might be in other forms of poetry. A fat sheep, in other words, is more likely to act as an emblem of a bucolic song than a fat victim is of Callimachus' verse. Indeed, it would not be unreasonable to see in this characteristic bucolic animal an embodiment of the kind of 'rich' (*pinguis*) literary stock which bucolic poetry repeatedly shepherds, and by which it should therefore, perhaps, come to be defined. At the very least, given the propensity of the *Eclogues* to represent bucolic songs in terms of ecphrastic objects,[85] and given that the verb *deducere* connotes the drawing off of wool from a sheep in particular,[86] the interrelationship between sheep and song here would seem to be very close indeed.

One might suggest, too, that the relationship this *deductum carmen* bears towards martial epic (here denoted by the theme of 'kings and battles') is not quite so antithetical either. Once again, the presupposition that the two are entirely distinct owes something to readings of Callimachus' *Aetia*, which in general assume that Callimachus is there complaining about those who criticise him for not having completed 'one continuous poem about kings and heroes in many thousands of lines' (εἵνεκεν οὐχ ἓν ἄεισμα διηνεκὲς ἢ βασιλ[η / ...]ας ἐν πολλαῖς ἤνυσα χιλιάσιν / ἢ ...]ους ἥρωας *Aet.* 1.3-5).[87] Taken on their own terms, however, the *Eclogues*, like the *Aetia*, make frequent mention of both kings and battles, including in the main body of *Eclogue* 6 itself.[88] What is more, these battles not only reflect the poetic contests that take place throughout these poems, but they almost invariably involve arguments over, and lead to the redistribution of, bucolic ground. Indeed, once this has been recognised, it is possible to get a better idea of the 'sad wars' (*tristia ... bella* 6.7) Publius Alfenus Varus is here said to have fought.[89] For the adjective *tristis* is used elsewhere in the *Eclogues* to describe both a certain type of bucolic song[90] and the feelings of those herdsmen who, like Moeris in *Eclogue* 9, have lost their plots of land as a result of the confiscations: 'now, conquered and <u>sad</u>, since chance overturns everything, we are sending these kids to him (and may it not turn out well)' (*nunc uicti, <u>tristes</u>, quoniam fors omnia uersat, / hos illi (quod nec uertat bene) mittimus haedos* 9.5-6).

That the *deductum carmen* Apollo here enjoins does not so much distance itself from such things as kings and battles as reconfigure them is further suggested by the literary programme Tityrus then proceeds to outline. As has already been mentioned, his promise to 'contemplate the muse of the fields on my slender reed' (*agrestem tenui meditabor harundine musam* 6.8) actively recalls Meliboeus' description of him contemplating the woodland muse in *Eclogue* 1 (*siluestrem tenui musam auena* 1.2). By replacing Meliboeus' *siluestris musa* with his own *agrestis musa* here, therefore, he points up his investment in the disturbances that are everywhere in evidence in the fields in that poem as well. We should not forget either that *Eclogue* 6 remains a 'song for Varus' and that the tamarisks and groves that will sing his name (6.9-11) are thereby inscribing into the environment the proprietorial rights, as well as the presence, of a land surveyor.

All in all, then, these lines perpetuate the very equation between poetry and place we have been observing throughout, in which bucolic contests and competition over bucolic land are two sides of the same coin. And it is precisely this affinity between bucolic poetics and the process of land confiscation that Apollo's notion of a *deductum carmen*, with its aspirations towards the cosmos and colonisation alike, sets out to enjoin.

5

Landscape

Most discussions of the role and depiction of nature in the *Eclogues* invoke at some stage or other the concept of landscape.[1] Unlike terms such as 'geography' and 'topography', however, the word 'landscape' does not boast a direct etymological link with the ancient world and there are those who would argue that such a connection is also missing for the concept as a whole. Indeed, it has recently been suggested that we should shift our focus away from the representation of landscape in the *Eclogues* altogether, on the grounds that it introduces too many post-classical connotations to our understanding of these poems.[2] This chapter will therefore begin with a brief survey of these claims and will outline some of the presuppositions that underlie them. For the most part, though, it will illustrate how an approach to the *Eclogues* which conceives of their depictions of nature as 'landscapes' engages with at least three important features of Virgil's bucolic poetry: its use of ecphrasis; its corresponding configuration of time; and the role it thereby constructs for its readers and viewers.

Landscape criticism

The criticisms that have been made of landscape-based readings of the *Eclogues* largely concern the relationship they cause these poems to bear towards time. In addition to the claim that the focus on landscape encourages an anachronistic interpretation of Virgilian bucolic, it has also been argued that such an approach removes 'time and its necessities' all together from this kind of verse.[3] Both these charges relate in part to the pictorial connotations of the word 'landscape'. For in as far as landscape entered the English language in the sixteenth century as 'a technical term for painters',[4] which derived its primary sense from the example of Dutch and Flemish painters,[5] it might be felt to be both anachronistic and liable to draw its configuration of nature more into line with the arts of space than with those of time. We shall come across a rather more nuanced view of landscape and its relationship to time in due course, but one should in any case acknowledge that its tendency to act and be interpreted in this way is also due to the close affinity it has been thought to bear towards Friedrich Schiller's influential essay of 1795-6, 'On Naive and Sentimental Poetry'. Indeed, Paul Alpers, whose work represents the most sustained and incisive critique of the approach to poetry that takes nature or

landscape as its defining characteristic, argues that if you elevate land-
scape to this status, you are unlikely to avoid being drawn into the 'field of
force' represented by this essay.[6]

One does not need to describe Schiller's essay at any great length in
order to illustrate how its characterisation of 'sentimental poetry' – which
is to say of poems that, like the *Eclogues*, are in some way or other 'about'
the natural world – ascribes to nature a number of properties that are
traditionally assumed to inform its representation in visual art. In short,
the sentimental perspective freezes nature and places a frame around it,
thereby detaching it from contemporary reality and rendering it liable to
recede, or even fracture, the moment anyone or anything from that reality
comes into contact with it. It is not difficult to find interpretations of
landscape that work to a similar effect. Jonathan Bate, for instance, in a
discussion of Schiller's essay, remarks that 'the framing of environment
into "landscape"' is one of many 'symptoms of the loss of integration with
nature'.[7] It is largely as a result of this kind of equation of landscape with
'sentimental poetry' that Paul Alpers has been led to argue that, if we take
landscape as the defining characteristic of the opening of *Eclogue* 1, 'these
lines appear to criticize and undermine the very notion of pastoral' and
that 'its idyllic landscape represents a fantasy that is dissipated by the
recognition of political and social realities'.[8]

Alpers appears to be of the opinion that one cannot avoid replicating
Schiller's terms no matter how one shapes ones notion of landscape or
nature. His own response to this problem is to relegate the importance of
this relationship to our understanding of this kind of poetry and to
concentrate on the figure of the herdsman instead.[9] But one wonders
whether this is strictly necessary. For, apart from anything else, and
despite what Alpers persistently assumes,[10] landscape does not offer the
only way in which to constitute and talk about nature and one might
suggest a whole range of models that promise to avoid recycling Schiller's
essay instead. But even landscape only reproduces the configuration of
nature presupposed by Schiller if one interprets the history of the term
and the effect of the pictorial connotations of this word in a particular
way. For a start, the version of landscape that recasts both nature and
poetry in Schiller's terms ultimately requires the belief that, whereas
poetry operates within the realm of time, painting and the other visual
arts are to be classified solely as arts of space.[11] Only if a picture really
does have nothing to do with time, that is, will the approach to poetry
which views it as a landscape or picture inevitably render that poetry
entirely static and its viewer irrevocably distant. But if the viewer or
reader is actively engaged in the poem or picture in question, this allows
for the very processes of movement and change that Schiller's model,
with its presupposition of a distanced and even excluded viewer, fore-
goes. As it happens, it is precisely this presumption of a moving and
engaged viewer that informs the numerous scenes from nature that were

being painted on Roman walls at around the time that Virgil was composing his *Eclogues*.

One Roman wall-painting that clearly encapsulates this mode of viewing, for instance, is the so-called 'Landscape with Polyphemus and Galatea', which was originally found in the Mythological Room in the Augustan villa at Boscotrecase, in southern Italy.[12] So far from serving to establish a distance between the paintings and the viewer, one can imagine that, as one entered this room, one would have felt very much 'in the picture'.[13] For on all sides the walls were painted, with red panels throughout and, on the west, with this painting, on the east with the 'Landscape with Perseus and Andromeda'.[14] The experience of entering such a room could consequently have been one of paradox: one is simultaneously bounded by the walls (the room itself is reasonably small)[15] whilst also being in the middle of far-ranging visual prospects. Such a double bind appears to have been a feature of what scholars now call the 'Second Style' of Roman painting, which prevailed in the second half of the first century BC and to which period this painting is tentatively assigned.[16] Christopher Dawson, for example, describes the time at which these paintings were being produced as, 'a restless period in which, as if affected by some form of claustrophobia, [the Italians] sought more and more to break through the walls of the rooms in which they lived'.[17]

One might suggest that the experience of being in rooms of this kind offers a paradigm for the experience of reading the *Eclogues* more generally.[18] Irrespective of the particular dynamic of the room in which it appeared, however, certain features of the 'Landscape with Polyphemus and Galatea' work in themselves against the assumption that paintings can only ever be static. Indeed, it would appear that this painting for one engages in a distinct play between stasis and movement. Peter von Blanckenhagen, for instance, describes the spectator's experience of looking at this picture in terms that emphasise the importance of movement and change. 'Just as in wandering through a real landscape we enjoy continuously changing vistas,' he writes 'so being led into the magic world of this painting our perceptions and interpretations continuously change their relations and values'.[19] Blanckenhagen also notes that there is not one single vantage point from which all the details in this picture cohere, but that each detail by itself is presented at the eye-level of the viewer.[20] In this way, each viewer is able to inhabit a variety of positions and perspectives within the painting and consequently to perform a variety of roles. We can look now from the perspective of one Polyphemus, now from the other, now from Galatea's viewpoint, and so it goes on.

Later in this chapter, we shall see how the contrasting perspectives of Polyphemus and Galatea frequently give shape to the representations of nature in the *Eclogues* as well. But what each of these examples in any case indicates is how it is by no means inappropriate to bring the term 'landscape' to bear upon depictions of nature in ancient culture, since something analogous to what we understand by this concept, with its emphasis on visual modes of depiction and on the role of the shaping perception of the viewer,[21] does seem to be available in both the literature and the art of this period.[22] Indeed, a fuller account of landscape reveals that it boasts a much more profound engagement with history and time than is usually allowed, in which it acts as a term of mediation not only between one period and another, but also between potentially discrete categories such as 'art' and 'reality'.[23] As Peter Coates writes in his book, *Nature*:

'Landscape' was once a far more precise term. For the medieval peasant, it meant a system of cultivated plots. In its original medieval sense, the related expression 'countryside' was also primarily associated with the peasantry. Deriving from the French *contra*, meaning 'opposite' or 'against', it was attached to a tract of land stretching before the observer. These largely vernacular ideas were eventually redefined by social elites, who transformed them into aesthetic and recreational concepts. English landscape preferences were acquired from 16th- and 17th-century Dutch and Flemish painters such as Pieter Brueghel and Peter Paul Rubens, who applied the term *landskip* to rural scenes. 'Landscape' was also applied to the painting itself – a sense retained in references to 'a landscape' by John Constable – a process Olwig refers to as 'the colonisation of nature by landscape scenery'.[24]

It is this capacity of 'landscape' to constitute simultaneously a site of similarity and difference, of coherence and divergence, and in so doing to act almost as a unit of exchange,[25] that renders it so valuable a term for capturing the equally complex sequence of exchanges in the *Eclogues*. Indeed, rather than assume that the introduction of this post-classical term to the classical world of the *Eclogues* has the same effect upon the ground of these poems as the sentimental perspective upon nature, one might argue instead that a better analogy is with the way in which certain Latin words such as *patria* ('fatherland'), *arua* ('ploughed lands') and *noualia* ('lands, or fields, brought under cultivation for the first time')[26] serve in the *Eclogues* to act upon the Greek land of the *Idylls* and in so doing to configure the relationship between these two related, yet different, works of poetry.[27]

This more engaged and dynamic understanding of the concept of 'landscape' promises to replicate in the case of the modern-day reader the often competitive, sometimes incursive, but never static approach to bucolic ground that is such a feature of the *Eclogues*' own relationship to the *Idylls* and other works from the literary tradition. Olwig's remark about 'the colonisation of nature by landscape scenery' (repeated by Coates in the passage cited above) captures one part of this process and points to possible parallels between the work of a reader of the *Eclogues* and that of a land surveyor. But to see how all this works in detail, the rest of this chapter will illustrate how two features of the pictorial connotations of landscape enable this more dynamic view of bucolic ground to emerge: in the first place, by drawing our attention to the role of ecphrasis in these poems; and in the second by giving due prominence to the temporal configuration of literary tradition it constructs and to the role of the viewer or reader in the process of bucolic transmission and exchange.

Ecphrasis in *Idyll* 1

Right from the very start, bucolic poetry has sought to express itself in terms of an exchange between the verbal and visual arts. In the poem which first introduces this form to literary history, *Idyll* 1,[28] a goatherd offers a finely-crafted bowl, as well as a goat for milking, in return for a song. What is more, he specifies exactly which song he wants in return for this bowl, as well as the standard to which he expects it to be sung: he wants to hear 'The Sufferings of Daphnis' (τὰ Δάφνιδος ἄλγεα), the song with which Thyrsis has achieved excellence in bucolic music, and he wants him to sing it as well as he did when he competed with Chromis from Libya (*Id.* 1.19-28). When the bowl and the goat are handed over at the end of the idyll, it signals that the version of this song recorded in *Idyll* 1 has met both these criteria.

Because of the determining role *Idyll* 1 was to play in the later development of the bucolic tradition, this exchange of a visual for a verbal artefact was to become not just a characteristic feature of bucolic verse, but also a way of figuring some of its key characteristics. Indeed, by considering both the description of the bowl in *Idyll* 1 and the manner in which it relates to the rest of the poem as a whole, one can see how this ecphrastic moment informs so many of the exchanges in the *Eclogues* as well.

The three scenes depicted on the bowl – of a woman standing unmoved between two suitors who compete in alternating verse; of an old fisherman; and of a young boy weaving a cricket cage while foxes steal food from his satchel and grapes from his vineyard – bear a teasing relationship to scenes described elsewhere in the *Idylls*. To a certain degree, these three vignettes can be taken (and have been taken) as emblems of Theocritus' bucolic verse,[29] with its frequent depiction of amoebaean and competitive contests, its focus on rural activities and the suggestion that the creation of small-scale but intricate works (symbolised here by the cricket cage) can be a distraction from more serious, or at least more routine, tasks. Yet the fit is by no means exact and not one of these scenes is directly reproduced elsewhere in the *Idylls*.[30] Thus, even as the bowl offers itself as an emblem of Theocritean bucolic, it is perhaps more accurate to suggest that the relationship between this visual artefact and the poem in which it appears is one of counterpoint rather than direct equation. This strategy of bringing together a sequence of close, but not quite interlocking, elements – between, for instance, one singer and another, one song and another, and between texts and their readers – is a characteristic of Theocritean and

Virgilian bucolic alike and is an important reason why ancient bucolic continues to shift and change without ever becoming entirely static. The introduction of this feature in the form of an ecphrasis, moreover, not only plays upon the capacity of this device to instantiate such a practice, but it also means that the terms in which it comes to be enacted in later poems, including the *Eclogues*, repeatedly reflect the terms of this inaugural, ecphrastic model. When the goatherd describes his bowl to Thyrsis as a 'goatherd's wonder' (αἰπολικὸν θάημα *Id.* 1.56), for instance, the sense of amazement he expresses comes to constitute a 'buzzword' for and signal of this kind of ecphrastic moment, even when it is not quite so obvious as here that an ecphrastic exchange is actually taking place.[31]

The ability of the goatherd's bowl to serve both as an emblem for bucolic verse and as a counterpoint to it is due in part to the role it fills as a kind of *bureau de change* between itself and bucolic song on the one hand, and between bucolic poetry and other forms of verse on the other.[32] The financial content of the transaction in which these two herdsmen engage is brought to the fore by the story the goatherd tells of how this particular bowl came into his possession: he bought it from a sailor from Calydnos and paid for it in the local, bucolic currency – a goat and a large cheese of white milk (*Id.* 1. 57-8). By offering it now to Thyrsis in part exchange for a performance of 'The Sufferings of Daphnis', the goatherd thereby brings the financial history of the bowl together with the cultural history of that song. For this song too has its beginnings (for the goatherd at least) in an exchange, and in particular in a song contest that took place at some unspecified moment in the past between Thyrsis and Chromis. It has been observed that the promise of a bowl in return for a song recalls the tripod Hesiod received as a prize for winning a song contest in Euboea[33] and so the financial element of this particular transaction could be said simply to render more explicit what was already latent in earlier, 'pre-bucolic', instances of cultural exchange. At the very least, because the goatherd reveals the high regard in which he holds the bowl before we have even had a chance to hear this exemplary song for ourselves, *Idyll* 1 ensures that bucolic poetry enters the literary record as a form that, from the first, both emerges from and engages in a range of cultural and financial transactions alike.

Its specific designation as an 'ivy-wood bowl' (κισσύβιον) means that one of the intertextual exchanges in which this bowl participates is with the 'ivy-wood bowl' from which Polyphemus drinks the wine that befuddles his wits in Homer's *Odyssey*.[34] The scenes depicted on the goatherd's bowl, moreover, recall similar scenes on the shield of Achilles in *Iliad* 18 and the Hesiodic shield of Heracles[35] and to this extent uphold Brian Breed's observation that ecphrasis constitutes one of ways in which poems such as the *Idylls* and *Eclogues* establish and articulate their relationship towards the epic.[36] Indeed, the very material out of which this bowl is fashioned contributes to the structuring of this relationship, since its initial designation as an 'ivy-wood bowl' establishes an intriguing point of departure for its subsequent description, which, as is also the case with the description of the herdsmen's cups in *Eclogue* 3, repeatedly presupposes an artefact of a rather more illustrious nature, such as a piece of metalwork or statuary.[37] Even on its own terms, then, one might suggest that this verbal description of a visual artefact – which in turn reflects back upon the kind of poetry that can produce such a description – indicates a close affiliation between the nature of pictorial representation and the nature of bucolic art. But the fact that this particular bowl is exchanged within the context of what would become an archetypal bucolic setting and for what is already here characterised as an archetypal bucolic song render this visual artefact all the more emblematic of bucolic. What is more, this analogy is sustained both within the ancient notion of ecphrasis itself – which was by no means restricted to literary accounts of visual works of art, but which could denote 'any poetic or rhetorical description, including descriptions of landscape (*topothesia*), buildings, battles, and storms'[38] – and through the inclusion of visual artefacts as defining features of the setting within which Thyrsis is to sing his song of Daphnis. For just before the goatherd proceeds to describe the bowl he will offer in exchange for Thyrsis' song, he suggests that the two of them 'sit here beneath the elm, opposite the statues of Priapus and the Nymphs' (δεῦρ' ὑπὸ τὰν πτελέαν ἐσδώμεθα τῶ τε Πριάπω / καὶ τὰν Κρανιάδων κατεναντίον *Id.* 1.21-2). In so doing, he introduces as immobile images two sets of characters who will later reappear – and, in the case of Priapus, act – in the song itself.[39]

This sequence of alignments between bowl, setting and song bears a number of implications for the narrative structure of all three alike. Judith Haber, for instance, draws an analogy between the border motifs on the bowl and the refrain in Thyrsis' song and argues that this equation affects both the nature of this song and our response to it:

> Like the ivy on the cup described by Thyrsis' goatherd companion (27-56), the refrain of the Daphnis-song serves to remove us from the events being portrayed, to foreground the formal qualities of the artist's performance, and to affirm the primacy of stasis and continuity over movement, disruption, and death. Any refrain, simply by being repeated, will perform a similar function; for this reason, refrains eventually become regular features of pastoral poems: they are, in effect, the poetic equivalent of the limits of the bower.[40]

Here again, then, we find the supposition that the presence of a pictorial element within a bucolic poem introduces a sense of stasis. And yet, while it is true that the freezing of an action or the interruption of the progress of a song is one of the effects ecphrasis often has, it is perhaps better to suggest that this is but a part, rather than the end, of the process. Indeed, as often as not, the tendency of ecphrasis to engender a sense of stasis takes place alongside a concurrent articulation of movement and change.

5. Landscape

The bowl of *Idyll* 1 is a case in point. For the description of this vessel through the eyes of a marvelling goatherd, who claims, for example, that the woman in the middle of the song contest 'sometimes laughs and looks towards this man, and at other times turns her mind again to the other' (ἀλλ᾽ ὅκα μὲν τῆνον ποτιδέρκεται ἄνδρα γέλαισα, / ἄλλοκα δ᾽ αὖ ποτὶ τὸν ῥιπτεῖ νόον *Id.* 1.36-7) serves to give life to, and reanimate, the scenes it contains.[41] One might argue, moreover, that this combination of the still and the moving is a feature that recurs in the numerous related ecphrastic moments that are staged in the *Eclogues* as well.

Ecphrasis and environment in the *Eclogues*

The exchanges of *Idyll* 1, exemplified as they are by the interchange between the goatherd's bowl and Thyrsis' song, are re-enacted on several occasions and in several different ways throughout the *Eclogues*. Not all of these re-enactments are as easy to spot as others, although in every case there is some kind of signal that the passage in question is once again bringing those exchanges, and with them the ecphrastic structures of representation they deploy, into play. In *Eclogue* 6, for example, the appearance of a 'Chromis' as one of the boys who binds Silenus and demands from him a song in return for his freedom points back to the singer against whom Thyrsis had previously pitted his 'Sufferings of Daphnis' in *Idyll* 1. As such, it highlights the extent to which the song of Silenus that ensues, like the song against which Theocritus' Chromis had once competed, shares certain ecphrastic qualities with the bowl for which Thyrsis once again performs his archetypal bucolic piece in the idyll.[42] Thyrsis himself, meanwhile, returns as a competitor in the song contest of *Eclogue* 7, where, recalling the setting of *Idyll* 1, he promises to erect a golden statue of Priapus in place of his current representation in marble (*Ecl.* 7.33-6). This simple gesture intimates a subtle parallel between the exchange of a bowl for a song in *Idyll* 1 and the verses the two singers exchange in the song contest of *Eclogue* 7. For on both occasions these visual images are embedded within the context in which they appear and therefore serve as icons of bucolic exchange itself. The promise Thyrsis makes of a golden statue for Priapus, that is, is intended to cap Corydon's promise of a marble statue for Diana. As such, it duly illustrates the degree to which the rules and practices of ecphrasis share a number of structural affinities with the rules and practices of amoebaean exchange.

Above all, though, it is the cups of *Eclogue* 3 and the basket of hibiscus the narrator has woven by the end of *Eclogue* 10 that most obviously recall the bowl of *Idyll* 1. All three of these ecphrastic objects, moreover, bear a discernible relationship towards the physical environment within which they are introduced. The 'sweet wax' (ἁδέι κηρῷ *Id.* 1.27) which seals the bowl of *Idyll* 1, for instance, aligns it with the 'sweet whispering' (ἁδύ τι τὸ ψιθύρισμα *Id.* 1.1) of the pine tree mentioned at the poem's outset. What is more (and as we have already seen), the inclusion of natural features around the bowl's borders replicates the setting within which the goatherd wishes Thyrsis to sing, where an elm and some oaks similarly mingle with visual representations of Priapus and the Nymphs. It is perhaps no surprise, then, that the two artefacts in the *Eclogues* which most obviously derive from this bowl also display a certain affinity with their immediate environment. The basket the narrator has woven by the close of *Eclogue* 10 is made of hibiscus, a shrub or plant that Corydon mentions as a part of his world in *Eclogue* 2,[43] while the cups of *Eclogue* 3 are fashioned out of beech, a tree that is in turn very much a feature of Menalcas' and Damoetas' natural surroundings.

In addition to providing the material for these physical artefacts, the natural world also acquires a number of the characteristics of an ecphrastic description in its representation. A clear instance of this is constituted by the cups of *Eclogue* 3, where depictions of nature, and in particular its ability to reflect and respond to different kinds of poetry, leads it to serve as a physical emblem of the aspirations of bucolic song. An equally important example, however, comes with the contrasting perceptions of bucolic space offered by the two herdsmen in *Eclogue* 1.

As we saw in the previous chapter, *Eclogue* 1 begins with a five-line vignette in which Meliboeus describes the situation of his fellow herdsman, Tityrus. Like the plants and trees which constitute the bordering motifs on the bowl of *Idyll* 1 and the cups of *Eclogue* 3, Meliboeus' description is so ordered as to weave a woodland frame around the recumbent Tityrus and his own imminent exile. One of the effects of this frame is to render the image produced by these lines analogous to a work of pictorial representation. Indeed, Tityrus himself encourages the perception of this alignment when he in turn refers to his situation as something Meliboeus can see. Speaking of the god who granted him this leisure, he remarks that this divinity 'permitted my cows to roam, <u>as you see</u>, and me myself to play what I wish on the reed of the fields' (*ille meas errare boues, <u>ut cernis</u>, et ipsum / ludere quae uellem calamo permisit agresti* 1.9-10). Meliboeus' reply in the line immediately following also indicates that the scene of Tityrus reclining beneath his tree and playing his pipe has, from his perspective at least, taken the form of an ecphrasis. For the moment he admits that he, a goatherd, 'wonders at' the scene before him (*Non equidem inuideo, <u>miror</u> magis* 1.11), he aligns this scene with that other 'goatherd's wonder' (αἰπολικὸν θάημα *Id.* 1.56), the bowl of *Idyll* 1.

Meliboeus' tendency to view the world he is leaving behind in terms so strongly resonant of the *Idylls* is one that persists throughout the eclogue. But because his account of this world begins by recalling the goatherd's view of his cup in particular, he thereby introduces the idyllic gaze to the *Eclogues* as one that has a marked propensity to pictorialise. The significance of this is hard to overstate. For, apart from anything else, it further aligns Meliboeus' way of looking at this world with the perspective of the land surveyors; it accordingly emblematises one of the ways in which the *Eclogues* regard, divide up and reorganise the literary tradition; and it makes Meliboeus all the more representative both of those who take the title of Theocritus' poems, *Idylls*, to indicate that we ought to regard them as 'little pictures'[44] and of those who approach bucolic poetry for its depiction of nature and who understand nature in terms derived from (or, at least, related to) Schiller's essay.

Fundamental to all these effects is the fact that, for Meliboeus, both the world upon which he gazes and the way in which he gazes upon it are the product of literary tradition. Thus, when he remarks that 'we are leaving the boundaries of the fatherland and the sweet fields. We are fleeing the fatherland' (*nos patriae finis et dulcia linquimus arua.* / *nos patriam fugimus* 1.3-4), the ground he is leaving behind is, as we saw in the previous chapter, primarily that of the *Idylls*; but at the same time, the manner in which he describes this departure is also reminiscent of Odysseus' statement to the Phaecians in Book 9 of the *Odyssey* that 'I do not think anything is sweeter to look upon than one's own land' (οὔ τοι ἐγώ γε / ἧς γαίης δύναμαι γλυκερώτερον ἄλλο ἰδέσθαι *Od.* 9.27-8). The effect of this allusion is that it renders Meliboeus' gaze, like Odysseus', fundamentally nostalgic. This nostalgic mode of viewing, moreover, is likewise a key characteristic of the sentimental viewer described by Schiller and in both cases it serves to render the poem, picture, object or environment under consideration distant, static and, potentially, lost. What is more, conjoined with the pictorial form this nostalgic view commonly assumes, it leads Meliboeus to view this world – as the land surveyors also appear to have viewed it and as those critics who regard *Eclogue* 1 as an account of the destruction of the bucolic locale tend to look at it too[45] – in terms of frames, boundaries and borders.

Despite its post-classical connotations, therefore, landscape remains an appropriate term to bring to a discussion of the configuration and role of nature in the *Eclogues*. This is so not least because of its ability to replicate and sustain the pictorial quality of many of these depictions, including their recognition of frames and borders. Indeed, the very fact that 'landscape' offers an anachronistic representation of the natural world can itself be regarded as a further point in its favour, since a number of the descriptions of nature contained in the *Eclogues* – including Meliboeus' in *Eclogue* 1 – are themselves belated in some way. Through this intrusion into and disruption of the original historical moment in which the *Eclogues* first appeared, moreover, landscape not only continues the practice of re-ordering time that is itself a distinctive feature of ecphrastic representation (ancient as well as modern),[46] but in so doing it also marks its capacity to participate in and embody the structures of ecphrasis more generally. Thus, just as Meliboeus' name indicates that he is both a traditional part of the bucolic world (in as far as it suggests 'he to whom the oxen are a concern')[47] and not a part of that world (in as far as this is

111

his first appearance in extant ancient bucolic), and just as his description of that world both recalls the *Idylls* and marks a departure from those *Idylls*, so too does the concept of landscape give us access to nature (including to the nature of the text), whilst also keeping us at a distance from it in anything like its pristine and original form.

The reason why landscape need not lead us to view these poems as frozen and static, moreover, is precisely because of its grounding in the shaping perception of any given viewer. More than anything else, this allows the representation of landscape, like the representation of any ecphrastic object, to serve as an expression of character. It has been argued, for instance, that the manner in which the goatherd describes his bowl in *Idyll* 1, with his emphasis on its miraculous craftsmanship and his apparent conviction that its various figures are all but living and moving, says almost as much about the goatherd himself as it does about his bowl.[48] In much the same way, Tityrus and Meliboeus in *Eclogue* 1 are distinguished from one another as characters to a considerable degree through the very different accounts they offer of what is ostensibly their shared environment. We shall look at this in more detail below, but one might first note in passing that it is because of a perceived distinction between landscape and nature on the one hand and character on the other that Paul Alpers for one rejects the apparently static view of this kind of poetry that derives from a focus on the former and turns to the figure of the herdsman to emphasise his welcome belief that these poems participate in processes of movement and time through their inclusion of narration instead.[49]

To return to *Eclogue* 1, this poem, structured as it is as a conversation between two herdsmen, has all the promise of a drama. But this drama is not so much one that takes place against a natural backdrop as it is a drama that actively involves the local environment, and in particular the two herdsmen's differing perceptions of it. Their views on such things as the geopolitical constitution of the world and of the events currently occurring across the countryside, concomitant as they are with the different positions each of them occupies in relation to the literary tradition (as we shall see below), are expressed first and foremost through their engagement with and representation of place. Nowhere is this more in evidence than in their conception of what constitutes 'here'. For Meliboeus, 'here' is the rustic world in which he currently finds himself: it is the thick hazels where his goat has left behind two twins on a naked rock (*hic* 14); and it is the place where Tityrus will continue to enjoy known streams (*hic* 51), from where bees buzz gently from a neighbours hedge (*hinc* 53) and from where the leaf stripper sings from a high rock (*hinc* 56). More broadly, it is the place from which Tityrus was absent when he went off to Rome (*hinc* 38) and from which Meliboeus must in turn depart as he heads off for Africa, Scythia, Britain or the Oaxes (*hinc* 64). Throughout this eclogue, that is, Meliboeus displays a predominantly local sense of place and this is emphasised further by his use of the demonstratives *hic, haec* and *hoc*, with which he points to 'this goat', 'these copses', 'these fields' and 'these crops'.[50] Even when he speaks in more abstract terms of 'this evil', it is rendered more concrete through its perceived presence in the countryside.[51]

For Tityrus, on the other hand, 'here' is not only the place where he is now and where he finally invites Meliboeus to spend the night (*hic* 79), but it is also Rome (*hic* 42 & 44). As such, his own use of *hic, haec* and *hoc* is far more comprehensive than his companion's. In addition to 'this leisure' and 'this city of ours',[52] for instance, he also uses it to point to 'this city' when he means Rome.[53] Indeed, his interlocking conception of place is clearly exemplified in the lines in which he states that it was not possible for him 'to recognise so present gods elsewhere' and where he reveals that it was 'here' in Rome that the amoebaean exchange took place which allowed him to remain 'here' on his land (1.40-5):

> Quid facerem? neque seruitio me exire licebat
> nec tam praesentis alibi cognoscere diuos.
> hic illum uidi iuuenem, Meliboee, quotannis
> bis senos cui nostra dies altaria fumant.
> hic mihi responsum primus dedit ille petenti:
> 'pascite ut ante boues, pueri; summittite tauros'.

What was I to do? Neither was it permitted for me to leave my servitude nor to recognise so present gods elsewhere. Here I saw that young man, Meliboeus, for whom each year our altars will smoke for twice six days. Here, he first gave a response to my petition: 'feed the oxen as before, boys; rear bulls'.

In addition to bringing together the rustic world of herdsmen with the urban world of Rome, Tityrus' conception of his environment encompasses the space of the text as well. For his use of 'here' (*hic*) as the first word of line 42 points not only to Rome and to what is for him the centre of his world, but to the midway point of the poem too. We shall see how this equation between natural and literary space reflects upon the two contrasting positions these herdsmen adopt in relation to the literary tradition shortly. But first we should also note how it helps cast the poem as a whole as an ecphrastic object. For the persistent use of positional markers such as 'here' (*hic; hinc*) throughout *Eclogue* 1 (and, indeed, in several other eclogues as well) anticipates the technique deployed for the ecphrasis of the shield of Aeneas in *Aeneid* 8, which similarly uses this kind of spatial marker to organise its description.[54] What is more, just as the description of this shield combines an account of what Vulcan had intentionally placed on this artefact along with an account of what Aeneas thinks he sees there, so too does the fact that the setting for this poem is described through the shaping perception of the poem's two protagonists mean that each of them is as much a maker of these images as a viewer of them.

Indeed, it is striking how extensively both Tityrus and Meliboeus figure a number of the concrete and the more abstract features of their respective situations through the language of visual perception. In the central line of the poem, for instance, in which Tityrus provides an aetiology for his continued existence as a herdsman and bucolic musician, he states that it was in Rome that he 'saw' the young man he will henceforth continue to worship (*hic illum uidi iuuenem* 42). A few lines prior to this, moreover, he also describes his liberation in terms that are distinctly visual. Casting himself as 'inert' – like, one might suggest, a picture – he is only freed from slavery once liberty has cast its glance retrospectively towards him (1.27-30):

> Libertas, quae sera tamen respexit inertem,
> candidior postquam tondenti barba cadebat,
> respexit tamen et longo post tempore uenit,
> postquam nos Amaryllis habet, Galatea reliquit.

Liberty, although it was late, looked back at me in my inertia, after my beard was falling whiter as I cut it. It caught sight of me nonetheless and came after a long time, now that Amaryllis has me and Galatea has left.

It is not difficult to see how this passage offers itself as an emblem of how the *Eclogues* might imagine themselves to have liberated the figures and scenarios of the *Idylls* from roughly two centuries of stagnation. What is striking all the same is how this act of liberation is rendered analogous to the practice of a viewer looking back upon an aging picture. For the freeing up of the literary tradition which these lines entail takes the explicit form of an inert picture brought back to life through the gaze of a much later viewer (which may or may not be aligned with the liberation promised by Octavian's political programme).[55] Tityrus' shift of literary models, moreover, signified here by his change of girlfriends, encapsulates his more active and dynamic engagement with his literary models than Meliboeus. For in his case, the posture of sitting beneath the shade of a tree making music is a sign that his epic journey, constituted here by his trip to Rome, has come to an end.[56]

For Meliboeus, on the other hand, this same setting is simultaneously all he has known and a point of departure. He too was once accustomed to stretch himself out in a green cave, for instance, from where he was afforded a view of his goats hanging from a cliff in a scene he is now unlikely ever to 'see' again (*non ego uos posthac uiridi proiectus in antro / dumosa pendere procul de rupe uidebo* 75-6). Other than that, though, he has no real past, either in literary history more generally or in the present poem. This is demonstrated not least by his ignorance of Rome, by the sense of timelessness he ascribes to Tityrus' situation[57] and by his inability to interpret correctly the message intended by the repeated striking of the oak tree. It is also emblematised by the way his goats bear only twins, which serve, as it were, as mirror images of one another that lack the capacity to adapt and survive in this new environment. Tityrus, by contrast, has already moved away from the oaks with which he is associated in *Idyll* 7 and now sits beneath the *fagus*, a tree that, as we have a seen, signifies continuity through change and participates in a more responsive and evolving conception of time and place. While the significant acts of perception which have liberated Tityrus from his former inertia and contributed to his current happy situation all lie in the past or present, moreover, Meliboeus' image-making conjoins past, present and future. He deploys the interjection *en* ('look!') and the ecphrastic 'buzzword' *miror* ('I wonder') on three occasions each in this poem, and in each case he does so once for the past, once for the present and once for the future: 'Look! I myself, in sickness, scarcely lead my goats' (*en ipse capellas / protinus aeger ago* 12-13); 'Look! Will I ever see my ancestral boundaries after a long time' (*en umquam patrios longo post tempore finis* 67); and 'Look where discord has driven the wretched citizens!' (*en quo discordia ciuis / produxit miseros* 71-2). The same is also the case with *miror* (the ecphrastic connotations of which Meliboeus emphasises by twice associating it with a verb that connotes seeing, *uidere*): 'I for my part do not look askance at you, rather I am amazed' (*Non equidem inuideo, miror magis* 11); 'I used to wonder why you, Amaryllis, were calling sadly upon the gods' (*Mirabar quid maesta deos, Amarylli, uocares* 36); and 'after so many things, seeing you, my kingdom, will I ever wonder at my crops?' (*post aliquot, mea regna, uidens mirabor aristas?* 69).

In this way, the various acts of seeing that take place or are recorded throughout this eclogue are indicative of the extent to which these two herdsmen inhabit different places, literary paradigms and temporalities alike. Indeed, the fact that the same phrase, 'after a long time' (*longo post tempore*), is used to describe both the liberation of Tityrus from his inertia (29) and Meliboeus' hope that he will one day see his ancestral boundaries again (67) expresses the degree to which they are at the end and the beginning respectively of a closely correlated generic and temporal trajectory. To this degree, the chiastic structure of *tu, nos, nos, tu* which Meliboeus deploys in his opening five lines is prophetic of the unfolding drama to come. For what we witness in this eclogue are two herdsmen whose paths have momentarily crossed, but whose pasts and futures diverge in what are more or less inverted images of one another.

This particular configuration of the relationship between Tityrus and Meliboeus is also underpinned by the propensity of these two herdsmen to express themselves in terms reminiscent of Polyphemus and Galatea respectively. This mythical paradigm is most openly brought into play when Tityrus tells his companion that freedom only caught sight of him 'now that Amaryllis has me and Galatea has left' (*postquam nos Amaryllis habet, Galatea reliquit* 30). By transferring his affections in this way, Tityrus is in the first instance fulfilling the promise Polyphemus makes to himself in *Idyll* 11 that he will abandon his pursuit of the sea-dwelling Galatea and will take up with one of the women who lives on the land instead.[58] But even as he makes this transfer, his actions signal that he himself, and not just his emotions, has made the transition from sea to land which such a change of lovers would entail. As a result, and like many an epic adventurer both before and after him, this movement from sea to land indicates that he has brought his journeying to a successful close. Meliboeus, by contrast, remains very much 'all at sea' and so it is he who thereby comes closest to playing the part of Galatea. Indeed, when Tityrus finally invites him to stay the night and lists some of the treats he can offer him, his words are very much those that the Cyclops uses to address the sea nymph in *Idyll* 11.[59] But like Galatea in that poem, who may or may not be within earshot, Meliboeus, who might also have passed on along his way, does not answer. Or rather, he has perhaps given his answer already. For just as Polyphemus complains that Galatea always flees from him in the idyll (φεύγεις *Id.* 11.24, 30 and 75), so too does Meliboeus introduce himself in the eclogue as someone who is presently in flight (*fugimus* 1.4).

The story of Polyphemus and Galatea is one to which the *Eclogues*, like the *Idylls*, return time and again.[60] For the most part, it helps characterise and configure the relationship between speakers in any given poem, such as that between Tityrus and Meliboeus in *Eclogue* 1, as well as between those who are directly present in the text and those, such as Alexis in *Eclogue* 2, and even, perhaps, readers such as we ourselves, who are not. The reasons why this story in particular is taken to be paradigmatic for these relationships are numerous, but one that is of especial relevance here is that it runs parallel to, and therefore provides a concurrent narrative for, the *Eclogues*' prominent mode of ecphrastic representation. In the first place, the apparent absurdity of the relationship between the ugly, land-based monster Polyphemus and the beautiful sea nymph Galatea symbolises the disconnection of certain characters such as Meliboeus from their surroundings, as well as the potential incompatibility of verbal and visual media. At the same time, through the topographical associations each of these two characters conveys, it brings metaphors of the sea into play in what is ostensibly a poetry of dry land. In so doing, it both highlights the relative stability or instability of certain characters within their immediate environment (again, Tityrus and Meliboeus come to mind) and the capacity of some of the supposedly solid and static images of the bucolic world these poems contain to become more fluid and unstable.

Eclogue 2 is one such example of a poem in which the relationship between texts and their readers resembles that which might pertain between a landscape and its viewer. It is also the poem in which the songs Polyphemus addresses to Galatea in the *Idylls* are most vividly re-enacted. In this eclogue, the part of Theocritus' Cyclops is taken by the shepherd Corydon. In keeping with this role, Corydon fashions an image of the bucolic world which he then presents to his equivalent of Galatea, a boy called Alexis, in the hope that it will win him over and encourage him to transfer his affections, along with his place of residence, to Corydon. In this way, bucolic poetry, through its self-presentation as a landscape, takes on a number of the characteristics of a visual object that in turn invites and requires the animating gaze of an engaged viewer.

Eclogue 2: Corydon as an artist

In many respects, *Eclogue* 2 carries on where *Eclogue* 1 breaks off. Its protagonist, Corydon, inherits from Tityrus the voice of Polyphemus, as well as a number of features of that herdsman's situation and surroundings. In much the same way that Tityrus sits beneath the shade of a wide-spreading beech and teaches the woods to re-echo 'beautiful Amaryllis' (*formosam ... Amaryllida* 1.5), Corydon wanders among the 'thick beeches, those shady peaks' (*inter densas, umbrosa cacumina, fagos* 2.3) and tosses his songs about 'beautiful Alexis' (*formosum ... Alexin* 2.1) towards the mountains and the woods (2.4-5). Whereas Tityrus has transferred his attentions from Galatea to Amaryllis, however, and thereby from the sea to the land, Corydon has moved in the opposite direction. Despite the affinities he bears to the wooer of Amaryllis in *Idyll* 3,[61] he cannot persuade himself to put up with her 'sad anger' or 'proud disdain' any longer (14-15).[62] Rather, and like Polyphemus, he looks at himself in the sea and, even as he does so, attempts to win over his version of Galatea instead.

This shift from the conventional and seemingly static images of the bucolic world produced by Meliboeus, the Galatea figure of *Eclogue* 1, to what (as we shall see) are the equally conventional and static images of that world offered up by Corydon, the Polyphemus figure of *Eclogue* 2, is accompanied by a concomitant shift from dialogue to monologue. One effect of this is that it marks a re-orientation of the kind of relationships in which these images then engage. For whereas the dialogue form of *Eclogue* 1 enables that poem to present two differing views of what is ostensibly the same setting and by this means to generate its sense of movement, drama and change, the monologue of *Eclogue* 2 presupposes both a counter image and a listener outside the text, whose animating participation therefore remains largely hypothesised and is not brought openly into play. Like the Galatea of *Idylls* 6 and 11, that is, Corydon's addressee, Alexis, does not reply to his soliloquy. Indeed, if he really is in the city with Corydon's rival Iollas – and this again would make his situation analogous to that of the sea-dwelling nymph – he would not feasibly be in a position to hear Corydon's words anyway.[63]

Be that as it may, Corydon in any case proceeds to create an image of the countryside which he invites Alexis to inhabit. The following lines offer a clear example of his propensity to turn nature into a picture that in turn invites and requires an engaged reader or viewer to bring it to life (2.45-55):

huc ades, o formose puer: tibi lilia plenis   45
ecce ferunt Nymphae calathis; tibi candida Nais,
pallentis uiolas et summa papauera carpens,
narcissum et florem iungit bene olentis anethi;
tum casia atque aliis intexens suauibus herbis
mollia luteola pingit uaccinia calta.   50
ipse ego cana legam tenera lanugine mala
castaneasque nuces, mea quas Amaryllis amabat;
addam cerea pruna (honos erit huic quoque pomo),
et uos, o lauri, carpam et te, proxima myrte,
sic positae quoniam suauis miscetis odores.   55

Be present here, o beautiful boy: for you, look!, the Nymphs are bearing lilies
in full baskets; for you a white Naiad, plucking pale violets and the tops of
poppies, is joining narcissus and the flower of the nicely fragrant dill; then,
weaving them in with marjoram and other fragrant herbs, she paints the soft
orchids with yellow marigold. I myself shall gather apples that are hoary
with tender down and chestnuts, which my Amaryllis used to love; I shall
add waxy plums (there will also be honour for this fruit), and I shall pluck
you, o bay trees, and you, myrtle, to put right next to them, seeing that, so
placed, you will mingle your fragrant odours.

Corydon signals he is about to paint a picture of the bucolic world for Alexis
from the moment he enjoins his beloved to 'look' (*ecce* 46). He then makes
good on this promise through the explosion of colour his canvas immedi-
ately displays, with its white Naiad, pale violets, yellow marigold, hoary
apples and the suggestion of numerous others pigments besides. But even
as these brightly coloured objects, along with the verbs of painting (*pin-
gere*) and weaving (*intexere*) to which they are attached, exemplify Cory-
don's creation of a visual image through verbal means, these same objects
and activities also reflect back upon the continuing status of this image as
a text. Flowers, plants and trees are common emblems of literary works
and their weaving together into garlands and the like is in turn a familiar
metaphor for the putting together of literary anthologies. Indeed, one of
the most famous of these, Meleager's *Garland*, includes an epigram to
Alexis which, as we shall see, is an important component of Corydon's
soliloquy more generally. What is more, the verbs of joining, mingling,
painting and weaving which decorate Corydon's description draw particu-
lar attention to the ecphrastic nature of his enterprise through their ability
to connote the workings and sensations of different media at one and the
same time. For just as the Nymphs bring together sights and smells when
they join narcissus and the flower of the nicely fragrant dill, and just as
Corydon achieves the same effect through his intermingling of bays and
myrtle, so too do the two verbs *pingere* ('to depict')[64] and *intexere* ('to
interweave') denote the creation of verbal and visual artefacts alike. The
Nymphs' practice of weaving together (*intexens*) these plants and flowers
and placing them in baskets (*calathis*) is, after all, but a version of the

118

basket of eclogues, the *fiscella*, the narrator has finished weaving (*texit*) by the time he brings the *Eclogues* as a whole to a close.

The verb with which Corydon describes how he will 'gather' fruit for Alexis, *legere*, similarly doubles up as a verb of 'reading' and we shall consider Corydon's role as a reader, as well as a maker, of literary images in the section to follow. But what Corydon's representation of bucolic activity in any case brings to the fore is the extent to which it is fashioned for, and therefore requires the presence of, Alexis as its reader, viewer and adjudicator. 'Be present here' (*huc ades*) Corydon asks of his beloved and it is by no means a coincidence that the very same instruction is also issued to Galatea in one of the fragments of song recited in *Eclogue* 9 (9.39-43). As Ian Du Quesnay observes, moreover, the offering over of this image of the natural world to Alexis also casts the object of Corydon's affections somewhat in the role of a god, at whose coming that world blossoms into life.[65] What is more, it draws him into line with a number of other figures in the *Eclogues* as well, including the 'beautiful Alexis' to whom the Corydon of *Eclogue* 7 addresses the following quatrain in the course of his contest with Thyrsis (7.53-6):

> Stant et iuniperi et castaneae hirsutae,
> strata iacent passim sua quaeque sub arbore poma,
> omnia nunc rident: at si formosus Alexis
> montibus his abeat, uideas et flumina sicca.

> Both the junipers and the shaggy chestnut trees stand erect, and every fruit lies strewn here and there beneath its own tree, now all things are laughing: but if beautiful Alexis departs from these mountains, you would see even the rivers run dry.

The sentiment of these lines is clear: the picture of the natural world Corydon constructs is close to being inert, with its trees still and erect, its fruit lying idly on the ground and even its rivers threatening to run dry; only the vivifying presence of beautiful Alexis can bring it all to life and make it laugh. Likewise in *Eclogue* 2 the natural world similarly requires the presence of Alexis if the Nymphs are to gather their flowers and Corydon his trees and fruit. Indeed, the use of the pronoun 'for you' (*tibi*) just before the scenes of image-making that follow emphasises further the importance of Alexis' involvement in such images. And even as it does so, it exemplifies yet another important and pervasive feature of the ecphrastic representation of the natural world in these poems: its configuration as a gift.

One sees this configuration, for instance, in the 'little gifts' (*munuscula*) the earth will pour out for the heaven-sent boy in *Eclogue* 4 (4.18). One sees it as well in *Eclogue* 1, a poem in which Tityrus alone uses the pronoun *mihi* ('to me') to signal the bounty he has received, while it is left to Meliboeus to use the corresponding *tibi* ('for you') to elucidate further the gifts with which his companion has been bestowed.⁶⁶ As with Alexis in *Eclogue* 2 and the unnamed child of *Eclogue* 4, moreover, what has been fashioned for Tityrus is an image of the natural world that also doubles up as an image of bucolic poetry.⁶⁷ 'For you' (*tibi* 47), Meliboeus remarks, your fields will remain and 'for you' (*tibi* 53) Theocritean song, carried by Hyblaean bees, will bring sleep with its gentle whispering. Yet another example of this analogy between the re-animating of a potentially static natural world and the giving and receiving of song comes in *Eclogue* 5. At the very end of that poem, and as a direct response to Menalcas' celebration of the newly deified Daphnis, in which he addresses the god with the promise that 'for you' (*tibi* 66, 68 and 74) he will establish altars, bowls and rituals, and 'for you' (*tibi* 79) the farmers will each year make their prayers, Mopsus in turn takes up this motif of an exchange of gifts, redirects it away from Menalcas' depiction of an exchange between a singer and his subject, and returns it to the paradigm of *Idyll* 1, in which a listener hands over a gift in return for the performance of a song. 'What gifts,' he asks his companion, 'What gifts shall I give to you in return for such a song?' (*Quae tibi, quae tali reddam pro carmine dona?* 5.81).

In *Eclogue* 2, Corydon similarly conceives of the image of the country-side he has produced for his beloved as a gift, but even as he does so he reveals that it thereby also constitutes his contribution to the contest he is having over Alexis with his city-dwelling rival Iollas. Indeed, in the lines that follow immediately after those cited above, he explicitly acknowledges that this is the case: 'you are rustic, Corydon' he complains; 'neither does Alexis care for your gifts, nor, if you contend with gifts, will Iollas concede' (*rusticus es, Corydon; nec munera curat Alexis, / nec, si muneribus certes, concedat Iollas* 56-7). In this way, a certain drama is attached to Corydon's depiction of the countryside, not solely because of the activities of gathering and weaving it involves, but also because of its participation in this kind of agonistic competition. What is more, even though *Eclogue* 2 creates the fiction of a contest between Corydon and Iollas for the prize of Alexis alone, the topographical affiliations of each participant render it emblematic of the tussle between the city and the country more generally, including the respective modes of poetry to which each plays host.

The image of the countryside Corydon promotes, moreover, is itself set against, and to a certain degree contested by, other images from the rustic world. As the opening of his soliloquy might be taken to suggest (8-13), the time when the reapers come in for their lunch and the cicadas start to chirp in the bush is not the time to wander around in the sun, but to sing one's songs at ease in the shade.⁶⁸ In much the same way, his eventual realisation that, while he has been singing, the south wind has destroyed his flowers and boars his fountains (58-9), marks not so much a contrast between Corydon's singing on the one hand and real work on the other, as an intimation that he has been weaving the wrong kind of flowers in his literary garland and has allowed to go to waste those that might have been of more help or value instead. Such is also the case when he berates himself for having left 'the leafy vine half-pruned on the elm' (*semiputata tibi frondosa uitis in ulmo est* 70) and enjoins himself to do something useful instead, such as 'prepare to weave a complete object with wicker and gentle rush' (*uiminibus mollique paras detexere iunco* 72). Apart from anything else, these activities in practice more or less replicate the plucking and weaving he imagines himself and the Nymphs carrying out for Alexis earlier in his soliloquy. The only real difference is that the *tibi* ('for you') no longer applies to Alexis, but to Corydon himself: it is as if he is trying to accept that he ought to fashion some images which might be of use to him and not only to one who is not even there to see them. Indeed, the range of ecphrastic images on show in this eclogue would appear to reflect the extent to which this poem brings together and replays all three of the scenes on the goatherd's bowl in *Idyll* 1. For Corydon is in many respects the boy who sits on his wall and weaves a cricket cage while the orchard he is supposed to be guarding is pillaged and he himself goes without his meal; he also plays the part of one of the two men from the opening scene, in which each tries endlessly to win his beloved from his rival through song, but without ever achieving any definite result; and finally, like the fisherman, he concentrates all his endeavour and attention on casting his net out to sea.

To the degree that Corydon revisits and re-enacts the scenes from the bowl in *Idyll* 1 (among others), he duly provides one model for how the potentially static images of bucolic poetry might be read and brought back to life. We shall look at this aspect of his soliloquy in more detail below. But it is worth prefacing this discussion with a summary of why it is so important that Corydon produces his ecphrastic images of the bucolic world and its poetry in the guise of the lovelorn Polyphemus. Put simply, this guise achieves two primary effects: it helps identify the extent to which Corydon's own acts of image-making and image-viewing serve as expressions of character; and it incorporates the soliloquy of this poem within a much broader intertextual story. It is necessary to recognise these effects, because it is for their apparent suppression of such agents of movement and change as characterisation and story-telling that Paul Alpers for one has criticised readings of the *Eclogues* and *Idylls* which focus on their depiction of landscape. What we are now in a position to respond is that 'landscape' not only encapsulates the incessant images of the natural world that are produced throughout these poems, but that it is also as capable of reflecting the presence of drama, action, movement and change as are the herdsmen upon whom Alpers suggests we turn our attention in their place. Indeed, the emphasis landscape places upon the shaping perception of the viewer renders this particular understanding of the distinction between setting and character somewhat beside the point. For it actively allows the depiction of the natural world to share in the processes of, and to this extent represent, bucolic verse as a whole, not least because both require the approval of a reader or viewer for them to come to life and be regarded as a success. In *Eclogue* 2, the rules of engagement are such that, for Corydon to defeat Iollas in his singing and win Alexis as his prize, he needs to paint a picture of the countryside which Alexis will like so much he will want to come and live inside.

As the poem's introductory lines imply, however, for as long as Corydon continues to wander through his landscape all alone (*solus*), the words he tosses to the mountains and the woods will continue to be 'unfounded' (*incondita*)[69] and his enthusiasm 'empty' (*inani*).[70] In the next chapter, we shall see how we ourselves, as readers, might be scripted to fill this void and to help this song achieve something akin to 'lift-off'. First, though, we shall look at another reader in this poem, Corydon himself, and will see how his propensity for image-making relates not only to his creation of poetry, but to his reading of it as well.

Eclogue 2: Corydon as a reader

When Corydon promises Alexis that he will gather apples and other fruits for him, his words play upon two of the connotations of the verb *legere*: 'to gather' and 'to read'. In so doing, they pick up on a motif that informs the whole of his soliloquy: namely, that Corydon is at least as much of a reader of rustic poetry as he is a rustic lover. What this promise also brings to the fore is the extent to which, for him, the act of reading is an act of mimesis. After all, his gathering – and therefore reading – of fruits, plants and trees is itself both a reflection of and a response to the Nymphs' gathering and weaving of flowers in the lines immediately before. Corydon's practice as a reader, indeed, is nowhere more clearly exemplified than in the mimetic relationship his actions and soliloquising bear to a poem that forms a part of precisely this kind of literary harvest: the epigram to Alexis in Meleager's *Garland* (*Anth. Pal.* 12.127):[71]

> Εἰνόδιον στείχοντα μεσαμβρινὸν εἶδον Ἄλεξιν,
> ἄρτι κόμαν καρπῶν κειρομένου θέρεος.
> διπλαῖ δ' ἀκτῖνές με κατέφλεγον· αἱ μὲν Ἔρωτος
> παιδὸς ἀπ' ὀφθαλμῶν, αἱ δὲ παρ' ἠελίου.
> ἀλλ' ἃς μὲν νὺξ αὖθις ἐκοίμισεν· ἃς δ' ἐν ὀνείροις
> εἴδωλον μορφῆς μᾶλλον ἀνεφλόγισεν.
> λυσίπονος δ' ἑτέροις ἐπ' ἐμοὶ πόνον ὕπνος ἔτευξεν,
> ἔμπνουν πῦρ ψυχῇ κάλλος ἀπεικονίσας.

I saw Alexis walking in the road in the middle of the day, just when the summer was being clipped of the tresses of her fruits. Two sets of rays burnt me; the rays of love, from the eyes of the boy, and the rays of the sun. The night put to bed again those rays that come from the sun, but the phantom of his form kindled those others all the more in my dreams. So sleep, which frees others from toil has created toil for me, having sculpted a figure of beauty in my soul that is a living fire.

5. Landscape

The manner in which Corydon tries to replicate the original conditions of this epigram and to place himself in the role of its narrator is paradigmatic for the way in which he reads other texts as well. By ranging over Alexis' 'traces' (*uestigia*) at the time of year when the reapers are in the fields and at the time of day when their lunch is being prepared (8-13), for instance, he recreates the season and the hour at which Alexis was seen to pass in the epigram. In much the same way, he takes on a number of the attributes of the epigrammatist too. For just as this latter is burnt by the sight of Alexis with rays that are kindled still further in his dreams, Corydon too 'was burning for Alexis' (*Corydon ardebat Alexin* 2.1) as he wanders around 'under a burning sun' (*sole sub ardenti* 2.13).

Corydon might well be described as the kind of reader who hopes to experience the 'reality effect' in his reading. The irony, though, is that the more he seeks to replicate the original experience of the epigram, the less original, and even the less real, his own experience comes to seem. Indeed, the motif of doubling, which is such a persistent feature of the epigram and to which the eclogue repeatedly returns, redoubles in this poem into a figure of imitation. In particular, the several recurrences of figures of two enable it to play out in exaggerated form some of the key characteristics of bucolic poetry as a whole, with its persistent investment in such dualistic modalities as dialogue and amoebaean exchange. In this second poem in the book of *Eclogues*, that is, which also invokes Theocritus' second idyll, Corydon – who proves to be a 'second' Meleager, a 'second' Damoetas (the singer of the second song in *Idyll* 6), a 'second' Polyphemus, and a 'second' singer of *Idyll* 3 – promises Alexis 'two young roe-deer' who drink their milk 'twice a day' (*duo ... capreoli; bina die* 40-2), even as 'the falling sun doubles the growing shadows' (*et sol crescentis decedens duplicat umbras* 67).

An element of change is therefore inscribed in the very process of reduplication itself and is one of the reasons why Corydon's attempts to replicate a number of scenes and motifs from literary tradition never quite achieve a strict mimesis. We shall come across others as we proceed, but it is in any case important to note the extent to which his engagement with literary history, here as elsewhere, is structured in terms of ecphrasis. For even as Meleager's epigram bears witness to Alexis' metamorphosis from a person seen on a road to a sculpted figure of beauty and a text, the contest in which Corydon is currently engaged marks an attempt to continue and reverse that process. After all, the person who succeeds in the battle between Corydon and Iollas and wins 'beautiful Alexis' (*formosus Alexis*) for himself will be the one who can bring this ecphrastic image back to life.

One might suggest, then, that 'looking' is an important and distinctive feature of the way in which Corydon reads this text in part because it is also an important motif in that text. The same can also be said of another key poem he repeats: Damoetas' 'Polyphemus song' in *Idyll* 6. In this case, Corydon explicitly records how this song was handed down to him in the form of an ecphrastic object: the pipe of Damoetas himself. The manner in which he describes its transmission, moreover, reflects the manner in which his own soliloquy repeats several of the themes, gestures and motifs of the song it contains (2.36-9):

> est mihi disparibus septem compacta cicutis
> fistula, Damoetas dono mihi quam dedit olim,
> et dixit moriens: 'te nunc habet ista secundum';
> dixit Damoetas, inuidit stultus Amyntas.

I own a pipe, fastened together with seven hemlock reeds of unequal length, which Damoetas once gave me as a gift, and, dying, said: 'now this pipe has you second'; Damoetas said this and stupid Amyntas looked askance.

Corydon has already shown himself to be a worthy heir to the dying Damoetas by claiming that Alexis, by ignoring him, is compelling him to die.[72] His receipt of this pipe in the form of a gift, moreover, draws him yet further into line with a range of other bucolic figures, since this is a familiar means of representing the passing on of song in bucolic verse.[73] But through his observation that Amyntas 'looked askance' (*inuidit*) when he saw Corydon receive this gift – a way of looking which Meliboeus for one refuses to adopt when he sees the scene of Tityrus' *otium* in *Eclogue* 1[74] – he draws attention to the ecphrastic structure of this exchange. This is important for two reasons at least: it reflects the theme of seeing that pervades the songs about the Cyclops in *Idyll* 6 (along with most other representations of this character in literary tradition); and it reflects the degree to which Corydon's attempts to read and re-create the experience of this song are also instigated through a further act of viewing.

After all, at no stage in his soliloquy does Corydon look more like the Cyclops than in the lines in which he recalls seeing his reflection on the shore (2.25-7):

> nec sum adeo informis: nuper me in litore uidi,
> cum placidum uentis staret mare. non ego Daphnin
> iudice te metuam, si numquam fallit imago.

Neither am I ill-formed: recently I saw myself on the shore, when the sea was standing still from the winds. I would not fear Daphnis, with you as judge, if an image never lies.

The reason Corydon looks like Polyphemus here is because Polyphemus casts a similar look at himself in *Idyll* 6 (*Id.* 6.34-8):

> καὶ γάρ θην οὐδ' εἶδος ἔχω κακὸν ὥς με λέγοντι.
> ἦ γὰρ πρᾶν ἐς πόντον ἐσέβλεπον, ἦς δὲ γαλάνα,
> καὶ καλὰ μὲν τὰ γένεια, καλὰ δέ μοι ἀ μία κώρα,
> ὡς παρ' ἐμὶν κέκριται, κατεφαίνετο, τῶν δέ τ' ὀδόντων
> λευκοτέραν αὐγὰν Παρίας ὑπέφαινε λίθοιο.

124

5. Landscape

For truly I do not have a bad form, as they tell me. For lately I looked into the sea, when it was calm, and fair was my beard, and fair shone out my one eye, as my judgement goes, and it reflected a gleam from my teeth that was whiter than Parian marble.

Through its replication of this particular scene, then, Corydon's act of (self-)mimesis within the eclogue serves also to reflect the structure of the relationship between this poem and the idyll. One consequence of this is that it endows the process of literary transmission with a number of the properties of ecphrasis and its distinctive modes of representation. One might note, for instance, how Corydon and Polyphemus both see their reflections in the sea only when it is calm and it would appear that the additional act of mimesis Corydon achieves – namely, his imitation of Polyphemus – depends upon time standing still as well. After all, Corydon's claim that this event took place 'recently' (*nuper*) simultaneously gestures towards this event's location in the past whilst also collapsing the distinction between himself and a cyclops who had similarly looked 'lately' (πρᾶν) at the sea. Such a structuring of time is, of course, a feature of ecphrasis too and one might note how even as the ecphrastic quality of this particular evocation of literary tradition is instigated through the distinctly visual properties of Corydon's 'look', it is also sustained and reflected in the 'image' in which that evocation results.

We shall return to the question of how far this image acts as an emblem of the lines in which it appears below, but one should also be aware of how its structuring as an ecphrastic object configures its relationship to the future as well. For when Corydon boasts that he would not fear to put his image up in contest even with Daphnis, he anticipates the very contest between Damoetas and Daphnis in *Idyll* 6 he is already imitating here. This folding over of the past into the future, and vice versa, is not simply a feature of this particular, and explicitly ecphrastic, evocation of literary tradition, but it is in play throughout the eclogue as a whole. It is signalled, for instance, by Corydon's own repeated wanderings among the beech trees and by his equally repetitive renditions of the texts he reads. Above all, though, it engages the temporal structure ascribed to the act of literary transmission by the conventional bucolic gesture of the handing over of a pipe. For even as this practice might seem to entail an element of linear progression, the status of the pipe itself as an ecphrastic object simultaneously disrupts – or, at least, reorientates – any such progression. Corydon's hemlock reed is an especially good case in point: not only does it connote its heritage in Damoetas' song in *Idyll* 6, but, by the close of *Eclogue* 5, when Menalcas likewise gives such a reed to Mopsus as a gift, it comes to connote its future history as well. Rolled up together in this single, static pipe, that is, are the present, past and future of Corydon's song alike.

This, somewhat recursive, structuring of literary tradition, with its complex reorientation of literary progression, need not entail that the songs and images involved are unable either to change or to evolve in the course of their transmission, but simply that this evolution is not in itself conjoined with a process of strict chronological progression. Of far more importance in this regard are the different structures of viewing through which each of these songs and images are engaged. This, after all, is where Polyphemus' 'form' (εἶδος) and Corydon's 'image' (*imago*) converge and move apart. Both, for a start, derive much of their nature from the competitive contexts within which they appear. Polyphemus' self-representation in *Idyll* 6, for instance, is informed both by his own need to refute what others say about him (ὥς με λέγοντι 34) – which in practice means what other texts say about him[75] – and Damoetas' need to answer in the voice of Polyphemus the song Daphnis addresses to Polyphemus in the lines before. When Polyphemus takes a look at himself in the sea, therefore, the image he sees reflects not just his own physical attributes, but also the relationship his present song bears to other 'Polyphemus songs' that have gone before.[76] Its nature, that is, is a product of these relations. The same could be said of Corydon's *imago* too, except that what distinguishes it from Polyphemus' is precisely the close relationship between them. For much of the comedy that derives from Corydon's claim to be 'not ill-formed' (*non informis*) relates to the manner in which his reflection here resembles nothing more than the famously ugly Cyclops. But it relates too to the way in which the differences between these two images are therefore emblematic of the differences between Corydon's soliloquy in *Eclogue* 2 and Damoetas' 'Polyphemus song' in *Idyll* 6. For it is precisely its role as an emblem of his verse that further undercuts Corydon's boast to be *non informis*, since the line in which this is expressed, with its awkward elisions and somewhat unseemly rhythm, is itself quite strikingly 'ill-formed'.[77]

This interchange between texts and images is one that persists throughout this eclogue. More than anything else, it helps structure the process of literary transmission, whether that process involves in any given moment the passing on of a pipe or the act of reading or writing. As often as not, moreover, this interchange is both instigated and reflected by Corydon's relationship towards his physical environment. Even as his own song fashions a sequence of images of the natural world for Alexis to view, inhabit and bring to life, that is, so too does he himself receive his texts in the form of natural emblems such as garlands, a pipe and the sea and so too does his corresponding viewing of those texts introduce him to a spatial environment that is buzzing with life. This is nowhere more in evidence than in his reading of Meleager's epigram, which in his case motivates and is motivated by a desire to see Alexis for himself. The traces of Alexis left behind in Meleager's text double up as footprints on the ground, so by reading them Corydon is projected into a landscape that is resonant with literary references (2.8-13):

nunc etiam pecudes umbras et frigora captant,
nunc uiridis etiam occultant spineta lacertos,
Thestylis et rapido fessis messoribus aestu
alia serpyllumque herbas contundit olentis.
at mecum raucis, tua dum uestigia lustro,
sole sub ardenti resonant arbusta cicadis.

Now even the flocks make for the shades and the cool places, now even the
thickets hide the green lizards, and Thestylis crushes fragrant herbs, garlic
and thyme, for the reapers weary from the rapid heat. But with me, while I
range over your traces, under a burning sun, the hedges re-echo with raucous
cicadas.

With this image we have come full circle. Having begun by looking at the
representation and construction of landscape in bucolic poetry, we have
ended with an example of how the *Eclogues* represent poems as landscapes
in themselves. It seems right to refer to the environment Corydon here
inhabits as a landscape, both because its representation is so thoroughly
informed by other literary texts[78] and because it comes into being as a
result of Corydon's reading, which is configured as an act of seeing
throughout. It also seems reasonable to suggest that *Eclogue* 2's charac-
terisation of other literary texts as landscapes reflects back upon, and
might therefore be applied to, *Eclogue* 2 itself. After all, it is as a result of
our own, repeated readings of this poem, that the landscapes Corydon
weaves come to be viewed and brought back to life and that he himself is
made to 'come continually among the thick beeches, those shady peaks'
(*tantum inter densas, umbrosa cacumina, fagos / adsidue ueniebat* 3-4)
time and time again. This particular configuration of the exchange be-
tween a text and a reader, of course, also points to a feature of the *Eclogues'*
modes of literary production and transmission that we have had occasion
to observe before: the importance to them of such structuring processes as
repetition and recursion. In the next chapter, we shall follow these ex-
changes and processes even further – all the way down, no less, to the
atomic structure which the *Eclogues* share with the physical universe.

6

Physics

It is one of the defining characteristics of ancient bucolic that its singers are almost always herdsmen as well.[1] For this reason alone, it is perhaps not surprising that this kind of poetry plays upon an analogy between herding and singing from the very start.[2] The *Eclogues* themselves, however, take this equivalence between these two activities further still and they do so not least by attributing something akin to an atomic structure to both. They relate the elements of a herdsman's flock, in other words, to the elements of a herdsman's song and to the elements that make up the physical universe alike. As a result, the process of herding one's flock – of releasing it from its pens, leading it out to pasture, allowing it to scatter far and wide, and then gathering it together again – comes to serve as a paradigm, not only for the shepherding of a verse and of the tradition from which it comes, but also for the creation and structuring of the cosmos as a whole. This final chapter will therefore look at how the *Eclogues* introduce and engage this relationship between the composition and constitution of bucolic poetry on the one hand and the composition and constitution of the physical universe on the other. In so doing, it will illustrate how this equation gives further definition to such key bucolic procedures as convening, beginning, organising and transmitting song, and will also demonstrate the important role readers play in the inauguration and perpetuation of bucolic verse.

Eclogue 6: first things

One of the clearest examples of where the *Eclogues* draw an equation between the atomic structure of the physical universe on the one hand and the structure of bucolic singing and herding on the other comes in the course of the so-called 'song of Silenus' in *Eclogue* 6. This song begins with an account of the beginnings of the universe and to this extent alone intimates a preliminary equation between its own starting point and that of physical matter. What is more, this song is said to have a greater effect on its environment than Orpheus does over Rhodope or Ismarus (29-30) and this further incorporates its representation of these 'first things' within a bucolic framework, since, as we have seen before, it thereby sets its own creation story up in competition with the cosmogony offered by Orpheus in Apollonius' *Argonautica*.[3] What really seals this equation between bucolic practice and natural process at the beginning of the song of Silenus and the beginning of the universe alike, however, is the way in which the elements that proceed to make up this universe are herded together as if they were animals in a flock (6.31-3):

> Namque canebat uti magnum per inane coacta
> semina terrarumque animaeque marisque fuissent
> et liquidi simul ignis; ut his ex omnia primis.

> For he was singing how through the great emptiness the seeds of lands, air and the sea had been gathered, and simultaneously of liquid fire; how all things came from these first things.

The key word here is *coacta*. For even though Lucretius also uses this verb to describe how the seeds of things were 'gathered together' at the preliminary stages of the creation of the universe,[4] it is more commonly deployed in the *Eclogues* to denote the gathering together of a herd. As such, it likens the atoms it here collates to the flock Menalcas instructs Tityrus to gather together in *Eclogue* 3 (*Tityre, coge pecus* 3.20) and to the sheep he orders some boys to herd up in that same poem (*cogite ouis, pueri* 3.98). More than anything else, though, it anticipates the scene that takes place when the song of Silenus itself draws to a close, when 'Vesper came into view from unwilling Olympus and ordered them to drive the sheep to the stables and to make a note of their number' (*cogere donec ouis stabulis numerumque referre / iussit et inuito processit Vesper Olympo* 6.85-6).

This last example brings the analogy between the gathering of atoms and the herding of animals into play within the context of a single poem. In doing so, moreover, it renders each of these activities emblematic of the ordering of bucolic verse. Just as the representation of the beginning of the universe stands at the beginning of Silenus' song and participates in a form of bucolic contest with Apollonius' Orpheus, that is, so too does the 'noting of the numbers' (*numerumque referre* 85) of the sheep and their herding into stables at its end both replicate the act of 'recording' the 'numbers' of poetry that the song of Silenus, with its catalogue of poetic themes, has only just performed and signal that the song itself has now come to an end.[5] Indeed, given that, as we saw in Chapter 4, the act of driving one's flocks home and putting them back in their stables serves to enact the restoration of bucolic order more generally, it is perhaps not surprising that in *Eclogue* 6 at least this act is equated with the ordering of the elements that leads to the formation of the universe.[6]

To this degree, then, *Eclogue* 6 fashions an equation between the archetypal bucolic act of herding and the archetypal creation story. When we come to *Eclogue* 7, we shall see how the evolution of a new poem out of the random distribution of elements from the literary tradition reflects the composition of the physical universe out of individual atoms. *Eclogue* 6 itself, meanwhile, persistently relates these 'first things', these primal elements, to 'first moments' and for this reason we shall proceed here to consider the temporality of the relationship between herding and cosmogony. For even though the creation of the earth is placed at the beginning of Silenus' song and the beginning of time, while the gathering together of sheep is enjoined at the end of that song and the end of the day, it is by no means the case that the latter persistently reflects, and to this extent invariably comes after, the former. Instead, the act of herding repeatedly shares in, and to this extent re-instantiates, the temporality of cosmological creation. One can see how the temporal relationship between bucolic poetry and cosmogony plays itself out if one considers the relationship between Silenus' song and the cosmos more generally. For Vesper, the star that orders this herding of the sheep to take place and, with it, the song as a whole to be brought to a close, is itself presumably one of the stars that the song had begun by shepherding into being (37). Likewise, in the lines that come immediately before the rising of this star, the cosmos which the song sings into existence is also cited as one of its primary destinations, as well as a key participant in its ongoing transmission (82-4). In this way, the song which had initially given shape to the cosmos now acquires its own shape in relation to that cosmos and thus each provides to a certain degree an aetiology for the other.

The language of aetiology is relevant here because the lines that seek to place the song of Silenus within the context of the cosmos themselves provide a history for this song and, in so doing, actively re-instantiate the terms of the cosmogony with which the song began. For just as Silenus had opened his cosmogony with a brief enumeration of 'the first things from which all things came' (*ut his ex omnia primis* 33), Tityrus, the narrator of *Eclogue* 6, now brings the song as a whole to a close with a brief rehearsal of the elements from which 'all the things he sings' in their own turn derive (6.82-4):

> omnia, quae Phoebo quondam meditante beatus
> audiit Eurotas iussitque ediscere lauros,
> ille canit, pulsae referunt ad sidera ualles.

> he sings all the things which, when Phoebus was once contemplating them, the blessed Eurotas heard and ordered the bay trees to learn, and the struck valleys carry them back to the stars.

One of the effects of this aetiology, of course, is to indicate that Silenus' song of origins is not itself original, but it has a history. A comparable aetiological structure informs its account of the creation of the cosmos as well, since this has both a discursive and a material history in the 'seeds' (*semina* 32) of things that precede it too. Indeed, the involvement of the river Eurotas, the bay trees, the valleys and the stars in the history and transmission of this song demonstrates the extent to which the processes

130

of poetry and nature are not simply analogous in this poem but that they actively interrelate. In this poem, in other words, literary and natural history are inextricably conjoined. One can see this, for instance, when Silenus places the time we might infer bucolic poetry appeared, 'when woods first begin to rise and when a few scarce animals wander through the unknowing mountains' (*incipiant siluae cum primum surgere cumque / rara per ignaros errent animalia montis* 39-40), like Lucretius,[7] at an early stage in the earth's evolution. More broadly, though, Tityrus' structuring of the song of Silenus as a sequence of 'now's and, especially, 'then's, explicitly aligns the order of events with the order of Silenus' singing.[8] The following lines in particular offer a good example of how the structure of this song and the structure of world history repeatedly interrelate (6.61-4):

> <u>tum</u> canit Hesperidum miratam mala puellam;
> <u>tum</u> Phaethontiadas musco circumdat amarae
> corticis atque solo proceras erigit alnos.
> <u>tum</u> canit, errantem Permessi ad flumina Gallum ...

> <u>then</u> he sings how the girl marvelled at the apples of the Hesperides; <u>then</u> he surrounds the sisters of Phaethon with the moss of a bitter bark and erects tall alders in the ground. <u>Then</u> he sings how Gallus, wandering at the streams of the Permessus ...

It is important to observe in this regard that Tityrus does not always have Silenus reproducing events in their strict chronological order.[9] In one couplet, for instance, he places Pyrrha before the Golden Age and refers to Prometheus' punishment before he mentions his crime: 'from here he relates the tossed stones of Pyrrha, the reign of Saturn, the birds of the Caucasus and Prometheus' theft' (*hinc lapides Pyrrhae iactos, Saturnia regna, / Caucasiasque refert uolucris furtumque Promethei* 6.41-2). This particular configuration of natural and human history is significant because it reproduces and reflects the nonlinear ordering of literary process in this eclogue more generally, in which the seemingly distinct acts of commissioning, performing and receiving song are forever anticipating, reflecting and folding into one another. *Eclogue* 6, after all, is a poem in which Apollo is identified first as the god who commissioned Tityrus to sing this kind of verse (3-5), then as its delighted reader (11-12), and finally as the author of the sequence of songs which, by way of the river Eurotas, bay trees, valleys, stars, Silenus and now Tityrus, he is here about to read (82-4).[10]

We shall come back to the role individual characters, including the various readers and recipients of this song, might play in this eclogue shortly. But first we should reiterate how, in this poem at least, the interrelationship of poetry and nature, and especially their shared atomic structure, plays itself out in relation to beginnings , or 'first moments', in particular. For *Eclogue* 6 shows a recurrent interest in beginnings and these beginnings repeatedly engage literary and natural elements alike. The very first word of the poem, for instance, is *prima* ('first') and the opening couplet as a whole proceeds to characterise the narrator, Tityrus', first steps as a singer through reference to the environment his muse first inhabited: 'Our Thalea first deigned to play with Syracusan verse and neither did she blush to inhabit the woods' (*Prima Syracosio dignata est ludere uersu / nostra neque erubuit siluas habitare Thalea* 6.1-2). Having then claimed for himself the same kind of seminal experience that Callimachus recounts in the prologue to his *Aetia*, when he 'first' placed a writing tablet on his knees (*Aetia* fr. 1.21-2 Pf.), Tityrus immediately aligns poetic and natural beginnings once again by undertaking to contemplate the 'muse of the fields' (*agrestis musa*), a type of song which, as we have seen, comes straight from the passage in the *De Rerum Natura* in which Lucretius discusses the origins of this kind of verse.[11]

Even aside from their engagement with natural process, the degree to which each of these literary beginnings alludes to other originary moments in literary history means that each of these beginnings is more accurately described as a 'beginning again'. Indeed, *Eclogue* 6 actively thematises its status as a 'beginning again'. Not only does it constitute the beginning of the second half of the *Eclogue* book, but it also begins by recalling how it itself evolves out of a still earlier, yet ultimately false, start. As Tityrus himself acknowledges, he was already in the process of singing about 'kings and battles' (*cum canerem reges et proelia* 3) when Apollo intervened and gave him the set of aesthetic instructions which have caused him to abandon (or, at least, re-conceive) that earlier project and to embark on the present poem instead. It ends, moreover, as we have seen, with an acknowledgement that it includes songs which have been sung many times before.

When one allows for the engagement of natural processes in the transmission and history of these songs, it seems all the more appropriate to speak of this sequence of 'beginnings again' in terms of recursion and recycling. After all, this equation between natural and poetic beginnings in the *Eclogues* is reflected further still by their mutual engagement in a shared vocabulary, in which the verbs *incipere* and *coepere* are used to denote the process of beginning in poetry and nature alike. In *Eclogue* 6 alone, for instance, *incipere* is used both of the moment when Silenus 'at once begins to sing' (*simul incipit ipse* 26) and of the moment in the earth's evolution when 'the woods first begin to rise' (*incipiant siluae cum primum surgere* 39), an event which, as we have seen, both anticipates and reflects Tityrus' own first experiments in verse, when his muse, Thalea, did not deign to inhabit the woods (1-2).

One of the effects of this characterisation of the various beginnings described and engaged in *Eclogue* 6 as 'beginnings again' is that it awards a dual temporality to this key bucolic act. It entails, in other words, that the practice of beginning both initiates and repeats. One might note, for instance, how these poems' persistent interest in the beginnings of bucolic song is matched throughout by an equally persistent desire for bucolic song to begin. 'Begin, Damoetas; you then follow, Menalcas' (*incipe, Damoeta; tu deinde sequere, Menalca* 3.58), Palaemon instructs the two opponents in *Eclogue* 3; 'you begin first ... begin' (*Incipe, Mopse, prior ... incipe* 5.10-12) Menalcas similarly enjoins his companion in *Eclogue* 5; 'Begin with me Maenalian verses' (*incipe Maenalios mecum, mea tibia, uersus* 8.21, etc.), Damon urges his pipe repeatedly in *Eclogue* 8; 'begin, if you have anything' (*incipe, si quid habes* 9.32), Lycidas tries to persuade his companion, Moeris, in *Eclogue* 9; and, finally, in *Eclogue* 10 the narrator issues the same injunction to Arethusa as he asks her to begin their song of the anxious loves of Gallus (*incipe: sollicitos Galli dicamus amores* 10.6). On several occasions, moreover, these dual concerns with the beginnings of bucolic song and with beginning bucolic song fold into one. Damoetas' first contribution to the song contest in *Eclogue* 3, for example, demonstrably begins with an assertion of the foundations of his verse: 'The <u>beginning</u> of my muse is from Jove: all things are from Jove' (*Ab Ioue <u>principium</u> musae: Iouis omnia plena* 3.60), a statement of first principles that nimbly grounds Damoetas' muse in the cosmos and a literary text – namely Aratus' *Phaenomena* – alike.

Through such means, the *Eclogues* repeatedly conjoin beginnings in nature and poetry in an inherently recursive structure, in which the present is folded into both the past and the future and in which the processes of poetry and nature initiate and instantiate one another in equal measure. To a certain degree, this configuration is but a further reflex of bucolic poetry's propensity towards ecphrastic modes of representation, which, as we saw in the previous chapter, are brought into play through this very exchange between poetry and nature and which thereby display a distinctively ecphrastic temporality. The explicit involvement of the natural world in this exchange, moreover, means that the working out of this ecphrastic impulse in the *Eclogues*, including its temporal relations, engages a number of natural processes, perhaps the most notable of which is echo. In *Eclogue* 6, for instance, these two devices of ecphrasis and echo are brought suggestively together in a section of the song of Silenus that Tityrus organises spatially ('from there ... to these', *hinc ... his* 41 and 43) and which Silenus himself treats in a similar manner when he 'joins to these [other stories]' a further tale. What is noteworthy about this tale in our context is that what it describes is precisely an instance of echo: 'how the whole shore echoed "Hylas, Hylas"' (*ut litus 'Hyla, Hyla' omne sonaret* 44).[12]

We saw in the previous chapter how echoes can look forward as well as back and one might add to this that, as Lucretius also acknowledges in his account of the *siluestris musa*, when he speaks of how echoes can turn one voice into many (*DRN* 4.577-89), they can be generative as well.[13] This is an important component in what one might call the 'ecology' of the *Eclogues*, not least because it arises out of the tendency of these poems to characterise songs as places which both they themselves and their future readers might inhabit. Indeed, in much the same way that *Eclogue* 2 casts itself and the texts it reads as spatial topographies, so too does *Eclogue* 6 open by presenting itself as a page that, if it is read with love, will take on the form of a living and responsive natural environment (*Ecl.* 6.9-12):[14]

> si quis tamen haec quoque, si quis
> captus amore leget, te nostrae, Vare, myricae,
> te nemus omne canet; nec Phoebo gratior ulla est
> quam sibi quae Vari praescripsit pagina nomen.

Nonetheless, if anyone will read these things too, if anyone will read them captured with love, of you our tamarisks, Varus, of you the whole grove will sing; neither is there any page more pleasing to Phoebus than one which has written the name of Varus at its top.

Here again, with the repetition of 'if anyone ... if anyone' (*si quis ... si quis*) and 'of you ... of you' (*te ... te*), echo forms a constituent part of this literary-natural topography. It is an echo, moreover, that is triggered above all by an act of reading. It is important to note this capacity of a reader to set such echoes in motion because this places her or him in an analogous position to the bay trees the Eurotas ordered to learn these things, to the valleys that transmit them to the stars and to the singer Tityrus himself. For, having received similar orders himself (*non iniussa cano* 9), when this herdsman undertakes to '<u>contemplate</u> the woodland muse on a slender reed' (*agrestem tenui <u>meditabor</u> harundine musam* 8), not only does his ensuing performance engage the origins of the form as described by Lucretius, but it also echoes, and to this degree provides a future for, the songs which Apollo 'was once <u>contemplating</u>' (*quondam <u>meditante</u>* 82) on the banks of the Eurotas.

It is important to note too how these echoes are instigated by an act of reading that, because it involves an exchange between poetry and nature, reflects the terms of ecphrasis. The significance of this is that it helps structure the temporal status of each reading experience as an historical intervention in what is otherwise an ongoing, recursive, but currently 'frozen' system. There are, after all, numerous 'echoes' between each of the poem's various parts, many of which explicitly invoke a language of perception and, thereby, ecphrasis. Thus, the marvelling of the natural world at Silenus' song, for instance (*nec tantum Rhodope <u>miratur</u> et Ismarus Orphea* 30), is in turn mirrored by the account of 'the girl [who] marvelled at the apples of the Hesperides' (*Hesperidum <u>miratam</u> mala puellam* 61) within that song. This combination of echoes and ecphrastic events, moreover, is precisely the means by which the poem as a whole sets in motion most, if not all, of its seminal 'first moments'. Even as many of these moments are echoes of earlier passages from works such as the *Idylls*, the *Aetia*, the *Argonautica* and the *De Rerum Natura*, that is, so too do they rely on a sequence of interlinking visual apprehensions. The song of Silenus, in other words, acquires as one of its beginnings the moment when Chromis and Mnasyllos 'saw' (*uidere*) Silenus himself asleep (14). Then, in line 21, Silenus in turn reflects their gaze when he 'sees' (*uidenti*) them tying him up, and he subsequently asserts the importance of perceiving and of being perceived to the eliciting of his song when he declares that to be perceived to be capable is power enough. 'Why are you binding chains?' (*Quo uincula nectitis?* 23), he asks them. 'Free me, boys; it is enough to be seen to have been able' (*soluite me, pueri; satis est potuisse uideri* 24). Finally, when Silenus has at last struck up his song, then, reader, you 'would have seen' (*uideres* 27) the fauns and the wild beasts dance in time, and the stiff oaks shake their peaks.

As this sequence of exchanges illustrates, readers and recipients of bucolic song are evidently of some importance for its production and transmission in the *Eclogues* more generally. In what follows, we shall therefore look at a number of further instances of how several of the characters who appear in these poems, whether as active participants or addressees, both participate in and contribute to its self-renewing and recursive structure.

People

The *Eclogues* are populated by a range of different characters. In addition to such familiar Theocritean figures as Tityrus, Corydon, Thyrsis, Amaryllis, Lycidas and Galatea, these poems also introduce new herdsmen such as Meliboeus, as well as those who, like Alexis, are not so obviously a part of the bucolic world. Perhaps the most notable members of this latter group are the poets and politicians Virgil includes from his contemporary reality: the land surveyor, Publius Alfenus Varus; the poet and politician, Gaius Asinius Pollio; the poet and soldier, Gaius Cornelius Gallus; the unnamed divine young man at Rome in *Eclogue* 1; and the unnamed poet and soldier who is the addressee of *Eclogue* 8. It has sometimes been assumed that the introduction of these particular characters to the bucolic world variously intimates, initiates and reflects the destruction of this world, but there are at least two reasons for suggesting that this is not so. In the first place, Theocritus too addresses or names a number of friends, patrons or other contemporary figures throughout the *Idylls*, which is enough to indicate that this practice is not in itself antithetical to the nature of bucolic verse. More important still is the role these figures play both as characters within and as recipients of the songs of the *Eclogues*. For as we shall see, not only does the inclusion of such characters within the world of these poems enable Virgilian bucolic to engage with a range of supposedly non-bucolic paradigms and settings, and in so doing expand its own horizons, but the consistent characterisation of these figures and recipients as gods, who as often as not are evoked as constituent elements in the beginning of bucolic verse, also helps establish and instigate the recursive and ecphrastic temporality we have already identified, not least by recasting it as a form of litany.

To begin with, though, we might first note how the act of reading is often represented in the *Eclogues* as an act of love. We have just seen in *Eclogue* 6 how the tamarisks and the whole grove will sing Varus' name 'if anyone will read these things <u>captured with love</u>' (*si quis / <u>captus amore</u> leget* 6.9-10) and we shall encounter this relationship between reading and loving again shortly in the passage from *Eclogue* 3 in which Damoetas asserts that his reader, Pollio, 'loves our muse' (*Pollio amat nostram ... musam* 3.84). The most extended example of this equation, however, comes in *Eclogue* 10, a poem that opens by expressing the hope that it will consist of songs 'which Lycoris herself might read' (*sed quae legat ipsa Lycoris* 10.2). For were Lycoris in practice to read this poem, her reading would serve to bring both her and Gallus together again within the textual space of the eclogue by causing her to take Gallus' part and share his *amores*. It would also lead her to speak the words with which the narrator affirms his love for Gallus at the end as if they were her own.[15] In all these cases, moreover, the idea that a reader might be brought together with a text through an act of love provides the preliminaries for a process which, in terms of human relations, might presage marriage, but which in terms of bucolic poetics (as we saw in Chapter 2) could thereby instigate and map the trajectory by which bucolic poetry hopes one day to ascend to the stars and become truly cosmological.

The capacity of the readers of the *Eclogues* to set such a trajectory in motion is due not least to their frequent casting in the role of a god and, alongside this, as prime movers in the transmission and production of bucolic verse. Indeed, it is striking how often the contemporary Romans named or addressed in the *Eclogues* participate, like Varus in *Eclogue* 6, in scenes that recall seminal moments from the prologue to Callimachus' *Aetia*. One might note, for instance, how Pollio is also awarded an analogous role to Callimachus' Apollo in the course of the song contest of *Eclogue* 3, when he is addressed as both a reader and a poet, and when the Muses are instructed to fatten a young cow and bull for him, as if in sacrifice (3.84-7):

DAMOETAS:
Pollio amat nostram, quamuis est rustica, musam:
Pierides, uitulam lectori pascite uestro.

MENALCAS:
Pollio et ipse facit noua carmina: pascite taurum,
iam cornu petat et pedibus qui spargat harenam.

DAMOETAS: Pollio loves our muse, even though she is rustic: Pierians, feed a young cow for your reader.

6. Physics

MENALCAS: Pollio himself also makes new poems: feed a bull, one which is already able to attack with its horn and scatter the sand with its feet.

The young man of *Eclogue* 1 similarly fulfils an aetiological function that is in several respects reminiscent of Callimachus' Apollo. Characterised from the outset as a deity who has allowed Tityrus' oxen to roam and Tityrus himself to play what he wishes on his reed (1.6-10), he is explicitly associated with beginnings when, in words that also recall Apollo's instruction to Callimachus to 'feed your burnt offering to be as fat as possible' (τὸ μὲν θύος ὅττι πάχιστον / θρέψαι fr. 1.23-4 Pf.), Tityrus recalls how this man 'first gave a response to my petition: "feed the oxen as before, boys; rear bulls" ' (*hic mihi responsum primus dedit ille petenti: / 'pascite ut ante boues, pueri; summittite tauros'* 1.44-5). In this same eclogue, moreover, the striking of the oak tree by lightning (1.14-15) reworks Callimachus' assertion in the prologue that 'it is not for me to thunder, but for Zeus' (βροντᾶν οὐκ ἐμόν, ἀλλὰ Διός *Aetia* fr. 1.20), while Gallus' initiation by the Muses on Mount Helicon in *Eclogue* 6 in turn evokes Callimachus' dream of his own initiation there.[16] Tityrus' response to this young man, meanwhile, is to treat him as a god and to celebrate his munificence by undertaking to observe a sequence of sacrifices in his honour every year: 'here I saw that young man, Meliboeus, for whom our altars will smoke for twice six days a year' (*hic illum uidi iuuenem, Meliboee, quotannis / bis senos cui nostra dies altaria fumant* 1.42-3). In this instantiation of a series of annual rites in commemoration of this young man's initiating intervention (*hic mihi responsum primus dedit ille*) is to be found an embodiment of the recursive temporality that is set in play whenever a reader sets these poems more generally in motion.

Another figure who is endowed with just about every one of the important attributes afforded to the Roman recipients of bucolic song in the *Eclogues* is the unnamed dignitary of *Eclogue* 8. As we saw in Chapter 2, this poem begins with a resonant, but frozen, picture of the Orphic power of bucolic song, wherein the contest between the herdsmen Damon and Alphesiboeus causes heifers and lynxes to stand in wonder, while streams still their courses (8.1-5). The narrator then breaks off from this scene to address an unnamed acquaintance, who is currently in the process either of overcoming the rocks of great Timavus or of hugging the coast of the Illyrian sea (*seu magni superas iam saxa Timaui / siue oram Illyrici legis aequoris* 8.6-7). The effect of this juxtaposition is to establish from the outset a preliminary distinction between the world of the poem on the one hand and the world inhabited by its recipient on the other. It is perhaps tempting to see in this a corresponding contrast between the fantastical, a-temporal world of bucolic poetry and the real world of Roman politics, time and action respectively. But, as was also the case with the simile involving the eagle and the doves at *Eclogue* 9.11-13, one might just as readily find here a contrast between two distinctive literary modes as well.

The epic quality of the river Timavus, for instance, which once formed a part of the route by which the Argonauts made their way home, is indicated by its epic epithet *magnus*,[17] while the literary credentials of the Illyrian sea are in their turn suggested by the verb *legere*. This, after all, is the first occasion in Latin literature in which this verb is used to designate the 'hugging' of a shore and it is just as likely that Virgil's first readers would initially have understood this word in its more familiar sense and assumed that his addressee was duly 'reading' that coastline as well.[18] These two connotations are, of course, also both in play in a similar passage in Book 2 of the *Georgics*, when Virgil invites his reader Maecenas to 'be present and hug the coast of the first shore' (*ades et primi lege litoris oram Geo. 2.44*).

Regardless, then, of who the poem's addressee might in practice have been and where he might have been sailing at the time of the composition of *Eclogue* 8, he is just as likely to have been travelling through these places in literature as in the context of a military campaign.[19] The crucial thing, though, is that, by inviting his addressee to receive the kind of poems that cause animals to stand and stare and streams to still their waters, the narrator is encouraging his addressee not only to inhabit this alternative environment but to do so whilst also navigating the rocks of Timavus or hugging the Illyrian shore. Which is to say, this reader is being asked to bring these two, supposedly distinct, settings together in much the same way that he is subsequently enjoined to 'allow this ivy to entwine around your temples among your conquering laurels' (*atque hanc sine tempora circum / inter uictricis hederam tibi serpere lauros 8.12-13*).[20] This kind of reading, in other words, is itself a form of ecology.

It is also the act that sets this literary environment in motion and gives it life. As with so many other instances in the *Eclogues*, the unnamed poet and soldier of *Eclogue* 8 receives this poem as an ecphrastic object or gift: 'receive songs' (*accipe ... / carmina 8.11-12*), he is told, and the static, frozen nature of what he is being given has already been represented by the opening depiction of the effects on the natural world of the contest he is about to read. His capacity to revivify this scene and to realise the Orphic powers of this kind of verse, moreover, is likewise already indicated in the words with which he is awarded this gift: 'receive songs <u>begun at your orders</u>' (*accipe <u>iussis</u> / carmina <u>coepta tuis</u> 8.11-12*). The idea that he himself 'ordered' these songs draws him into line with Apollo (and possibly Varus)[21] in *Eclogue* 6, because of whom Tityrus does not sing 'things unordered' (*non iniussa cano 6.9*); with Vesper and Eurotas in that same poem, who similarly issue orders that enable the transmission of those songs (*iussit ... iussit 6.83 and 86*); and with the godlike young man of *Eclogue* 1, who 'permitted' (*permisit 1.10*) Tityrus to play his reed.

Like those others, moreover, he too is addressed as if he were a god – most notably through the 'prayer-like' *seu ... siue* of lines 6-7[22] – and he too is cited as a constituent element in the poem's beginnings. Its songs were begun at his orders (8.11-12) and the verb which is used to denote this, *coepta*, is recycled a few lines later to describe how one of the competing herdsmen, Damon, does then proceed to sing: 'Damon, leaning on a smooth olive, <u>begins</u> as follows' (*incumbens tereti Damon sic <u>coepit</u> oliuae* 8.16). More than this, though, he is actively invoked as a *principium*, or beginning, in himself: 'From you is my beginning, with you shall I cease' (*a te principium, tibi desinam* 8.11). This form of address, through its recollection of Damoetas' first words in the song contest of *Eclogue* 3 and thereby of the opening of Aratus' *Phaenomena* alike, aligns him also with Jupiter, who, according to Aratus, fills the whole of the universe.[23] As such, it reasserts once again his capacity to give life to the contest of Damon and Alphesiboeus and, in so doing, to realise the Orphic powers of this poetry depicted at its start and to set in motion its cosmological potential.

To the extent that this particular reader remains anonymous, he might be called upon to serve as a paradigm of each and every recipient of the *Eclogues* more generally. At the very least, it is worth noting that, along with several of the other Romans named or addressed in these poems, he is characterised as a poet himself (8.9-10), as well as an instigator and receiver of verse.[24] This is important not least because it aligns the process of reading with the process of singing, which is to say, it characterises it as an inherently creative act. We shall see this again in relation to the, similarly anonymous, child reader of *Eclogue* 4, whose reading has the capacity to start the order of generations anew. First, however, we shall turn to *Eclogue* 7, a poem which illustrates how bucolic poetry is not only capable of absorbing chance elements, such as unexpected readers, into its midst but that it is precisely the introduction of such new and random elements which instils it with its sense of order.

Eclogue 7: chance collocations

While the song of Silenus begins with a scene of atoms being herded up like sheep, *Eclogue* 7 turns the analogy around and opens with a scene of pasture animals being gathered together like atoms (7.1-5):

> Forte sub arguta consederat ilice Daphnis,
> compulerantque greges Corydon et Thyrsis in unum,
> Thyrsis ouis, Corydon distentas lacte capellas,
> ambo florentes aetatibus, Arcades ambo,
> et cantare pares et respondere parati.

By chance, Daphnis had sat down beneath a clear-sounding ilex, and Corydon and Thyrsis had driven their flocks together into one, Thyrsis his sheep, Corydon his she-goats distended with milk, both flowering with youth, both Arcadians, well-matched at singing and prepared to respond.

These lines re-enact one of bucolic poetry's most persistent and distinctive conventions: the coming together of two or more herdsmen and their flocks prior to an exchange of song.[25] They are also conventional in a second sense too, since this particular gathering of herdsmen and their flocks replays similar scenes from elsewhere in the tradition. In particular, it recalls the coming together of herdsmen at the start of *Idylls* 6 and 8, two poems whose influence extends over *Eclogue* 7 more broadly,[26] although the verbs *considere* and *compellere* are also used to designate acts of convening in other eclogues as well.[27] Indeed, so conventional is this scene in the second as well as the first sense of that term that it contains barely a feature or detail that cannot be paralleled elsewhere in the *Eclogues* or in the bucolic tradition as a whole.

One corollary of this is that, even as Daphnis 'sits down together' beneath his ilex and Corydon and Thyrsis 'drive their flocks together' in the opening lines of *Eclogue* 7, a number of other poems and songs also duly take their place within the space of this poem. Corydon, for instance, enters this poem fresh from *Eclogue* 2 and will here be required to play the part of Polyphemus and to address Alexis all over again;[28] Thyrsis, meanwhile, recalls the figure who produced the paradigmatic bucolic piece, the 'Sufferings of Daphnis', in *Idyll* 1; while Daphnis is the archetypal figure of the bucolic and, as such, acts as a generic marker for the exchanges of *Eclogue* 7 more generally. His presence here, moreover, also ushers in those two idylls whose influence upon the eclogue has already been noted and which is rendered all the more explicit in the lines that follow: *Idyll* 6, a poem in which Daphnis is matched by Damoetas in a song contest and from which derives the practice of bringing the two singers' flocks together into one place; and *Idyll* 8, a poem in which Daphnis defeats Menalcas and from which comes the equation of two singers whose flocks consist of different animals, but who are identical in age and appearance and who are both able to play the pipe and sing.[29]

What is noteworthy about this particular collocation of traditional elements is that they are introduced and organised as if they were free-floating atoms coming together in physical space. This analogy depends in part upon the constant interchange of terms and properties between poetry and nature that is in evidence from the very start. When the two singers, Corydon and Thyrsis, are said to be 'flowering with youth' (*ambo florentes aetatibus*), for example, this is but the flip side of an equation between poetry and nature that also sees the tree under which Daphnis sits share its epithet, 'clear-sounding' (*arguta*), with the flute to which Corydon refers later in the eclogue (*arguta ... fistula* 24). More than anything else, though, it the deployment of a recognisably Lucretian vocabulary in these lines that points up this association between the preliminaries to a song contest and the primal motions and elements that underpin the physical world. After all, the phrase that describes the union of Corydon's goats with Thyrsis' sheep, *in unum*, and that also translates a phrase Theocritus uses in a comparable context, εἰς ἕνα χῶρον (*Id.* 6.1), brings the *De Rerum Natura* immediately into play, where it is used to represent the collocation of diverse elements in physical space.[30]

The particular application of this Lucretian language to the herding together of sheep and goats indicates the extent to which these animals and their differing combinations constitute and embody the poetic world of any given eclogue in much the same way that atoms constitute and embody the physical world described in the *De Rerum Natura*. Indeed, Lucretius himself provides a precedent for this analogy both when he deploys an image of sheep grazing on a hill as a way of illustrating the barely discernible movement of atoms (*DRN* 2.308-22) and when, in a passage that also uses the phrase *in unum*, he compares the combination of letters that make up the words of his poem with the combination of atoms that constitute the physical universe (*DRN* 2.686-94).

In *Eclogue* 7, the driving of Corydon's and Thyrsis' flocks 'into one' (*in unum*) therefore achieves two, interrelated, effects: it renders the space of this poem equivalent to the space of Lucretius' universe; and it transforms those flocks into analogues of Lucretius' atoms and the letters of the alphabet alike. Like those atoms and letters, moreover, the different combinations of these animals are suggestive of different physical and literary entities. We shall see one way in which this is so shortly below, but first we should observe how the force that supposedly brings all these elements together at the outset of the *Eclogues* likewise finds its parallel in Lucretius' universe. Introduced in the very first word of *Eclogue* 7, *fors*, or 'chance', serves in the *De Rerum Natura* to characterise the, occasionally random, motions of atoms as well as the, often mistaken, judgements people make about the world that results (to look ahead to the closing lines of this eclogue).[31] At the same time, it plays an important role in other eclogues as well, especially in relation to a herdsman's ability to hear and play music and to remain on one's land. In *Eclogue* 9, for instance, Moeris complains how the former farmers have been told to migrate and observes from this how 'chance overturns everything' (*fors omnia uersat* 9.5). In *Eclogue* 1, meanwhile, Meliboeus twice calls Tityrus 'fortunate' (*fortunatus*) because he is able to stay where he is and carry on listening to the sounds of nature and the song of the leaf-stripper (*Ecl.* 1.46-58). It is in *Eclogue* 7, though, that the principle of chance most obviously shapes both the poetry and the topography of bucolic song. Here, it atomises familiar elements (most notably in the distinction between Corydon's and Thyrsis' flocks in line 3 that follows on immediately after their conglomeration) and redistributes those elements into new combinations. This dual movement is suggested, above all, by those compound words that begin with the prefix (or near-prefix) *con-*. For while *considere* ('to sit together') and *compellere* ('to drive together') here bring these various elements together, *contendere* ('to contend') and, to some degree, *contra* ('against' or 'opposite'), both of which appear a few lines later, pull them apart.[32]

In the opening five lines of *Eclogue* 7, then, we find an analogy between the random collocation of atoms in cosmological space that serves to fashion a world and the act of convening that stands as a prelude to the performance of bucolic song. The very next word, *huc* ('to here'), moreover, actively characterises the scene of this gathering as a place which another character, who is to some degree 'off-stage', is invited to enter. In accordance with a number of the other instances we have considered, this is the character who, once again through an act of visual perception, will set the contest itself in motion.[33] In accordance with the sequence of chance encounters that structure this eclogue's opening rehearsal of bucolic convention, meanwhile, his own participation introduces yet another random element to the events about to take place. Not the least of the surprises in store is that this figure, who will also prove to be the poem's narrator, is none other than Meliboeus, the herdsman who was sent into exile in his very first appearance in bucolic poetry in *Eclogue* 1 (7.6-17):

> huc mihi, dum teneras defendo a frigore myrtos,
> uir gregis ipse caper deerrauerat; atque ego Daphnin
> aspicio. ille ubi me contra uidet, 'ocius' inquit
> 'huc ades, o Meliboee; caper tibi saluus et haedi;
> et, si quid cessare potes, requiesce sub umbra.   10
> huc ipsi potum uenient per prata iuuenci,
> hic uiridis tenera praetexit harundine ripas
> Mincius, eque sacra resonant examina quercu'.
> quid facerem? neque ego Alcippen nec Phyllida habebam
> depulsos a lacte domi quae clauderet agnos,   15
> et certamen erat, Corydon cum Thyrside, magnum;
> posthabui tamen illorum mea seria ludo.

To here, while I protect my tender myrtles from the cold, the man of the flock, my he-goat himself, had wandered off. And I catch sight of Daphnis. He, when he sees me, says 'be quick and come here, o Meliboeus; your he-goat and kids are safe; and, if you are able to hang around at all, rest under the shade. To here your bullocks will come through the meadows to drink of their own accord, here the Mincius has covered its green banks with tender reed and bees resound from the sacred oak'. What was I to do? I used to have neither an Alcippe nor a Phyllis at home to shut up the lambs once they had been weaned off their milk, and it was a big contest, Corydon against Thyrsis; I held my serious things at less worth than their game.

Meliboeus' encounter with Daphnis here is in several respects reminiscent of his encounter with Tityrus in *Eclogue* 1. Like Tityrus, for instance, Daphnis appears to be enjoying a state of leisure (*otium*) that contrasts with Meliboeus' labours (or *negotium*); he hails Meliboeus in the exact same terms which Tityrus uses the first time he addresses him, *o Meliboee* (7.9 and 1.6); and, when he encourages Meliboeus to 'rest under the shade' (*requiesce sub umbra* 10), he reworks Tityrus' invitation to the Meliboeus of *Eclogue* 1 to 'rest here with me this night' (*hic tamen hanc mecum poteras requiescere noctem* 1.79) as the shadows begin to lengthen (*maioresque cadunt altis de montibus umbrae* 1.83). Given that the opening lines of this poem have already drawn an equation between the convening of bucolic elements that leads to the exchange of song and the collocation of atoms that constitutes the physical universe, one might suggest that the relationship between these two poems can be accounted for in terms of Lucretian physics as well. Which is to say, they share a number of common elements, but in each instance these elements have been randomly dispersed, like Lucretius' atoms, into different combinations.

We can see how this kind of atomic structure informs the configuration both of *Eclogue* 7's own nature and of its relationship to other poems more generally if we return for a moment to the analogy between animals and atoms which this eclogue draws at its outset. For, given that Daphnis is consistently characterised in bucolic poetry as a herder of cows, the inclusion of Corydon's goats and Thyrsis' sheep means that *Eclogue* 7 starts off with something close to a full set of pasture animals. This is important for two reasons: it affords the poem the same kind of atomic structure as other key bucolic works, such as *Idyll* 1 and *Eclogue* 1, which boast the same set of animals; and it is matched by the cows, goats and sheep that Meliboeus also brings to the poem in the lines cited above. To take the first of these first, one might suggest that the differences between these three poems is expressed not least through the different distribution of cows, goats and sheep. In *Idyll* 1, for instance, these three types of animal are allotted to three different characters: Daphnis has cows, Thyrsis sheep and both are represented as singing (the latter the former's song). Only the goatherd is forbidden to make music (*Id.* 1.15-18). In *Eclogue* 1, by contrast, the character who is entitled to sing, namely Tityrus, combines Daphnis' and Thyrsis' flocks of cows and sheep (and to this degree their roles), while the goatherd, Meliboeus, like his counterpart in the idyll, is unable to sing in a formal sense, but can only converse. In *Eclogue* 7, on the other hand, the cowherd does not participate in the contest and the goatherd defeats the shepherd.

We shall see shortly how the goatherd's victory on this occasion could be assigned to the particular fallout of atoms in this eclogue, but in order to do so we should first observe how the arrival of Meliboeus on the scene introduces a further degree of chance and disorder to the poem's convenings. On the face of it, he would seem to be the right man for the job, since as a herder of goats (7-9), cows (11) and sheep (15), he already possesses all the elements that have come together to instigate the contest about to begin (like a reader with all the right references). At the same time, the manner in which he organises his flocks is anything but exemplary: his he-goat had wandered off without him noticing; he is prepared to allow his cattle to find their own way to the Mincius; and he chooses not to shut up his lambs at home himself. Added to this, he is characterised as something of a comic character. Whether or not one accepts Van Sickle's delightful

143

suggestion that his claim to have been protecting his myrtles from the cold is but a rustic euphemism for taking a snooze,[34] his encounter with Daphnis clearly derives some of its terminology and choreography from Roman comedy.[35]

Rather than being antithetical to the production and transmission of bucolic verse, however, it is precisely as a result of these accidental encounters and chance collocations that the poem's sense of bucolic order is both generated and asserted. For once all these random elements are finally in place, Meliboeus continues with a connective that, through its repeated use in the *De Rerum Natura* but relative absence from other instances of what Wendell Clausen calls 'the higher style of poetry',[36] constitutes a wonderful, and wonderfully quixotic, assertion of Lucretian causality: *igitur* ('therefore') (*Ecl.* 7.18-20):

> alternis igitur contendere uersibus ambo
> coepere, alternos Musae meminisse uolebant.
> hos Corydon, illos referebat in ordine Thyrsis.

It was therefore in alternate verses that both began to contend, and alternate verses that the Muses wished to remember. Corydon was relating these, Thyrsis those in order.

Like the physical universe itself, order emerges out of disorder. What is more, the element of chance (*fors*) with which the poem begins does not disappear from this point on, but rather it carries through to the somewhat arbitrary decision announced at the poem's end, when Meliboeus breaks off from his account of the contest to proclaim (*Ecl.* 7.69-70):

> Haec memini, et uictum frustra contendere Thyrsin.
> ex illo Corydon Corydon est tempore nobis.

This is what I remember, and that Thyrsis, conquered, competed in vain. From that time it has been 'Corydon, Corydon' for us.

This is an abrupt and controversial conclusion to say the least and readings of the poem from the past hundred years or so have focused almost exclusively on the question of why Corydon wins.[37] Rather than rehearse all those arguments again here, we might consider instead how this seemingly arbitrary verdict reflects the equally random grounds on which the contest itself was fought. For one might suggest that Thyrsis had been predisposed to lose this contest even before it had begun. After all, and as Rory Egan remarks: 'The sequence of tenses, with the perfect participle *uictum* followed by the present infinitive *contendere*, suggests that Thyrsis continued to compete even *after* he was defeated'.[38] It is a beaten man, in other words, who here contends with Corydon. Throughout the contest, both singers try to ground their quatrains in the topography of the poem's preliminary environment,[39] but for Thyrsis the random distribution of elements that make up that environment combine to work against him. To take just one example of this: when one of those arbitrary elements, Meliboeus' he-goat, happens to wander over to join the gathering of herdsmen, animals and texts convened at the poem's outset, he shows a partiality to Corydon's flock of she-goats that no arbitration panel is likely to overthrow. On this occasion, one might suggest, the atoms simply haven't fallen for him and the constitution of both the physical and poetic universe is, as a consequence, already adversely predisposed.

To this degree, *Eclogue* 7 offers a good example of how the practice of bucolic convention and the generation of bucolic order are not only analogous to, but actively participate in, the structures of atomic physics. It illustrates too how an individual recipient of bucolic song – who, in this case, and in keeping with the equation between singers and listeners that is sustained throughout the book, is also the poem's narrator – can serve both as a random element within and as an arbitrary influence upon the production and transmission of that song. In this way, Virgilian bucolic incorporates chance – and therefore novelty – as a prominent feature of its configuration of bucolic process, even as it simultaneously invests in a recursive and often ritualistic temporality. Indeed, in keeping with the *Eclogues*' own use of repetition and recursion, we shall in turn draw things to a close by revisiting the theme with which we began: the desire of bucolic poetry to ascend to the stars and become truly cosmological. For in the course of the present chapter, we have come across a number of instances in which the *Eclogues*' engagement with 'first things' initiates its trajectory towards the cosmos, not least through its association of the creation and organisation of bucolic poetry with the creation and organisation of the physical universe. We have also seen, moreover, how the reader or receiver of bucolic song is often cited as a key component of these 'primal elements'. We shall therefore now end with a brief look at *Eclogue* 4, a poem in which the act of reading sets the order of generations revolving anew and which promises to elevate the recipient of bucolic song to the table of a god and the couch of a goddess.

Eclogue 4: ornaments of time

Eclogue 4 is a poem in which a number of the features of Virgilian bucolic discussed in this chapter and throughout this book are brought vividly into play. Not the least of these are that it conjoins poetry and nature; it casts the reader as both a recipient and an instigator of song, with the capacity to give life to other literary works and to the natural world alike; it characterises itself as an ecphrastic object whose temporal configuration takes the form of a litany; and it identifies the cosmos as its ultimate venue and destination. Each of these features will become more apparent as we proceed.

The equation between poetry and nature is introduced from the very start, with the invocation to the Sicilian Muses and the calibration of literary scale in terms of tamarisks, copses and woods (1-3). In the lines that follow, a further element is then added to this mix: time (4.4-5):

> Vltima Cumaei uenit iam carminis aetas;
> magnus ab integro saeclorum nascitur ordo.

The final age of the Cumaean song has now come; a great order of generations is being born anew.

Here, time, poetry and nature all interrelate. The time the poem celebrates is an age that is defined by a particular song (*carminis aetas*) and this song is in turn defined by its grounding in a particular place (*Cumaei ... carminis*). Likewise, the 'great order of generations' heralded in line 5 is suggestive of literary, natural and human history alike, since the recurrence of the word *ordo* in other eclogues indicates that it can denote bucolic as well as cosmological 'order' and its epithet *magnus* ('great') in any case picks up on the 'greater things' which this poem has already expressed the desire to narrate (*paulo maiora canamus* 1).[40] A key constituent of this sequence of interrelationships, moreover, is the child, the *puer*, at whose birth (*nascenti* 8), this order of things is 'born anew' (*ab integro ... nascitur* 5). Whoever else this child might have been,[41] and whatever other qualities the specific details of his genealogy might have afforded him, *Eclogue* 4 emphasises the extent to which his influence on the workings of the physical universe is achieved not least through his role as a reader.[42] 'As soon as you are able to read the praises of heroes and the deeds of a parent and to recognise what virtue is' (*at simul heroum laudes et facta parentis / iam legere et quae sit poteris cognoscere uirtus* 26-7), the narrator tells him, the plain will turn yellow with corn, the grape will redden without any cultivation and hard oaks will sweat dewy honey (28-30). Like several of the other readers addressed in these poems, that is, his readings evidently have the capacity to bring the natural world back to life. Indeed, in the lines that follow, in which 'another Argo' (*altera ... Argo* 34) is caused to set sail and Achilles will again be sent to Troy (36), it becomes clear that this child has a similarly animating effect upon the texts he reads as well, which, as these examples suggest, include Homer's *Iliad*, Apollonius' *Argonautica* and Catullus 64. It is no surprise, then, that this child, like a number of other readers in the *Eclogues*, is afforded the status of a god.[43]

It is a feature of his characterisation as a god, moreover, that, again like many of those other readers, poetry is presented to this child in the form of physical objects and in particular as gifts. The ivy, cyclamen, Egyptian bean and acanthus the earth will bear for him, for a start, are all emblems of poetry culled from nature and parcelled up as 'little gifts' (*munuscula* 18-20).[44] By receiving these poems in the form of gifts given to a god, therefore, he at once instils in them a temporality that is at the same time both ecphrastic and liturgical. Indeed, the relationship of these two temporal configurations is highlighted further still when it emerges that it is precisely by way of an ecphrastic act of visual perception that this child not only acquires the life of the gods for himself, but that he thereby comes to revive the literary tradition by, quite literally, giving his own life to it. After all, the association this poem draws between the child's moral development, and in particular his acquisition of 'virtue' (*uirtus*), and the texts he reads means that literary history as a whole comes to acquire the contours of an individual life. What is more, the trajectory of this history is brought to a close and the golden age is reinstalled precisely when this reader will confirm his acquisition of *uirtus* by becoming a *uir* ('man' 37). 'This child will receive the life of the gods' (*ille deum uitam accipiet* 15), the narrator announces, categorising this life as a gift through the verb *accipere*, 'and he will see heroes mixed with gods' (*diuisque uidebit / permixtos heroas* 15-16), an observation which duly characterises that child's reading as a form of viewing. What comes next, however, is equally important, since it points up the element of reciprocation and recursion in this poem's representation of the ecphrastic configuration of reading: 'and he himself will be seen by them' (*et ipse uidebitur illis* 16). By embodying and, in effect, giving his life to these ecphrastic texts, the child in turn takes on some of the properties of those texts and thereby becomes an ecphrastic object in his own right.[45] Indeed, the narrator had already signalled as much when he refers to this child as 'this ornament of time' (*decus hoc aeui* 11) just a few lines before.

Here, then, one can discern yet another way in which the *Eclogues'* use of ecphrasis feeds into their equally persistent investment in the processes of repetition and recursion. The manner in which the child reads other texts in the tradition, that is, proves to be paradigmatic both for the manner in which the poem then proceeds to read this child and for the manner in which we in turn read this poem. To take the first of these stages first, one might suggest that the multicoloured ram and lambs that appear as signs of the golden age are to this degree ecphrastic emblems of the child's reading, just as the golden age itself marks the completion of his literary education. Quite apart from anything else, their ecphrastic and emblematic qualities are clearly delineated. 'When a mature age will have made you a man' (*ubi iam firmata uirum te fecerit aetas* 37), the narrator informs this child, there will be no more trading by sea, the whole earth will bear everything itself, and all forms of agriculture will cease. What is more (4.42-5):

> nec uarios discet mentiri lana colores,
> ipse sed in pratis aries iam suaue rubenti
> murice, iam croceo mutabit uellera luto;
> sponte sua sandyx pascentis uestiet agnos.

Neither will wool learn to simulate diverse colours, but the ram itself in the meadows will change its fleece, now with pleasing reddish purple dye, now with saffron dye; and scarlet will clothe the feeding lambs of its own accord.

The potential of these animals to stand as visual representations of verbal artefacts is signalled not least by their vivid colours, by the adjective *uarius* ('diverse'), which is a common marker of ecphrastic descriptions,[46] and by the verb *uestire* ('to clothe'), which evokes, among other comparable objects, the *uestis*, or coverlet, that adorns the marriage bed described in Catullus 64 and that, like the texts the *puer* is reading, also represents 'the virtues of heroes' (*heroum ... uirtutes* Cat. 64.51). In addition to these animals' more general role as ecphrastic objects, moreover, they also act as emblems of bucolic verse in particular. Sheep are in any case recurrent features of this kind of verse, although their programmatic significance is enhanced still further here by the qualification that the lambs are 'feeding' (*pascentis*), since the feeding of one's flocks is repeatedly associated with the production of song in the *Eclogues*.[47] What is more, as the culmination of the child's reading programme, which begins with the attempt made on the sea with ships, the surrounding of towns with walls, and the cutting of furrows in the earth (32-3), and which progresses by way of the voyage of the Argonauts to the sending of Achilles to Troy (34-6), the description of these animals serves also to reflect the relationship between bucolic and epic. After all, as an emblem of the golden age, it marks in general terms the goal of natural and literary history alike. More specifically, however, it signals bucolic poetry's status as the proper destination for heroic epic by representing itself in terms reminiscent of the object of the Argo's quest: which is to say, as a marvellously coloured fleece.

Just as the child's practice of reading the texts and lives he inherits through a combination of visual perception, re-enactment and re-embodiment results in its own concretisation in the form of these ecphrastic and emblematic sheep, moreover, so in turn does the narrator of the poem read the child and represent his life through much the same process.[48] Indeed, the moment he has described these miraculous animals, the narrator proceeds at once to imagine himself drawing off some of the threads of this ovine image and, by way of the Parcae's spindles, to work them into a prophecy of his own future song (4.46-7):

'Talia saecla' suis dixerunt 'currite' fusis
concordes stabili fatorum numine Parcae.

'Hasten such generations' the Parcae said to their spindles, concordant with the stable power of the fates.

This constitutes an obvious reference to the Parcae's prophetic song about Achilles in Catullus 64 and it is worth noting how, just as the Parcae spin their yarn as they work with wool (*lana* 64.311 and 318) and fleeces (*uellera* 64.319 and 320) in Catullus, the narrator of *Eclogue* 4 also has access to each of these materials in the ram that constitutes the ecphrastic embodiment of the child's reading.[49] The product of the child's reading, in other words, is at one and the same time the source of the narrator's song. Indeed, there are several respects in which the narrator reads the child in much the same way that the child reads the deeds of heroes and the life of the gods. Even as the child receives the life of the gods by looking at them, for instance, so too does the narrator point up the visual effects of the child's birth. 'See how the firmament is nodding with its convex weight, and the lands and the tracts of the sea and the deep sky' he declares, 'see how all things rejoice in the coming age!' (*aspice conuexo nutantem pondere mundum, / terrasque tractusque maris caelumque profundum; / aspice, uenturo laetentur ut omnia saeclo!* 50-2). Likewise, in much the same way that the child reshapes the trajectory of literary tradition in accordance with the trajectory of his own life, the narrator also attempts to give shape to the future of literary history by aligning it with the shape of his own life. 'O may the final part of a long life remain to me', he prays, 'and as much breath as will be enough to tell of your deeds' (*o mihi tum longae maneat pars ultima uitae, / spiritus et quantum sat erit tua dicere facta* 53-4), a wish that at the same time also replicates the child's reading of 'the praises of heroes and the deeds of a parent' by celebrating the child's own deeds in an encomiastic manner. Finally, just as the child's reading is to culminate in the realisation of bucolic scenes of natural abundance and freedom from travelling, trading and labour, a state symbolised by the multicoloured ram and lambs, so too is the result of the narrator's telling of the child's deeds to result in victory in a bucolic contest over the god Pan and those children of gods, Orpheus and Linus.

The extension of this analogy between the way the child reads other texts from the literary tradition and the way *Eclogue* 4 reads the child, combined with the poem's orientation towards the future more generally, would seem to suggest that this eclogue allows for future readers, including us, to get in on the act as well. Indeed, one such reader, Pollio, is openly addressed by the narrator, where he is told that his consulate will bear witness to the dawning of this new age (11-17). Both we and Pollio, moreover, could be said to receive this poem, as the poem receives the child, and as the child receives the texts he himself reads, in the form of an ecphrastic object, whether that object assumes the form of the woods of which the narrator promises to sing from the very start (3) or of words on a page. At the same time, one might also suggest that the very anonymity of the child makes him a kind of 'everyman', a model for all readers and singers of the *Eclogues*, not least because his title of *puer* is used to denote any number of the inhabitants of Virgil's bucolic world, its singers and auditors alike.[50]

What this all seems to promise, then, is that we too might be able to set in motion the order of generations anew, to sing in accord with the cosmos, defeat Orpheus and Linus in song and take our place at the banquets and in the beds of the gods. In order to realise this promise, we would do well to heed the advice given at the end of the poem which, appropriately for a poem that is oriented so relentlessly towards the future, enjoins its addressee to begin (4.60-3):

> Incipe, parue puer, risu cognoscere matrem
> (matri longa decem tulerunt fastidia menses)
> incipe, parue puer: qui non risere parenti,
> nec deus hunc mensa, dea nec dignata cubili est.

> Begin, small boy, to recognise your mother with a laugh (ten months have conveyed long weariness to your mother) begin, small boy: he who does not laugh at a parent, neither does a god deem him worthy of his table, nor a goddess for her couch.

The question of who were the real-life parents of this particular child is something that has been endlessly discussed.[51] But regardless of whether there really was such a child or such parents, one might note how the poem invests repeatedly in the notion of genealogy as a way of structuring its representation of the workings of literary tradition, including of the child's and the narrator's reading of it. The narrator proclaims, for instance, that the child 'will rule over a world pacified by his father's virtues' (*pacatumque reget patriis uirtutibus orbem* 17) and that he will read the 'deeds of a parent' (*facta parentis* 26). He himself, meanwhile, hopes that, by telling of this child's deeds, he will be able to defeat Orpheus and Linus in song, even if Orpheus' mother, Calliope, and Linus' father Apollo are there to help them (*huic mater quamuis atque huic pater adsit* 56). Viewed in terms of *Eclogue* 4's own literary ancestry, moreover, one might suggest that the child's mother is Lucretius' *De Rerum Natura* and the father Catullus 64. It is from Lucretius, after all, that the phrase 'to recognise your mother' (*cognoscere matrem*) derives[52] and it is surely no coincidence that this phrase appears in a passage that first describes how parents are able to recognise their children because they do not look the same either as themselves or as other children and that then illustrates this with an example of a cow who looks in vain for a calf that has been killed in sacrifice.[53] One might posit Catullus 64 as the father because of this poem's role as the primary model throughout, but in particular because the 'father's virtues' (*patriis uirtutibus* 17) point to Catullus' poem in which virtues (*uirtutes*) are also very much the theme. Were the child to recognise this lineage, moreover, he too, through his practice of setting in motion and even embodying the texts he reads, would, like Peleus in Catullus 64, eat at the table of a god and share his couch with a goddess.

And so it is left to us to recognise with a smile this poem's literary relations: above all, its witty reworking of a line from *Idyll* 11 to represent its golden age ideal of goats finding their own way home, the original of which depicts Polyphemus' flock having to do the same because their herdsmen is too wrapped up in his song and his love to bother to lead them there himself;[54] its evocation of Catullus 64 in its proclamation of the importance of heroic virtue, a poem which offers an equally strenuous, though in practice heavily ironised, affirmation of that same quality;[55] its allusion to Lucretius' account of the soul of a cow in its representation of the structure of the envisioned golden age;[56] and its flock of multicoloured sheep, which serve, somewhat flamboyantly, to emblematise the same. Were we to recognise these relations, that is, and, in common with other depictions of the act of reading in these poems, do so with love, we too might inaugurate the 'order of generations', the *ordo saeclorum* all over again, see the lives of heroes and gods, feast with the gods, sleep with the goddesses and, all in all, participate in poetry that finds its place among the stars.

With prospects such as this, it is small wonder that, in the ancient world, few forms of poetry were treated with a higher regard than those which dealt, either implicitly or explicitly, with the cosmos.

Notes

Introduction

1. I discuss innovative place names and geographical epithets in Chapter 3.

2. The defeat of Orpheus and Linus is anticipated at *Ecl*. 4.53-9. Other prophecies of better songs to come include 8.7-10 and even 9.67.

3. See Hardie (2006) 296-8, including n. 53.

4. See *Ecl*. 2.22, 3.86, 4.7, 5.67 and 71, 6.37, 8.29, 9.14, 10.74.

5. These difficulties extend at least as far back as the fourth-century grammarians Aelius Donatus and Servius, both of whom exclude certain of the *Eclogues* from those poems they regard as 'properly bucolic' (*proprie bucolica*) and 'pure rustic pieces' (*merae rusticae*) respectively.

6. I owe this point to Monika Asztalos.

7. One might assume, for instance, that the recurrence of the name 'Meliboeus' in *Eclogues* 3 and 7 recycles the theme of his exile and dispossession there as well.

8. Alpers (1979) 6.

9. See esp. Alpers (1979) 204-9 and (1996) 28-37.

10. Alpers (1996) 32.

11. Alpers (1979) 6 and (1996) 22. One might suggest, however, that, even as Alpers' demotion of nature promises to remove Schiller from the bucolic landscape, his understanding of 'pastoral convenings' as 'characteristically occasions for song and colloquies that express and thereby seek to redress separation, absence, or loss' (Alpers [1996] 81) restores to this influential figure his bucolic homestead, and with it his long-standing hegemony over interpretations of this kind of poetry, once again.

12. One might here cite Raymond Williams' remark that 'Nature is perhaps the most complex word in the language' (Williams [1976] 184).

13. Longinus' treatise *On the Sublime* constitutes an obvious example of this practice in ancient literary criticism. For a brief survey of this tradition both before and after Virgil, see Berg (1974) 1-6.

14. Garrard (2004) 44, for instance, describes 'On Naive and Sentimental Poetry' as 'a prototype of ecocritical theory'. Important examples of ecocritical studies grounded in Romanticism include Bate (1991), Kroeber (1994) and Bate (2000).

15. Given what I shall shortly say about the role assigned to readers in these poems and the cultural topography they themselves inhabit, it would be disingenuous of me to try to expel Romantic presuppositions entirely.

16. Cited and discussed by Bate (1991) 36-9 and Kroeber (1994) 22-3.

17. Moeris claims that he and Menalcas were both in danger of losing their lives at *Ecl*. 9.14-16. My reasons for viewing the land confiscations in the terms of bucolic exchange are given in Chapter 4.

18. Bate (2000) 107, for instance, claims that 'an ecosystem does not have a centre, it is a network of relations'.

19. On the ways in which Tityrus' teaching of the woods in *Eclogue* 1 relates to

153

Lucretius' account of how nature first taught music to mankind at *DRN* 5.1382f., see Van Sickle (2000) 44, Breed (2006) 99 and Hunter (2006) 124.

20. Marranca (1996) xiv.

21. For detailed accounts of the *Eclogues'* structural organisation, see Maury (1944), Otis (1964) 128-31, Berg (1974) 107-13, Rudd (1976) 119-44, Van Sickle (1978/2004).

22. Garrard (2004) 56. Putnam (1970) 295 offers a case in point.

23. *Ecl.* 8.6-13. See pp. 137-9 below.

1. Catasterisms

1. Varro discusses the possible relationship between *caelum* and *caelatum* at *DLL* 5.18. See also p. 21 below.

2. The herdsman Mopsus uses this same verb when he relates how he 'described poems' (*carmina descripsi*) on the bark of a beech tree at *Ecl.* 5.13-14.

3. I would like to thank Monika Asztalos for drawing my attention to the way this second figure on the cup bears some of the hallmarks of a didactic author.

4. Segal (1967) 284f., for instance, argues that the cups introduce a 'cleavage' between two realms: of the 'practical' and 'rustic' on the one hand and the 'aesthetic' and 'poetic' on the other.

5. Clausen (1994) ad 3.13 remarks that 'Evidently Menalcas had been defeated in a singing-match with Daphnis and then had destroyed the prize, the bow and arrows, that Daphnis had won' but does not mention *Idyll* 8 in this context.

6. Clausen (1994) notes some of the parallels between *Eclogue 3* and *Idyll* 8 on p. 92 and in his notes on lines 32-4 and 80-1. *Idyll* 8 is not now thought to be by Theocritus, although in Virgil's day it was still attributed to him. But could Virgil's alteration of *Idyll* 8's 'father and mother' (15-16) to 'father and stepmother' (33) suggest that he too knew better?

7. Clausen (1994) 93 observes how 'Menalcas and Damoetas repeatedly avail themselves of Plautine language or language reminiscent of comedy'. See also Currie (1976) and Wills (1993).

8. Clausen (1994) ad loc.

9. This point is also made by, among others, Clausen (1994) ad loc. and Faber (1995).

10. See also Segal (1967) 289.

11. Praxiteles is mentioned at *Id.* 5.105.

12. There are two possible literary precedents for this Alcimedon: a Myrmidon who rescues Achilles' horses after the death of Patroclus at *Il.* 17.466f.; and the addressee of Pindar's *Olympian* 8, the winner of a wrestling competition. Whether one emphasises the Homeric quality of the former or the martial pedigree of either, both would seem suitable models for the craftsman of *Eclogue* 3.

13. Lucretius *DRN* 2.976-7. I derive my rendition of this phrase from Ronald Latham's 1951 Penguin translation.

14. Fenton (2004) 72 observes that Damoetas' reply is metrically identical with its Theocritean model.

15. *Ecl.* 2.36-9.

16. See Hunter (1999) ad *Id.* 4.1-2.

17. Clausen (1994) 88: 'The Third *Eclogue* is modelled on the Fifth *Idyll*, with incidental reference to the Fourth, First, Eighth, and Third', with references.

18. See also Breed (2006) 54 on the responsion between the two descriptions and the way in which they 'amount to a miniature or preliminary amoebean contest'.

19. Thomas (1983) 178.

20. Wills (1998) 292.

21. See Wills (1998) 292 n. 29, who also notes how this line 'advertises the subsequent imitation of *Ecl.* 3.41-1 to the opening of the Coma'.

22. I owe this point to Marianne Soon Ophaug.

23. The verb *condere* is used to denote composition at *Ecl.* 6.6-7: *namque super tibi erunt qui dicere laudes, / Vare, tuas cupiant et tristia <u>condere</u> bella* ('for others will remain for you, who will desire to tell of your praises, Varus, and to <u>found</u> sad wars'). An even closer parallel can be found at *Ecl.* 10.50-1, which is discussed in the next paragraph.

24. See Clausen (1994) ad 3.60, where he notes Cicero's translation of this line, *A Ioue Musarum primordia*, as well as Theocritus' reworking of Aratus at the opening of *Idyll* 17.

25. Campbell (1982-83) 124. Clausen (1994) ad 3.40 lists the seven alternatives provided by the Verona scholiast: Eudoxus, Archimedes, Hipparchus, Euctemon, Hesiod and Euclid.

26. Bing (1990).

27. Theocritus employs a similar tactic in *Idyll* 16. Addressed to Hieron II of Syracuse, this poem has a strong intertextual relationship with Pindar's poems to Hieron I. See Hunter (1996) 82-90.

28. Attempts to solve these riddles are legion, but include Wormell (1960), Clay (1974), Campbell (1982-83) and Dix (1995).

29. See also *Ecl.* 1.10, 2.32 and 34, 5.2 and 48, 6.69.

30. See also Dix (1995) 260.

31. See *OLD* s.v. *ex(s)tinguo* 1.

32. Clausen (1994) ad loc.

33. This claim might also be compared with Simichidas' boast at *Id.* 7.91-3 that fame has perhaps brought his songs all the way to the throne of Zeus.

34. See also *DRN* 1.78-9, about Epicurus, and *Geo.* 2.490-2, which perhaps evokes Epicurus as well. *Pedes* similarly signifies both metrical and physical feet at *Ecl.* 9.1.

35. See also Mizera (1982) 368.

36. For the chain of allusions between Virgil, Lucretius and Homer, see Mizera (1982) 368.

37. Hardie (1986) 7-8 and 22.

38. The mountains that toss their voices to the stars, for instance, recall the mountains that, struck by the shouting of an army, also throw back their *uoces ad sidera* at *DRN* 2.327-8, while their confirmation to Menalcas that Daphnis is now a god (*deus, deus ille, Menalca!*, 5.64) reworks Lucretius' similar assertion about Epicurus to his patron Memmius (*deus ille fuit, deus, inclute Memmi, DRN* 5.8).

39. Clausen (1994) ad 5.23 notes Rohde's suggestion that Orpheus might have been one of the models for the image of Daphnis dead at the start of *Eclogue* 5.

40. Hunter (1999) ad loc. notes that: 'As Virgil saw (and made explicit), Daphnis here writes his own epitaph'.

41. See also Breed (2006) 57-61.

42. One might note that, just as it is sometimes assumed that the god alluded to in *Eclogue* 1 is Octavian, so is the newly deified Daphnis of *Eclogue* 5 sometimes supposed to have been Octavian's adopted father, Julius Caesar. See, for instance, Otis (1964) 135 and Coleman (1977) 173.

43. This line is also recalled in Menalcas' opening speech in this poem, in which he acknowledges Mopsus' ability 'to blow into light reeds' (*tu calamos inflare leuis*, 5.2).

44. In practice, this scene replays several other such exchanges as well, including, for example, Hesiod's investiture by the Muses at *Theogony* 30-1, mentioned below.

45. On this act of mutual endowment, see also Hubbard (1998) 99 and Breed (2006) 68.

46. Compare, for instance, the description of Daphnis and Menalcas at *Id.* 8.3-4.

2. Cosmology

1. I discuss the land confiscations in more detail in Chapter 4.

2. Clausen (1994) 268, for instance, concludes of this poem that: 'Poetry fails in the end'. Other pessimistic readings include Putnam (1970) 293-341, Van Sickle (1978/2004) 183-8, Boyle (1986) 15-16 and 24-30 and Lee (1989) 70-6. More optimistic readings, which emphasise the ability of bucolic song to address the misery caused by the land confiscations are offered by Segal (1965), Coleman (1977) 275 and Alpers (1979) 136-54. Perkell (2001) offers a convenient summary of approaches to this eclogue and of the interpretative assumptions that underlie them.

3. *Ecl.* 9.27-9 is based on *Id.* 3.3-5 while *Ecl.* 9.39-43 combines verses scattered throughout *Id.* 11 (namely 19, 42 and 45-9).

4. Clausen (1994) ad 9.29, adducing Callimachus *Hymn* 4.252. Their musical qualities are emphasised here through their depiction as *cantantes* ('singing').

5. Hardie (1986) 16f. Clausen (1994) ad 9.32 remarks that 'much, too much perhaps, has been made of the distinction between *poeta* and *uates*' but still supplies a useful bibliography.

6. It is worth noting that, while the fragment to Varus uses the Greek word *cycni*, Lycidas on this occasion uses the Roman word *olores*, which is perhaps more appropriate for the two Latin poets, Varius and Cinna.

7. For the association between these two constellations and wet and stormy weather, see Hunter (1999) ad *Id.* 7.53-4. See also *Aeneid* 1.535, for 'cloudy Orion' (*nimbosus Orion*), and *Aeneid* 9.668, for the 'rainy Kids' (*pluuialibus Haedis*).

8. I understand the *te* ('you') of line 44 to refer to Moeris, although others argue that Menalcas should be understood here. For a summation, with bibliography, of this discussion, see Perkell (2001) 73-4.

9. Clausen (1994) ad 51-2, Breed (2006) 1-4 and Hunter (2006) 132-4 all mention the relationship between these lines and Callimachus 34.2-3 G.-P. (= *Anth. Pal.* 7.80).

10. This acrostic is discussed in Domenicucci (1996) 47-60.

11. Clausen (1994) ad 9.47.

12. See also Alpers (1979) 144.

13. Both poems, for instance, involve an exchange between a younger and an older singer. Linguistic echoes include 5.40 and 9.19-20.

14. Hunter (2006) also relates *Ecl.* 9.57-8 to *Id.* 2.38.

15. On this debate see, among others, Rudd (1976) 122-3 and Clausen (1994) ad 9.57-8.

16. This is the only occasion on which the verb *deponere* appears in the *Eclogues* outside *Eclogue* 3.

17. Hence the repetition of the word for 'road', *uia*, five times in this poem (1, 23, 59, 64) but nowhere else in the *Eclogues* (the one slight exception being *obuia* at 6.57).

18. Hunter (2006) 134 speaks of the movement towards 'the revelation of poetry "in composition" here'.

19. For the careful arrangement of these fragments within the poem see, for instance, Perkell (2001) 76.

20. The verb *uenire* is important here. It recurs four times in this eclogue (2, 13, 62, 67) and features in the last line of all three of the *Eclogues'* last poems: 8, 9, 10. As we shall see in the next section, it can be applied to stars and points especially to the planet Venus.

21. Aratus *Phaen.* 783-7. This acrostic was discovered by Jacques (1960).

22. This acrostic was identified by Brown (1963) and is discussed and accepted by Thomas (1988) ad *Geo.* 1.427-37.

23. Richard Thomas has pointed out to me that *pura* also forms part of the acrostic that spells out the 'Publius' part of Virgil's name at *Geo.* 1.433. Both the acrostic in that passage and at *Ecl.* 9. 43-51, moreover, move across alternate lines.

24. Marianne Soon Ophaug has pointed out to me that Propertius also 'draws down the moon' at 1.1.19 and 2.20.21.

25. I discuss these two connotations of the verb *deducere* on pp. 96-101 below.

26. As I suggested earlier in relation to the *haedi* ('kids') of *Eclogue* 9, there are quite possibly other heavenly bodies hidden in these poems as well.

27. See Hunter (1999) 243.

28. For this belief, see Krevans (1983) 218.

29. See, for instance, Syme (1939/1960) 218-20, Du Quesnay (1977) 31 and Clausen (1994) 121-2. Berg (1974) 158-9 is more sceptical.

30. Coleman (1977) ad loc. plays down the importance of this point.

31. Aratus *Phaen.* 133-6. See also Hesiod *Works* 256. It is possible that Hesiod's account in the *Works and Days* (197-200) of the departure of Shame and Nemesis from the earth is also relevant here, not least because Nemesis was in ancient astrology often associated with Saturn, who is mentioned alongside Virgo in these lines. On this association, see Beck (2007) 75. Slater (1912) 115 suggests that the return of Virgo in *Eclogue* 4 specifically reverses the departure of Justice (*Iustitia*) at the end of Catullus 64, where 'all banished justice from their greedy minds' (*iustitiamque omnes cupida de mente fugarunt* Cat. 64.398).

32. Hesperus appears at 8.30 and 10.77, Lucifer at 8.17 and Vesper at 6.86.

33. See *Ecl.* 8.17: *Nascere, praeque diem ueniens age, Lucifer, almum* ('Be born, Light Bringer, and, coming in advance, lead in the nurturing day') and 10.77: *ite domum saturae, uenit Hesperus, ite capellae* ('Go home, replete she-goats, go home, Hesperus comes').

34. Clausen (1994) ad 9.47.

35. Coleman (1977) ad 10.77.

36. Compare Cat. 62.3, 'now is the time to leave the rich tables' (*iam pinguis linquere mensas*) with *Ecl.* 10.77, 'Go home, replete she-goats, go home, Hesperus comes' (*ite domum saturae, uenit Hesperus, ite capellae*).

37. Compare Cat. 62.3, 'now is the time to rise' (*surgere iam tempus*), with *Ecl.* 10.75, 'let us rise' (*surgamus*).

38. Vesper's rising from Olympus in the final line of *Eclogue* 6 but the first line of Catullus 62 is in itself emblematic of this point. The Daphnis fragment of *Eclogue* 9, however, offers at least one counterexample of a bucolic song sung at night.

39. For the parallels between *Eclogue* 4 and Catullus 64 see, for instance, Slater (1912), Herrmann (1930) 62-7, Berg (1974) 162-6, Du Quesnay (1977) 68-75, Arnold (1994-5) 149-51, Hubbard (1998) 78-83, Breed (2006) 139-44.

40. Might one also see in retrospect the banter and abuse of *Eclogue* 3 as in some way the bucolic counterpart to the often obscene and ribald 'Fescennine verses' addressed to the bride as she made her way to her husband's house? On the place of such verses in the wedding ceremony and Catullus 61, see Hurley (2004) 81.

41. See also Berg (1974) 193-4.

42. Berenice cut off this lock as a gift to the gods in exchange for the safe return of her new husband from war.

43. On the relationship between *Ecl.* 3.60 and *Id.* 17.1-2 see p. 19 above.

44. On the relationship between *Eclogue* 4 and *Idyll* 17, see Du Quesnay (1977) 52-68 and Clausen (1994) 122-5.

45. *Id.* 17.126-34. See Du Quesnay (1977) 67.

46. *Idylls* 3 and 11 are especially good examples of bucolic poetry reworking the notion of the paraclausithyron, although *Eclogue* 10 is perhaps the locus classicus for an attempt to relate these two literary forms. On the relationship between bucolic and elegiac poetry see, for instance, Fantazzi (1966), Papanghelis (1999) and Fantuzzi (2003).

47. *Ecl.* 2.67. See Chapter 5 below.

48. Clausen (1994) ad 5.23 notes that Orpheus might also have been one of the models for the image of Daphnis dead at the start of Mopsus' song in *Eclogue* 5, while Ross (1975) 92f. argues that the Hebrus at *Ecl.* 10.64 also points to Orpheus.

49. See, for instance, Putnam (1970) 255.

50. *Mirari* is used elsewhere of Daphnis' wonder at seeing the threshold of Olympus at *Ecl.* 5.56 and of Ismarus' and Rhodope's marvelling at Orpheus at *Ecl.* 6.30. *Stupere*, meanwhile, describes the stupefaction of the lands upon seeing a new sun shining at *Ecl.* 6.37.

51. See also Breed (2006) 77-81.

52. The same line, that is, to which Damoetas alludes at *Ecl.* 3.60.

53. *Eclogue* 8 is the only poem that makes use of this literary device.

54. Breed (2006) 43 and 45-6 has a number of interesting things to say about the role of the refrain in Damon's song in particular.

55. Homer *Il.* 18.593. See Clausen (1994) ad 5.73.

56. For these reversals, see Breed (2006) 36-41.

57. *Ecl.* 8.107. For the *deductio in domum* in Catullus 61, see Hurley (2004) 76f.

58. Putnam (1970) 277 offers the interesting suggestion that the singer 'prays not negatively against Nysa ... but positively for himself – for the power to have *adunata* become real through the quasi-magical force of his song'.

59. It is worth noting too how images from this introductory scene are recycled in the two herdsmen's songs. Alphesiboeus, for instance, in the kind of gender reversal typical of his song, matches the 'heifer' (*iuuenca*) of line 2 with a 'bullock' (*iuuencus*) at line 85, recycles the verb 'to change' (*mutare*) from line 4 at line 70, and returns to the theme of forgetfulness (*immemor* 2) at line 88 (*nec ... meminit*).

60. I discuss this in more detail in Chapter 6 below.

61. On 'convenings' and 'pastoral convention', see Alpers (1996) ch. 3.

3. Geography

1. *Ecl.* 1.66, 3.41, 4.17, 6.34, 8.9. It is therefore as conspicuous as two other terms that are to some degree constitutive of the *Eclogues'* specific nature: *Pierides*, 'Pierians' (3.85, 6.13, 8.63, 9.33, 10.72) and *fagus*, 'beech tree' (1.1, 2.3, 3.12, 5.13, 9.9 – not counting *fagina* at 3.37).

2. Even though the word *orbis* at *Ecl.* 3.41 probably signifies the firmament as a whole rather than the earth in particular, it nonetheless tells a similar story. For the figure of the astronomer on the cup who 'described the whole firmament with his rod to the nations' (*descripsit radio totum qui gentibus orbem* 3.41) stands in part as a representative of the kind of poetry to which Menalcas at least might aspire, but which he here agrees with Damoetas to let be.

3. For the ongoing debate about the whereabouts of the Oaxes, see, for instance, Myers (1938), Wellesley (1968) and Clausen (1994) ad 1.65.

4. The word *hic* ('here') at *Ecl.* 1.42, the central line of the poem, points directly to Rome.

5. One finds, for instance, tender lambs (1.8, 1.21, 3.103), apples (2.51), myrtles (7.6), reeds (7.12), grass (8.15), undergrowth (10.7), feet (10.49) and trees (10.53).

6. *Poenos ... leones* 5.27; *Armenias ... tigris* 5.29. See Clausen (1994) ad loc.

7. Clausen (1994) ad 8.44.

8. As Wallace (1974) 21 remarks: 'A great number of the place names about the region of the Valley of the Muses [that is, around Helicon] are duplicated in the Pieria region of Makedonia east of Mt Olympos'.

9. This list is derived entirely from Clausen (1994). For more details, see his commentary on *Hyblaeus* (1.54) and *Hybla* (7.37); *Sicanus* (10.4); *Actaeus* (2.24); *Caucasius* (6.42); *Cyrneus* (9.30); *Cydonius* (10.59); *Libethrides* (7.21); *Sithonius* (10.66); and *Cynthius* (6.3).

10. Clausen (1994) ad 4.1. It is possible that this epithet also gestures towards the poet Asclepiades of Samos, who appears as 'Sicelidas' at *Idyll* 7.40, although Mayer (1986) 52 rejects this on the grounds that this name, unlike Virgil's epithet, has a heavy initial syllable.

11. See Clausen (1994) ad 10.4.

12. Clausen (1994) ad 6.30.

13. See Clausen (1994) ad loc. *Syracosius* is not entirely Virgil's invention, although he seems to have been the first to introduce it to poetry: Cicero, for one, uses it in his (prose) *Lucullus* 123.

14. A helpful discussion is provided by Flintoff (1974).

15. See Clausen (1994) ad 9.30.

16. *Sicelides Musae* (4.1); *Nymphae Libethrides* (7.21); *Syracosio uersu* (6.1); *Maenalios uersus* (8.21, etc.); *Chalcidico uersu* (10.50).

17. Coleman (1977) ad 10.50 tentatively suggests that Theocles, who was associated with the invention of elegiac poetry and who came from a city close to Chalcis, might also be evoked here.

18. See Clausen (1994) ad 7.21.

19. Berg (1974) 189 also thinks Parthenius could be intended here. Mayer (1986) 51 suggests that Virgil 'found the Arcadian mountain Parthenius in Callimachus' *Hymn to Delos* (4.71)'.

20. It is worth mentioning that the Pierians also appear at *Id.* 10.24 and 11.3.

21. The Pierians are also associated with growth in *Eclogue* 10, when the narrator asks them to 'make these songs very great for Gallus' (*Pierides: uos haec facietis maxima Gallo* 10.72).

22. See note 1 above. Calliope and Thalea, whom Hesiod names among the Muses at *Theogony* 74-9, appear at 4.57 and 62 respectively.

23. For this aspect of *Eclogue* 6, see also Hunter (2006) 26, who observes that it 'needs little argument to see that the competition between localities is also a competition between the poets and poems that celebrate them'.

24. See Clausen (1994) 176 for the reference to Orpheus' song in the *Argonautica* and his note ad 6.29 for the allusion to Theocritus.

25. On the topography and hydrography of Hesiod's and Callimachus' Helicon respectively, see Wallace (1974) and Pfeiffer (1949) 9-11 and esp. (1951) 102-3. For its relevance to *Eclogue* 6 in particular, see Clausen (1994) ad 6.64.

26. Hesiod *Theog.* 5-8.

27. This is also suggested by Propertius 2.10.25-6: 'my songs do not yet know the Ascraean springs, but Love has washed them only in the stream of the Permessus' (*nondum etiam Ascraeos norunt mea carmina fontis, / sed modo Permessi flumine lauit Amor*).

28. See Clausen (1994) ad loc.

29. See Clausen (1994) ad 6.72 for discussion and further bibliography.

30. Clausen (1994) 200.

31. Breed (2006) 117-35 offers an excellent reading of *Eclogue* 10 and its use of geographical markers.

32. [Moschus] 3.76-7.

33. Except for a few fragmentary lines, the other primary model for this poem, Gallus' *Amores*, has not survived.

34. The story of Arethusa is told in more detail by Ovid in his *Metamorphoses* (5.572-641).

35. For this line of argument, see Van Sickle (1978/2004) 189-90. It has been analysed and adapted by Breed (2006) 121.

36. See also Breed (2006) 118-19.

37. Compare *Id.* 1.115-30.

38. The role of soldier-lover seems to have been one that the politician and elegiac poet Cornelius Gallus took on in 'real life' too, but this does not affect the point being made here about literary codes. See Conte (1986) 112, n. 15.

39. Could the battle between these two poetic codes also be gestured towards here by the use of the adjective *aduersus* in particular, suggesting, as it were, a 'battle in *verses*'?

40. Like Conte (1986) 111-12, n. 15, I take *Martis* with *amor* rather than *armis*.

41. Clausen (1994) 291.

42. *Patria* is used of (and by) Meliboeus at *Ecl.* 1.3, 4 and (as *patrius*) 67; and of Lycoris at 10.46.

43. See *Ecl.* 1.70-1.

44. Du Quesnay (1981) 41-2.

45. Berg (1974) 187 was unfortunately much mistaken when he remarked that it 'is impossible to miss the good-natured humour in all this'.

46. Compare *Ecl.* 10.77 and 1.74.

4. Topography

1. I discuss this aspect of *Eclogue* 4 in Chapter 6.

2. Copses (*arbusta*) appear in every one of the first five eclogues (1.39, 2.13, 3.10, 4.2, 5.64), but not once in the second half. For tamarisks as symbols of the *Idylls*, see Clausen (1994) xxix and 130.

3. Maggiulli (1995) 363 makes a similar point, arguing that the *siluae* determine the scenery in its vastness and complexity, the *arbusta* circumscribe its genre and height, while the *myricae* delimit the species.

4. Clausen (1994) xxvii, xxix.

5. Tamarisks (*myricae*) appear at 4.2, 6.10, 8.54, 10.13.

6. See, for instance, *Ecl.* 8.6-8, 9.57-8.

7. On the relationship between city and country in the *Eclogues*, see now Skoie (2006).

8. On *Eclogue* 2, see Du Quesnay (1979), who notes that Theocritus similarly transfers elegiac figures and motifs to the countryside in poems such as *Idylls* 3 and 11.

9. Daphnis assumes a status similar to Odysseus when he recites his own epitaph at *Ecl.* 5.43-4. He 'loves' Menalcas at 5.52 (*amauit nos quoque Daphnis*) and leisure at 5.61 (*amat bonus otia Daphnis*).

10. *Ecl.* 8.70: 'with songs Circe changed the companions of Ulysses' (*carminibus Circe socios mutauit Vlixi*).

11. At *Id.* 2.15 the singer, Simaetha, asks that her spells be as powerful as Circe's.

12. On the place of the *Phaedrus* in the bucolic tradition, see, for instance, Murley (1940), Gutzwiller (1991) 73-9 and Hunter (1999) 14, 145-6.

13. Henderson (1998a) 165 makes the claim that: 'Epics built The City, and their narrators manned the nascent walls.'

14. Herdsmen order their flocks home at *Ecl.* 4.21, 7.44, 10.77.

15. Hunter (2006) 122-3 suggests that the point of contrast here is between Roman and Greek forms of poetry.

16. Hunter (2006) 122-3.

17. For the idea of the epic as a unitary form, see Hardie (1993) esp. 3-10.

18. In Catullus, for instance, *tristis* indicates the sadness of lovers at 2.10, 64.126, 65.24, 66.30, 68.56.

19. See, for instance, Putnam (1970) 385f., Leach (1974) 167-70, Boyle (1986) 33-5, Hardie (2006) 278.

20. One thinks here of the remark made by the Renaissance theorist, the elder Scaliger, that 'pastoral works continually draw back material of every kind to the nature of the fields' (*pastoralia ... cuiuscumque generis negotium semper retrahunt ad agrorum naturam*). It is cited by, among others, Conte (1994) 116 and Martindale (1997) 108.

21. Skoie (2006) 304-5 discusses the details of this relationship.

22. The herdsman who lies down to die at the entrance to Amaryllis' cave at the close of *Idyll* 3 effects a similar combination of roles.

23. Van Sickle (2000) 28. Hunter (1999) 144-199 illustrates in detail how *Idyll* 7 structures itself in relation to the *Odyssey*, even to the scenes of ease and relaxation at its close.

24. For a useful survey of the different instruments of the *Eclogues* and the plants that constitute them, see Smith (1970).

25. For this sequence of exchanges, see also Breed (2006) 66-9.

26. For more on this, see Chapter 6.

27. For such acts of inscription, see now Breed (2006) and Hunter (2006) 136-9.

28. On the creation of competitive environments in Latin and Hellenistic poetry more generally, see Hunter (2006) ch. 1.

29. Pöschl (1964) 10. For this pose see, for example, *Id.* 1.12-13 and 21-5, 5.45-9, 7.88-9.

30. Tityrus appears twice in the *Idylls*: at *Id.* 3.2-5, where he is asked to look after the narrator's goats; and at *Id.* 7.72-82, where he sings of Daphnis and Comatas. Amaryllis is the recipient of the love song in *Idyll* 3 and her death is briefly lamented at *Id.* 4.35-40.

31. See also Breed (2006) 99.

32. Hunter (2006) 116.

33. No stringed instruments, though, are to be found in the *Eclogues*.

34. Masters (1992) 27, Hinds (1998) 12-13.

35. For the temporality of this passage, see also Breed (2006) 96-8.

36. He reverts, however, to his original role at *Ecl.* 5.12: 'Tityrus will look after the kids as they feed' (*pascentis seruabit Tityrus haedos*).

37. One might suggest that a similar trick is played in the *Lament for Bion* 58-63, where Bion outdoes Theocritus' Cyclops by winning over Galatea with his song.

38. Van Sickle (2000) 25. See also Breed (2006) 111.

39. Clausen (1994) ad loc. observes that this tree 'is found before Virgil only in Catullus 64.288-91'.

40. It appears at *Ecl.* 1.1, 2.3, 3.12 (and 3.37 as *faginus*), 5.13 and 9.9. Ross (1975) 72 calls the *fagus* 'beyond all others perhaps, the tree of the *Eclogues*'.

41. For the relationship between *fagus* and φηγός see, among others, Williams (1968) 317-21 and Clausen (1994) ad 2.3.

42. See also Maggiulli (1995) 420.

43. This is all the more so given that the *quercus* itself is commonly associated with Jupiter in Virgil. See Maggiulli (1995) 420-4.

44. Clausen (1994) ad loc.

45. On the oat reed (*auena*) here, see Page (1898) ad loc., Smith (1970) 497-8 and passim, Clausen (1994) ad loc.

46. Cairns (1999), Hunter (1999) 111 and (2006) 116.

47. See also Putnam (1970) 29.

48. The verb *agere* is also used to denote the performance of bucolic song at *Ecl.* 9.37.

49. This association of the *agrestis calamus* with the sanction of a god rather neatly inverts Lucretius' characterisation of the *agrestis musa* as music that mimics nature and the *siluestris musa* as music attributed to the gods. The same inversion is also in evidence in *Eclogue* 6, where Tityrus' decision to contemplate the *agrestis musa* comes at the behest of a god.

50. On this tradition, see Hardie (1993) ch. 4.

51. So Van Sickle (1978/2004) 149-50.

52. Examples of this are too numerous to list here, but see, among others, *Ecl.* 2.5, 4.3, 5.28, and, perhaps above all, 10.8.

53. In both the *Eclogues* and the *De Rerum Natura*, moreover, the *siluestris musa* is introduced before the *agrestis musa*.

54. Compare *DRN* 4.584 (*dulcisque querelas*) with 5.1384 (*dulcis ... querelas*).

55. *DRN* 4.585 = 5.1385: *tibia quas fundit digitis pulsata canentum*.

56. Coleman (1977) ad *Ecl.* 1.31-2 calls *peculium* a 'very unpoetical word'.

57. For an overview, see Winterbottom (1976) and Clausen (1994) 30 n. 4.

58. See also Saunders (2006) 9. The reading of *Eclogue* 1 offered in Hunter (2006) ch. 4, esp. 119-20, has many points of contact with my own.

59. See *Ecl.* 3.21, 4.59, 7.69.

60. One might also note the litigious connotations of the verb *petere*, which I have here translated as 'petition'.

61. Henderson (1998b) 216-18.

62. Clausen (1994) 32 n. 67 overstates the case when he remarks that 'Love for a native place, profound sorrow for its loss, the pleasure of undisturbed possession – these Roman sentiments are unknown to Theocritus', not least because the *Odyssey* provides an obvious Greek precedent for this sentiment. The idea of a fatherland (πατρίς), does appear in Theocritus (at *Id.* 28.17 and *Ep.* 9.4), but it is not called upon to perform quite this function.

63. Cf. *Ecl.* 1.3: *patriae finis* and 1.67: *patrios ... finis*.

64. A *saepes* ('hedge', 'fence' or 'barrier'), for instance, reappears at *Ecl.* 8.37. Likewise, the *limen* or 'threshold' makes an appearance at 5.56, 8.92 and 8.107.

65. The nouns *limus* ('mud' 8.80) and *limen* ('threshold' 8.92 and 107) are similarly placed in close proximity in *Eclogue* 8.

66. See, for instance, 4.33 (on ploughing) and 4.40-1 (on diverse agricultural activities).

67. Farmers are mentioned in the form of *agricolae* at 5.80 and 9.61 and as *coloni* at 9.4. Meanwhile, one finds a leaf stripper (*frondator*) at 1.56, reapers (*messores*) at 2.10 and 3.42, a ploughman (*arator*) at 3.42 and 4.41, and a vineyard worker (*uinitor*) at 10.36.

68. Villas are mentioned at *Ecl.* 1.82. Stables, pens and folds appear at 1.33 (*saeptum*), 3.80, 6.60, 6.85 (*stabulum*), 7.39 (*praesepe*).

69. The concept of 'home', *domus*, appears in this specific sense at 4.21, 7.15, 7.44, 10.77; but also in a related sense at 1.35, 3.33, 8.68f.

70. For *numeri* explicitly signalling the 'numbers' of poetry, see *Ecl.* 9.45.

71. For stables and folds in the *Idylls*, see, for instance, 7.153 and 11.12 (both of Polyphemus).

72. Crops, for instance, appear at 1.71, 5.33 and 9.48 (as *segetes*) and at 3.77, 3.80, 9.48 and 10.76 (as *fruges*); harvests (*messis*) at 5.70 and 8.99; orchards at 8.37; gardens at 7.34, 65 and 68; and irrigated meadows at 3.111.

73. See *DRN* 5.1367.

74. The presence of agriculture and cultivated fields in the *Eclogues*, as well as of soldiers and battles, contradicts Aelius Donatus' famous categorisation of these poems as representations of human society at its most primitive stage, before the advent of such things as 'cultivated fields' (*rura culta*) and 'wars' (*bella*). See Donatus, *Vita Verg.* 23-4 Diehl.

75. The further qualification of the *OLD*, that these *arua* should be understood as ploughed fields 'esp. as opposed to a meadow, etc.' is relevant here.

76. Admittedly, the *OLD* cites only later examples of *nouale* in this sense.

77. For the different connotations of *colonus*, see Mynors (1990) ad *Geo.* 1.299. As Mynors there observes, 'in *G.* 2.385 and five times in [the *Aeneid*] the special colouring "colonist" is clear'.

78. Conte (1992) remains the starting point for any discussion of these 'proems in the middle'.

79. Nauta (2006) 320.

80. For a start, Virgil has turned Callimachus' poet into a shepherd and has given him a history as an author that Callimachus' novice supposedly lacks. See also Breed (2006) 92.

81. *Patria*, for instance, recalls *Ecl.* 1.3-4 and 10.46; the qualification that he can only do this if he lives long enough recalls *Ecl.* 4.53-4 (but see also 8.7-8); the *Aonius uertex* looks back to *Ecl.* 6.64f. and 10.12; while the claim to be first likewise looks back to a similar concern in the *Eclogues* (cf. 1.44, 2.32, 4.18, 6.1, 8.24 and so on).

82. Compare *Geo.* 3.14-15 with *Ecl.* 7.12-13.

83. The *OLD* cites a number of pre-Virgilian examples for the use of *deducere* to mean 'to establish in residence (in a colony, or sim.), settle' and 'to found (a colony, or sim.)'.

84. Cheese: *caseus* 1.34; plants: *eruum* 3.100, *uerbena* 8.65; pine wood: *taeda* 7.49; fields: *arua* 5.33; olive oil: *oliuum* 5.68; amber: *electrum* 8.54.

85. See Chapters 5 and 6 below.

86. Nauta (2006) 320.

87. Yet, as Acosta-Hughes and Stephens (2002) 242 suggest, Callimachus might instead be saying that while his poem too is about kings and it too is thousands of verses long, the difference is that it isn't 'continuous'.

88. The reference to the 'kingdom of Saturn' (*Saturnia regna* 6.41) is one example.

89. Critics have long been puzzled by Virgil's attribution of battles to Varus, for whose military exploits the historical record is all but silent. See Clausen (1994) ad 6.6-7, where he mentions the consequent attempt to establish a different Varus as the addressee here.

90. See, for instance, *Ecl.* 2.14, where Corydon suggests it would have been better to endure the 'sad anger of Amaryllis' (*tristis Amaryllidis iras*).

5. Landscape

1. The bibliography on the theme of landscape in Virgil is extensive, but includes: Snell (1953), Flintoff (1974), Leach (1974) and (1988), Jenkyns (1989) and (1998).

2. The most important statements of this position come in Alpers (1979) and (1996).

3. Alpers (1996) 31-2.

4. This is part of the etymology for the term provided by the 1989 edition of the *OED*.

5. Coates (1998) 111.

6. Alpers (1996) 32.

7. Bate (2000) 73.

8. Alpers (1996) 24.

9. Alpers (1996) 22: 'This book will argue that we will have a far truer idea of pastoral if we take its representative anecdote to be herdsmen and their lives, rather than landscape and idealized nature.'

10. It is indicative that when one looks up 'nature' in the index to Alpers (1996) one is instructed to '*See* landscape' instead.

11. See, most famously, Lessing (1766/1984) 91: 'It remains true that succession of time is the province of the poet just as space is that of the painter.'

12. It is now in the Metropolitan Museum of Art in New York. For other detailed accounts of this painting see Leach (1974) 90-4, (1988) 339-44, and Blanckenhagen (1990) 28-33.

13. For an extensive discussion of this villa and its paintings see Blanckenhagen (1990).

14. The reconstruction of this room is conjectural. See Blanckenhagen (1990) 8.

15. 10 ft 6 in x 17ft 8 in (3.2 m x 5.4 m). See Blanckenhagen (1990) 8.

16. Blanckenhagen (1990) 3 sets the paintings of the Augustan villa at Boscotrecase in the transitional period between the Second and Third Styles of Roman painting. For the general dating of the Second Style, see Dawson (1944) 47 and Martin (1992) 155.

17. Dawson (1944) 48.

18. Skoie (2006) 311-22 offers an interesting account of how this relationship might have worked in practice.

19. Blanckenhagen (1990) 30-1.

20. Blanckenhagen (1990) 30.

21. See also Schama (1995) 10: 'at the very least, it seems right to acknowledge that it is our shaping perception that makes the difference between raw matter and landscape'.

22. Leach (1988) 23 is explicit in her belief that landscape has its origins in the Roman period: 'My current investigation is limited to the literature of the Republic and Augustan Age, in which the artistic history of landscape has its origins and most intensive development'. Likewise, Jenkyns (1998) 4 argues that 'it would be perverse, for example, to deny that [Virgil] felt deeply about the landscape and antiquity of Italy'.

23. See also Andrews (1999) 7: 'Landscape ... is mediated land, land that has been aesthetically processed'.

24. Coates (1998) 111.

25. For the idea of landscape as (among other things) 'a medium of exchange between the human and the natural, the self and the other', see Mitchell (1994) 5.

26. One of the anonymous readers for the press rightly suggests that *uilla* could be added to this list as well.

27. Accordingly, terms and practices such as 'geography' and 'topography', which both enjoy an etymological link with the ancient world, could be said to relate to that world rather as the *fagus* ('beech tree') in the *Eclogues* relates to the φηγός ('oak tree') in the *Idylls*.

28. For a history of collections of Theocritus' poems, see Gow (1952) lix-lxii, Gutzwiller (1996), and Hunter (1999) 26-8. Hunter (1999) 60 remarks that 'Idyll 1 seems always to have been placed first in ancient collections of Theocritus' poetry, and it is not hard to see why'.

29. Halperin (1983) 186-9 divides the *Idylls* into three groups to accord with the three scenes on the bowl.

30. Hunter (1999) 77: 'The cup is not a simple representation of the bucolic world ... because the ecphrastic relation here constructed between a described object and the poem in which it occurs is not that of "original" and "copy" '.

31. Breed (2006) 79: 'Pleasure and amazement are both ecphrastic buzzwords'.

32. See also my discussion of the cups in *Eclogue* 3 in Chapter 1.

33. Hunter (1999) 76.

34. For the κισσύβιον and its various manifestations in literary history, see Halperin (1983) 167-76, Gutzwiller (1991) 90 n. 28, and Hunter (1999) ad *Id.* 1.27.

35. Details can be found in Halperin (1983) 176-183, Gutzwiller (1991) 91-4, and Hunter (1999) 76-85.

36. Breed (2006) 80.

37. Hunter (1999) 76.

38. Laird (1993) 18, with further bibliography.

39. Hunter (1999) ad *Id.* 1.21. The Nymphs are mentioned in Thyrsis' song at lines 66 and 141, Priapus at 81f.

40. Haber (1994) 18.

41. Gutzwiller (1991) 91, n. 38: 'The goatherd's entire description is concerned with presenting the figures dramatically as if they had living form, not with delineating the cup as a work of art'.

42. For the parallels between Silenus' song and ecphrases elsewhere in the *Eclogues*, see Breed (2006) ch. 4.

43. The two occurrences of hibiscus in the *Eclogues* are at 2.30 and 10.71.

44. See, for instance, Berg (1974) 13-14, who says about the scenes on the bowl in *Idyll* 1 that 'These static vignettes, these *eidullia*, are the stuff of Theocritean poetry'.

45. Among the numerous critics who read the *Eclogues*, and especially *Eclogue* 1, in this way see above all Putnam (1970) and Boyle (1986) 15-35.

46. For more extended discussions of ecphrasis, including its negotiation of time, see Lessing (1766/1984) and Krieger (1992).

47. So Servius ad *Ecl.* 4.4-10.

48. Gutzwiller (1991) 91-2.

49. See, for instance, Alpers (1996) 327-8. Fowler (1991) 27 makes the relevant remark that, in ecphrasis, 'description is rarely "pure", because the way that narrative impurity is introduced is often through the figure of the observer'.

50. *hanc* [*capellam*] (13); *haec arbusta* (39); *haec tam culta noualia* (70); *has segetes* (71).

51. *malum hoc* (16).

52. *haec otia* (6); *huic nostrae* [*urbi*] (20).

53. *haec* [*urbs*] (24).

54. Breed (2006) 78-9 makes this point about Aeneas' shield as well, although in his case he contrasts it with the use of temporal markers in Silenus' song in *Eclogue* 6.

55. For *libertas* ('liberty') as a contested political term at this time, see Syme (1939/1960) 154f. and Clausen (1994) ad 1.27.

56. Van Sickle (2000) 28.

57. See also Breed (2006) 108-10.

58. *Id.* 11.75-9.

59. Compare *Ecl.* 1.79-83 with *Id.* 11.42-9.

60. Aside from the replaying of this relationship in *Eclogue* 2 (for which, see the following sections), some of the more obvious references to Polyphemus and Galatea in the *Eclogues* are to be found at *Ecl.* 3.64-5, 7.37-40 (Corydon again), 9.39-43.

61. For the details of this relationship, see Du Quesnay (1979) passim, but esp. 43-5 and 51-9.

62. Line 52 – 'chestnuts, which my Amaryllis <u>used to love</u>' (*castaneasque nuces, mea quas Amaryllis <u>amabat</u>*) – also suggests that Amaryllis is a former lover.

63. See also Du Quesnay (1979) 47-8 and 53.

64. For *pingere* as an ecphrastic marker related to ποικίλος, see Jackson (2002) 8 and 15.

65. Du Quesnay (1979) 42, with bibliography.

66. Tityrus uses *mihi* at lines 7, 35 and 44, while Meliboeus uses *tibi* at lines 26, 47 and 53. *Nobis* ('to us') is a pronoun which, somewhat appropriately, they share: Tityrus uses it at line 80, Meliboeus at 6, 16 and 18. The importance of these pronouns to the rhetorical technique of the *Eclogues* is suggested by the fact that *tibi* appears in all ten of these poems and *mihi* in all bar *Eclogue* 6.

67. Note also Tityrus' remark that a 'god has fashioned this leisure for us' (*deus nobis haec otia fecit* 1.6).

68. Cicadas suggest the time and the place for bucolic song at, for instance, *Id.* 7.138-40 and 16.94-6.

69. For the cosmological and other connotations of the verb *condere* and its compounds, see p. 17 above.

70. The adjective *inanis* ('empty') can be used of both the cosmic void (so *Ecl.* 6.31) and of paintings (so *Aen.* 1.464).

71. The relationship between *Eclogue* 2 and Meleager's epigram is discussed briefly by Du Quesnay (1979) 59.

72. *Ecl.* 2.7: *mori me denique cogis?*

73. Hubbard (1998) passim.

74. See again *Ecl.* 1.11.

75. Hunter (1999) 257.

76. For a detailed discussion of how Damoetas' song picks up on Daphnis' song to Polyphemus in particular, see Hunter (1999) 246 and 253-9.

77. See Coleman (1977) and Clausen (1994) ad loc. for a discussion of the prosody of this line.

78. In addition to its recreation of the time of year and the time of day at which the narrator saw Alexis in the epigram, the figure of Thestylis recalls the sorceress' assistant in *Idyll* 2, the hidden lizards of line 9 evoke the sleeping lizards to which Lycidas refers at *Id.* 7.22, while both the 'raucous' noise of the cicadas and the 're-echoing' of the hedges replicate aspects of Tityrus' setting in *Eclogue* 1 (the woods similarly 're-echo' [*resonare*] at 1.5 while the wood-pigeons are also 'raucous' [*raucae ... palumbes*] at 1.57).

6. Physics

1. See, for instance, Alpers (1996) 22 and passim.

2. One thinks, for example, of how Polyphemus 'was shepherding his love with his singing' in *Idyll* 11 (ἐποίμαινεν τὸν ἔρωτα / μουσίσδων *Id.* 11.80-1).

3. See p. 64.

4. *DRN* 2.1059-60: *semina rerum /... coacta.*

5. See again p. 95.

6. See again pp. 94-5.

7. See again *DRN* 5.1379-98.

8. Temporal markers are prominent throughout *Eclogue* 6. See, for instance, *cum* ('when'): 3, 39, 39; *iam* ('now') 21, 37, 56; *nunc* ('now'): 6, 52; *tum* ('then'): 27, 28, 35, 61, 62, 64.

9. See also Clausen (1994) ad loc. and Breed (2006) 82.

10. On the relationship between Silenus' song and Apollo's, see Stewart (1959) 196, Knox (1990) 185-93, and Clausen (1994) ad loc.

11. Cited on pp. 88-9.

12. For the details of this particular echo, see Breed (2006) 89. In his ch. 4 Breed offers an excellent discussion of how Silenus' song might itself be viewed as an ecphrastic object.

13. Cited on pp. 83-4.

14. One might note too the etymological derivation of *pagina* ('page' or 'column') from *pagus*, which signifies a demarcated country district.

15. For this reason if no other, it is worth recalling Servius' anecdote ad *Ecl.* 6.11 that Cicero once heard the mime actress Cytheris, who is generally assumed to be the 'real woman' behind Gallus' Lycoris, recite Virgil's *Eclogues* in the theatre.

16. Compare *Ecl.* 6.64-73 with Call. *Aet.* fr. 2 Pf.

17. Clausen (1994) 243 describes the Timavus as 'a river of legend, down which Jason and the Argonauts had sailed on their improbable return'. For an 'epic' description of the Timavus, see *Aen.* 1.242-9.

18. See also Clausen (1994) ad 8.7: 'the first extant occurrence of *lego* in this sense ... the phrase is used metaphorically in *G.* 2.44'.

19. For the debate on the identity of the addressee, see Clausen (1994) 239-40 and now also Thibodeau (2006).

20. As Clausen (1994) ad loc. observes: 'The intertwining word-order is no doubt intentional.'

21. The precise source of these orders remains unclear.

22. Nauta (2006) 312.

23. See again Aratus *Phaen.* 1-4.

24. One thinks above all of Pollio (3.84-9) and Gallus (6.64-73 and 10 passim).

167

25. For the association between 'convening' and 'convention' in bucolic and pastoral poetry, see Alpers (1996) ch. 3.

26. For details of the relationship between *Eclogue* 7 and *Idylls* 6 and 8, see, for instance, Clausen (1994) 213 n. 16 and ad 1-5, 7, 18-20, 45-60 and 59-60.

27. Compare *Ecl.* 2.30 (*compellere*), 3.55 and 5.3 (*considere*).

28. Other relevant poems introduced under his name here include *Idyll* 4 and Erucius *Anth. Pal.* 6.96, to which the *Arcades ambo* of line 4 is probably related: see Clausen (1994) ad loc.

29. See *Id.* 6.1-5 and 8.1-5.

30. Clausen (1994) ad loc.

31. The two Lucretian phrases identified in this discussion, *si forte* and *in unum*, can be found in close proximity at *DRN* 1.391-7, 3.533-4 and (without the *si*) at 6.274-5.

32. See Putnam (1970) 227 (on *contra*) and 252 (on *contendere*).

33. Fenton (2004) 93-4 makes the interesting observation that *Eclogue* 7 does not only adhere to the pattern found in *Eclogues* 1, 2, 6 and 8 of starting with a five-line introduction but, like 6 and 8 in particular, it then breaks off to address a further character who, initially at least, is off-stage.

34. Van Sickle (1978/2004) 166-7.

35. See Clausen (1994) on *atque* (7.7) and *ille ubi me contra uidet* (7.8). He observes too that the question Meliboeus asks himself at 7.14, *Quid facerem?* ('What was I to do?') is colloquial and can be found, for instance, in Terence. It is also, of course, the question Tityrus asks himself at *Ecl.* 1.40.

36. Clausen (1994) ad 7.18.

37. See Clausen (1994) 210-12 for a review of the various arguments.

38. Egan (1996) 234.

39. Topographical and other related features that recur from the preliminaries in the contest include: *arguta* (1 and 24), *sacra* (13 and 24), *Arcades* (4 and 26), *iuuenci* (11 and 44), *umbra* (10 and 46), *uiridis* (12 and 46), *frigor* (6 and 51), *ripae* (12 and 52) and *myrtus* (6 and 62).

40. The word *ordo* ('order') also appears at *Ecl.* 1.73 (of vines) and 7.20 (of song).

41. For a brief survey of some of the most common candidates, see Coleman (1977) 150-2.

42. On the *puer* as a reader, see especially Arnold (1994-5).

43. Discussions of the child's theological attributes are numerous. Clausen (1994) 126-9 offers a useful overview.

44. On these plants, see, for instance, Putnam (1970) 146-7, Berg (1974) 169, and Arnold (1994-5) 147.

45. As Arnold (1994-5) 145-6 observes, 'the *puer* is at once the subject of the text to be read and himself a product of reading texts'.

46. See Faber (1998) in relation to the 'diverse coverlet', the *uestis ... uariata*, of Cat. 64.50-1.

47. One thinks especially of *Ecl.* 1.45 and 6.5, but see also 1.77, 3.85-6, 96, 5.12 and 9.23. Arnold (1994-5) 149 makes a similar observation.

48. Gómez Pallarès (2001) argues that *Eclogue* 4 might be thought of as an ecphrasis in as far as it responds to the visual iconography of contemporary Rome.

49. This process is clearly also in play in Apollo's instruction to Tityrus to 'feed his sheep fat, to sing a drawn-down song' in *Eclogue* 6 (*pastorem, Tityre, pinguis / pascere oportet ouis, deductum dicere carmen* 6.4-5). One might note in this regard that the Parcae in Catullus similarly 'draw down' (*deducens*) their threads as they sing at 64.312.

50. See also Berg (1974) 168. Prominent examples include 1.45, 3.111, 5.19, 9.66 (of singers), 6.24 (of recipients), and 5.49 (of Daphnis).

51. See again Coleman (1977) 150-2.

52. As we saw on pp. 48-9 above, it also points to Cat. 61.212: *dulce rideat ad patrem* ('may he smile sweetly at his father').

53. *DRN* 2.349. See also Hardie (2006) 296 n.51, where he illustrates the admixture of Catullus and Lucretius throughout *Eclogue* 4.

54. Compare *Ecl.* 4.21-2 with *Id.* 11.12-13.

55. On Catullus' representation of heroic virtue, see now O'Hara (2007) 44-7. Hubbard (1995) 12-19 offers a finely nuanced reading of the relationship between Catullus 64 and *Eclogue* 4, although he focuses on its more troubling, rather than comic, elements.

56. See again p. 1 above.

Bibliography

Abbreviations of journal titles follow *L'Année Philologique*. For the *Eclogues*, I have used R.A.B. Mynors' 1969 Oxford Classical Text with only minor modifications throughout.

Acosta-Hughes, B. and S.A. Stephens (2002) 'Rereading Callimachus' *Aetia* Fragment 1', *CPh* 97: 238-55.
Alpers, P. (1979) *The Singer of the Eclogues: A Study of Virgilian Pastoral* (University of California Press).
———— (1996) *What is Pastoral?* (University of Chicago Press).
Andrews, M. (1999) *Landscape and Western Art* (Oxford University Press).
Arnold, B. (1994-5) 'The Literary Experience of Vergil's Fourth Eclogue', *CJ* 90: 143-60.
Barchiesi, A. (1997) 'Virgilian Narrative: Ecphrasis', in C.A. Martindale (ed.) *The Cambridge Companion to Virgil* (Cambridge University Press) 271-81.
Bate, J. (1991) *Romantic Ecology: Wordsworth and the Environmental Tradition* (Routledge).
———— (2000) *The Song of the Earth* (Picador).
Beck, R. (2007) *A Brief History of Ancient Astrology* (Blackwell Publishing).
Berg, W. (1974) *Early Virgil* (Athlone Press).
Bing, P. (1990) 'A Pun on Aratus' Name in Verse 2 of the Phainomena?', *HSPh* 93: 281-5.
Blanckenhagen, P.H. von and C. Alexander (1990) *The Augustan Villa at Boscotrecase* (Philipp von Zabern).
Bowersock, G.W. (1971) 'A Date in the Eighth Eclogue', *HSPh* 75: 73-80.
———— (1978) 'The Addressee of Virgil's Eighth Eclogue: A Response', *HSPh* 82: 201-2.
Boyle, A.J. (1977) 'Virgil's Pastoral Echo', *Ramus* 6: 121-31.
———— (1986) *The Chaonian Dove: Studies in the Eclogues, Georgics, and Aeneid of Virgil* (Brill).
Braund, S.M. (1997) 'Virgil and the Cosmos: Religious and Philosophical Ideas', in C.A. Martindale (ed.) *The Cambridge Companion to Virgil* (Cambridge University Press) 204-21.
Breed, B.W. (2006) *Pastoral Inscriptions: Reading and Writing Virgil's Eclogues* (Duckworth).
Brown, E.L. (1963) *Numeri Vergiliani. Studies in Eclogues and Georgics* (Collection Latomus 63).
Buell, L. (2005) *The Future of Environmental Criticism: Environmental Crisis and Literary Imagination* (Blackwell Publishing).
Cairns, F. (1999) 'Virgil Eclogue 1.1-2: A Literary Programme?', *HSPh* 99: 289-93.
Cameron, A. (1995) *Callimachus and his Critics* (Princeton University Press).
Campbell, J.S. (1982-3) 'Damoetas's Riddle: A Literary Solution', *CJ* 78: 122-6.

Bibliography

Cartault, A. (1897) *Étude sur les Bucoliques de Virgile* (Éditions Colin).

Clark, K. (1949/97) *Landscape into Art* (John Murray).

Clarke, K. (1999) *Between Geography and History: Hellenistic Constructions of the Roman World* (Oxford University Press).

Clausen, W. (1994) *A Commentary on Virgil: Eclogues* (Oxford University Press).

Clay, J.S. (1974) 'Damoetas' Riddle and the Structure of Vergil's Third Eclogue', *Philologus* 118: 59-64.

Coates, P. (1998) *Nature: Western Attitudes Since Ancient Times* (Polity Press).

Coleman, R. (1977) *Vergil: Eclogues* (Cambridge University Press).

Connolly, J. (2001) 'Picture Arcadia: the Politics of Representation in Vergil's *Eclogues*', *Vergilius* 47: 89-116.

Conte, G.B. (1986) *The Rhetoric of Imitation: Genre and Poetic Memory in Virgil and Other Latin Poets*, ed. C. Segal (Cornell University Press).

—— (1992) 'Proems in the Middle', *YCIS* 29: 147-59.

—— (1994) *Genres and Readers: Lucretius, Love Elegy, Pliny's Encyclopedia*, trans. G.W. Most (John Hopkins University Press).

Coupe, L. (ed.) (2000) *The Green Studies Reader: From Romanticism to Ecocriticism* (Routledge).

Currie, H. MacL. (1976) 'The Third *Eclogue* and the Roman Comic Spirit', *Mnemosyne* 29: 411-20.

Dalzell, A. (1987) 'Language and Atomic Theory in Lucretius', *Hermathena* 143: 19-28.

Dawson, C.M. (1944) *Romano-Campanian Mythological Landscape Painting* (Yale University Press).

Derrida, J. (1978/87) *The Truth in Painting*, trans. G. Bennington and I. McLeod (University of Chicago Press).

Desport, M. (1941) 'L'Echo de la Nature et la Poésie dans les Eglogues de Virgile', *REA* 43: 270-81.

—— (1952) *L'Incantation Virgilienne: Essai sur les Myths du Poète Enchanteur et leur Influence dans l'Oeuvre de Virgile* (Delmas).

Dix, T.K. (1995) 'Vergil in the Grynean Grove: Two Riddles in the Third Eclogue', *CPh* 90: 256-62.

Domenicucci, P. (1996) *Astra Caesarum: Astronomia, Astrologia e Catasterismo da Cesare a Domiziano* (Edizioni ETS).

Du Quesnay, I.M. Le M. (1977) 'Vergil's Fourth *Eclogue*', in F. Cairns (ed.) *Papers of the Liverpool Latin Seminar 1976* (Francis Cairns) 25-99.

—— (1979) 'From Polyphemus to Corydon: Virgil, Eclogue 2 and the *Idylls* of Theocritus', in West and Woodman (eds) *Creative Imitation and Latin Literature* (Cambridge University Press) 35-70.

—— (1981) 'Vergil's First Eclogue', in F. Cairns (ed.) *Papers of the Liverpool Latin Seminar 1981* (Francis Cairns) 29-182.

Egan, R.B. (1996) 'Corydon's Winning Words in *Eclogue* 7', *Phoenix* 50: 233-9.

Elder, J.P. (1961) '*Non iniussa cano*: Virgil's Sixth Eclogue', *HSPh* 65: 109-25.

Faber, R. (1995) 'Virgil Eclogue 3.37, Theocritus 1 and Hellenistic Ekphrasis', *AJPh* 116: 411-17.

—— (1998) '*Vestis ... Variata* (Catullus 64.50-1) and the Language of Poetic Description', *Mnemosyne* 51: 210-5.

—— (2000) 'The Literary Metaphor of the Chisel (*Tornus*) in Eclogue 3.38', *Hermes* 128: 375-9.

Fantazzi, C. (1966) 'Virgilian Pastoral and Roman Love Poetry', *AJPh* 87: 171-91.

172

Bibliography

Fantazzi, C. and C.W. Querbach (1985) 'Sound and Substance: A Reading of Virgil's Seventh Eclogue', *Phoenix* 39: 355-67.

Fantuzzi, M. (2003) 'Pastoral Love and "Elegiac" Love, from Greece to Rome', *Leeds International Classical Studies* 2.3 (www.leeds.ac.uk/classics/lics/).

Farrell, J. (1991a) *Vergil's Georgics and the Traditions of Ancient Epic: The Art of Allusion in Literary History* (Oxford University Press).

―――― (1991b) 'Asinius Pollio in Vergil Eclogue 8', *CPh* 86: 204-11.

―――― (1992) 'Literary Allusion and Cultural Poetics in Vergil's Third Eclogue', *Vergilius* 38: 64-71.

Fenton, A. (2004) *Cultural and Poetic Response in Vergil's Eclogues*, Diss. Penn.

Ferrari, G.R.F. (1987) *Listening to the Cicadas: A Study of Plato's Phaedrus* (Cambridge University Press).

Flintoff, E. (1974) 'The Setting of Virgil's Eclogues', *Latomus* 23: 814-46.

Fowler, D.P. (1991) 'Narrate and Describe: The Problem of Ecphrasis', *JRS* 81: 25-35.

Fraistat, N. (ed.) (1986) *Poems in their Place: The Intertextuality and Order of Poetic Collections* (University of North Carolina Press).

Garrard, G. (2004) *Ecocriticism* (Routledge).

Goldhill, S. (1991) *The Poet's Voice: Essays on Poetics and Greek Literature* (Cambridge University Press).

Gómez Pallarès, J. (2001) 'Sobre Virg., *Buc.* 4.18-25, *Puer Nascens*, y la Tradición de la Écfrasis en Roma', *Emerita* 69: 93-114

Gow, A.S.F. (1952) *Theocritus*, 2 vols, 2nd edn (Cambridge University Press).

Gutzwiller, K.J. (1991) *Theocritus' Pastoral Analogies: The Formation of a Genre* (University of Wisconsin Press).

―――― (1996) 'The Evidence for Theocritean Poetry Books', in M.A. Harder, R.F. Regtuit and G.C. Wakker (eds) *Theocritus*, Hellenistica Groningana 2 (Egbert Forsten) 119-48.

Haber, J. (1994) *Pastoral and the Poetics of Self-Contradiction: Theocritus to Marvell* (Cambridge University Press).

Halperin, D.M. (1983) *Before Pastoral: Theocritus and the Ancient Tradition of Bucolic Poetry* (Yale University Press).

Hardie, P.R. (1986) *Virgil's Aeneid: Cosmos and Imperium* (Oxford University Press).

―――― (1993) *The Epic Successors of Virgil: A Study in the Dynamics of a Tradition* (Cambridge University Press).

―――― (2006) 'Cultural and Historical Narratives in Virgil's *Eclogues* and Lucretius', in M. Fantuzzi and T. Papanghelis (eds) *Brill Companion to Greek and Latin Pastoral* (Brill) 275-300.

Heidegger, M. (1971) *Poetry, Language, Thought*, trans. A. Hofstadter (Harper and Row).

Henderson, J. (1998a) *Fighting for Rome* (Cambridge University Press).

―――― (1998b) 'Virgil's Third *Eclogue*: How Do You Keep an Idiot in Suspense?', *CQ* 48: 213-28.

―――― (1998c) 'Virgil, *Eclogue* 9: Valleydiction', *PVS* 23: 149-76.

Herrmann, L. (1930) *Les Masques et les visages dans les Bucoliques de Virgile*, Travaux de la Faculté de philosophie et lettres de l'Université de Bruxelles 1 (Editions de la Revue de l'Université de Bruxelles).

Hinds, S. (1998) *Allusion and Intertext: Dynamics of Appropriation in Roman Poetry* (Cambridge University Press).

Hubbard, T.K. (1995) 'Intertextual Hermeneutics in Vergil's Fourth and Fifth Eclogues', *CJ* 91: 11-23.

Bibliography

———— (1998) *The Pipes of Pan: Intertextuality and Literary Filiation in the Pastoral Tradition from Theocritus to Milton* (University of Michigan Press).

Hunter, R.L. (1996) *Theocritus and the Archaeology of Greek Poetry* (Cambridge University Press).

———— (1999) *Theocritus: A Selection* (Cambridge University Press).

———— (2006) *The Shadow of Callimachus: Studies in the Reception of Hellenistic Poetry at Rome* (Cambridge University Press).

Hurley, A.K. (2004) *Catullus* (Bristol Classical Press).

Jackson, P. (2002) *Verbis Pingendis: Contributions to the Study of Ritual Speech and Mythopoeia* (Universität Innsbruck).

Jacques, J.M. (1960) 'Sur un Acrostiche d'Aratos', *REA* 62: 48-61.

Jenkyns, R. (1989) 'Virgil and Arcadia', *JRS* 79: 26-39.

———— (1998) *Virgil's Experience. Nature and History. Times, Names and Places* (Oxford University Press).

Jeskins, P. (1998) *The Environment and the Classical World* (Bristol Classical Press).

Kerridge, R. and N. Sammells (eds) (1998) *Writing the Environment: Ecocriticism and Literature* (Zed Books).

Klingner, F. (1967) *Virgil: Bucolica, Georgica, Aeneis* (Artemis).

Knox, P. (1990) 'In Pursuit of Daphne', *TAPhA* 120: 183-202.

Krevans, N. (1983) 'Geography and the Literary Tradition in Theocritus 7', *TAPhA* 113: 201-220.

Krieger, M. (1992) *Ekphrasis: The Illusion of the Natural Sign* (John Hopkins University Press).

Kroeber, K. (1994) *Ecological Literary Criticism. Romantic Imagining and the Biology of Mind* (Columbia University Press).

Laird, A. (1993) 'Sounding out Ecphrasis: Art and Text in Catullus 64', *JRS* 83: 18-30.

Lawall, G. (1967) *Theocritus' Coan Pastorals: A Poetry Book* (Centre for Hellenic Studies).

Leach, E.W. (1974) *Vergil's Eclogues: Landscapes of Experience* (Cornell University Press).

———— (1988) *The Rhetoric of Space: Literary and Artistic Representations of Landscape in Republican and Augustan Rome* (Princeton University Press).

Lee, M.O. (1989) *Death and Rebirth in Virgil's Arcadia* (State University of New York Press).

Lessing, G. E. (1766/1984) *Laocoön: An Essay on the Limits of Painting and Poetry*, trans. E.A. McCormick (John Hopkins University Press).

Ling, R. (1977) 'Studius and the Beginnings of Roman Landscape Painting', *JRS* 67: 1-16.

———— (1991) *Roman Painting* (Cambridge University Press).

Lipka, L. (2001) *Language in Vergil's Eclogues* (Walter de Gruyter).

Llewellyn, N. (1984) 'Virgil and the Visual Arts', in C.A. Martindale (ed.) *Virgil and his Influence* (Bristol Classical Press) 117-40.

McKay, A.G. (1969) 'Virgilian Landscapes into Art: Poussin, Claude and Turner', in D.R. Dudley (ed.) *Virgil* (Routledge and Kegan Paul) 139-60.

Maggiulli, G. (1995) *Incipiant Siluae Cum Primum Surgere: Mondo Vegetale e Nomenclatura della Flora di Virgilio* (Gruppo Editoriale Internazionale).

Marranca, B. (1996) *Ecologies of Theater: Essays at the Century Turning* (Johns Hopkins University Press).

Martin, C. (1992) *Catullus* (Hermes Books).

Bibliography

Martindale, C. A. (1997) 'Green Politics: the *Eclogues*', in C.A. Martindale (ed.) *The Cambridge Companion to Virgil* (Cambridge University Press) 107-24.

Masters, J. (1992) *Poetry and Civil War in Lucan's Bellum Civile* (Cambridge University Press).

Maury, P. (1944) 'Le Secret de Virgile et l'Architecture des Bucoliques', *Lettres d'Humanité* 3: 71-147.

Mayer, R. (1983) 'Missing Persons in the Eclogues', *BICS* 30: 17-30.

——— (1986) 'Geography and Roman Poets', *G&R* 33: 47-54.

Mitchell, W.J.T. (1994) 'Imperial Landscape' in W.J.T. Mitchell (ed.) *Landscape and Power* (University of Chicago Press).

Mizera, S.M. (1982) 'Lucretian Elements in Menalcas' Song, *Eclogue* 5', *Hermes* 110: 367-71.

Murley, C. (1940) 'Plato's *Phaedrus* and Theocritean Pastoral', *TAPhA* 71: 281-95.

Myers, J.L. (1938) 'Oaxes. Virgil Ecl. 1.66', *CR* 52: 59.

Mynors, R.A.B. (1990) *Virgil: Georgics*, edited with a commentary (Oxford University Press).

Nauta, R.R. (2006) 'Panegyric in Virgil's *Bucolics*', in M. Fantuzzi and T. Papanghelis (eds) *Brill Companion to Greek and Latin Pastoral* (Brill) 301-32.

Nicolet, C. (1991) *Space, Geography, and Politics in the Early Roman Empire* (University of Michigan Press).

O'Hara, J.J. (1996) *True Names: Vergil and the Alexandrian Tradition of Etymological Wordplay* (University of Michigan Press).

——— (2007) *Inconsistency in Roman Epic: Studies in Catullus, Lucretius, Vergil, Ovid and Lucan* (Cambridge University Press).

Otis, B. (1964) *Virgil: A Study in Civilized Poetry* (Oxford University Press).

Page, T.E. (1898) *Bucolica et Georgica P. Vergili Maronis* (Macmillan).

Pandiri, T.A. (1985) 'Daphnis and Chloe: The Art of Pastoral Play', *Ramus* 14: 116-41.

Papanghelis, T.D. (1999) 'Eros Pastoral and Profane: On Love in Virgil's *Eclogues*', in S.M. Braund and R. Mayer (eds) *Amor, Roma: Love and Latin Literature* (Cambridge Philological Society) 44-59.

Parry, A.M. (1957) 'Landscape in Greek Poetry', *YCIS* 15: 3-29.

Perkell, C.G. (1996) 'The "Dying Gallus" and the Design of Eclogue 10', *CPh* 91: 128-40.

——— (2001) 'Vergil Reading his Twentieth-Century Readers: A Study of *Eclogue* 9', *Vergilius* 47: 64-88.

Perutelli, A. (1995) 'Bucolics', in N. Horsfall (ed.) *A Companion to the Study of Virgil* (Brill) 27-62.

Pfeiffer, R. (1949) *Callimachus I: Fragmenta* (Oxford University Press).

——— (1951) *Callimachus II: Hymni et Epigrammata* (Oxford University Press).

Pöschl, V. (1964) *Die Hirtendichtung Virgils* (Carl Winter).

Putnam, M.C.J. (1970) *Virgil's Pastoral Art: Studies in the Eclogues* (Princeton University Press).

Romm, J.S. (1992) *The Edges of the Earth in Ancient Thought* (Princeton University Press).

Rose, H.J. (1942) *The Eclogues of Vergil* (University of California Press).

Rosenmeyer, T.G. (1969) *The Green Cabinet: Theocritus and the European Pastoral Lyric* (University of California Press).

Roskill, M. (1997) *The Languages of Landscape* (Penn State University Press).

Ross, D. O. (1975) *Backgrounds to Augustan Poetry: Gallus, Elegy, and Rome* (Cambridge University Press).

Bibliography

——— (1987) *Virgil's Elements: Physics and Poetry in the Georgics* (Princeton University Press).

Rudd, N. (1976) *Lines of Enquiry: Studies in Latin Poetry* (Cambridge University Press).

Saunders, T.A. (2006) ' "Using Green Words" or "Abusing Bucolic Ground" ', in M. Skoie and S. B. Velázquez (eds) *Pastoral and the Humanities: Arcadia Re-Inscribed* (Bristol Phoenix Press) 3-13.

Schama, S. (1995) *Landscape and Memory* (HarperCollins).

Schiller, F. (1795-6/1985) 'On Naive and Sentimental Poetry', in H.B. Nisbet (ed.) *German Aesthetic and Literary Criticism: Winckelmann, Lessing, Hamann, Herder, Schiller and Goethe*, trans. J.A. Elias (Cambridge University Press).

Schultz, C.E. (2003) 'Latet Anguis In Herba: A Reading of Vergil's Third Eclogue', *AJPh* 124: 199-224.

Segal, C.P. (1965) 'Tamen Cantabitis, Arcades: Exile and Arcadia in Eclogues One and Nine', *Arion* 4: 243-4.

——— (1967) 'Vergil's Caelatum Opus: An Interpretation of the Third Eclogue', *AJPh* 88: 279-308.

Skoie, M. (2006) 'City and Countryside in Vergil's *Eclogues*', in R.M. Rosen and I. Sluiter (eds) *City, Countryside, and the Spatial Organization of Value in Classical Antiquity*, Mnemosyne Supplementum (Brill) 297-325.

Skutsch, O. (1969) 'Symmetry and Sense in the Eclogues', *HSPh* 73: 153-69.

Slater, D.A. (1912) 'Was the Fourth Eclogue Written to Celebrate the Marriage of Octavia to Mark Antony?: A Literary Parallel', *CR* 26: 114-19.

Smith, P.L. (1965) '*Lentus in Umbra*: A Symbolic Pattern in Vergil's Eclogues', *Phoenix* 19: 298-304.

——— (1970) 'Vergil's *Avena* and the Pipes of Pastoral Poetry', *TAPhA* 101: 497-510.

Snell, B. (1953) 'Arcadia: The Discovery of a Spiritual Landscape', in *The Discovery of the Mind*, trans. T. Rosenmeyer (Harvard University Press) 281-309.

Stewart, Z. (1959) 'The Song of Silenus', *HSPh* 64: 179-205.

Syme, R. (1939/1960) *The Roman Revolution*, rev. edn (Oxford University Press).

Tarrant, R.J. (1978) 'The Addressee of Virgil's Eighth Eclogue', *HSPh* 82: 197-9.

Thibodeau, P. (2006) 'The Addressee of Virgil's Eighth *Eclogue*', *CQ* 56: 618-23.

Thomas, R.F. (1982) *Lands and Peoples in Roman Poetry: The Ethnographical Tradition* (Cambridge Philological Society).

——— (1983) 'Virgil's Ecphrastic Centerpieces', *HSPh* 87: 175-84.

——— (1988) *Virgil: Georgics*, 2 vols (Cambridge University Press).

Thomson, J.O. (1955) 'Geographica Vergiliana', *G&R* 2: 50-8.

Thornton, B. (1988) 'A Note on Vergil *Eclogue* 4.42-45', *AJPh* 109: 226-8.

Van Sickle, J. (1978/2004) *The Design of Virgil's Bucolics*, 2nd edn (Bristol Classical Press).

——— (2000) 'Virgil *vs.* Cicero, Lucretius, Theocritus, Plato, and Homer: Two Programmatic Plots in the First Bucolic', *Vergilius* 46: 21-58.

Wallace, P.W. (1974) 'Hesiod and the Valley of the Muses', *GRBS* 15: 5-24.

Wellesley, K. (1968) 'Virgil's Araxes', *CPh* 63: 139-41.

Williams, G. (1968) *Tradition and Originality in Roman Poetry* (Oxford University Press).

Williams, R. (1973) *The Country and the City* (Oxford University Press).

——— (1976) *Keywords: A Vocabulary of Culture and Society* (Fontana).

Wills, J. (1993) 'Virgil's *cuium*', *Vergilius* 39: 3-11.

——— (1998) 'Divided Allusion: Virgil and the Coma Berenices' *HSPh* 98: 277-305.

Bibliography

Winterbottom, M. (1976) 'Virgil and the Confiscations', *G&R* 23: 55-9.

Wood, C. S. (1993) *Albrecht Altdorfer and the Origins of Landscape* (University of Chicago Press).

Wormell, D.E.W. (1960) 'The Riddles in Virgil's Third Eclogue', *CQ* 10: 29-32.

Wright, J.R.G. (1983) 'Virgil's Pastoral Programme: Theocritus, Callimachus and *Eclogue* 1', *PCPhS* 29: 107-60.

Zanker, G. (1985) 'A Hesiodic Reminiscence in Virgil, *E.* 9.11-13', *CQ* 35: 235-7.

Index

Index

Daphnis 11-12, 17, 20, 21-7, 29-30,
34-41, 45, 48, 52-3, 54, 56, 57, 63,
65-9, 75-7, 79, 80, 106-9, 120, 124-6,
139-44
deductum carmen 96-101
Donatus, *Vit. Verg.* 23-4: 163
doves 31-2, 62, 77-8, 91, 93, 137

eagles 31, 32, 77-8, 91, 137
earth, the 2, 24, 43, 44, 48, 59-60, 63, 94,
119, 130-2, 146-7
echo 24, 26, 74, 82-5, 87-90, 117, 127,
133-4
ecological literary criticism (ecocriticism)
4-7
ecology 4-7, 11, 72, 133-4, 138
economy (see also markets, and trade
and transactions) 5, 12
ecphrasis 6, 100, 102, 103, 106-17,
118-25, 133-6, 138, 142, 145, 147-9
elegy 8, 45, 46, 48, 57, 64-7, 70-1, 75, 77,
79, 136
elms 29, 43, 86, 93, 108, 110, 121
ending and endings 11, 17, 19-20, 22-3,
25, 27, 38-41, 43-50, 53, 57, 59, 63,
65-6, 72, 75-6, 79, 88, 94-5, 110,
114-16, 119, 125, 129-30, 144-5,
147, 150
epic 8, 23, 24, 65, 70, 71, 74-7, 79 85, 97,
100, 107, 114, 116, 138, 148
Erucius, *Anth. Pal.* 6.96: 168
Euphorion 62, 64
Eurotas 80, 130, 131, 134, 138
evolution and growth 5, 6, 8, 23, 26,
28-9, 50, 51, 57, 58, 63, 79, 83, 86,
93, 115, 123, 126, 129, 131, 132
exchange 5, 10-18, 26-30, 31, 33, 38-40,
46, 55-6, 58, 68-70, 77-9, 90-2, 98,
105-6, 106-8, 109, 113, 120, 123-4,
127, 133, 134-5, 140, 143
amoebaean exchange 18, 27, 46, 109,
113, 123
bureau de change 107

farm buildings 78, 86, 94-5, 128, 165
farmers and farmhands 84, 94, 96, 120,
141
farming, see agriculture
fatherland 69-71, 75, 82, 87-8, 90, 92-4,
98, 105, 111
fields 18, 34, 37, 73, 80, 82, 86-7, 87-90,
93, 95-6, 97, 98, 99, 100, 105, 110,
111, 113, 120, 123, 132
first things 1, 9, 13, 18, 20, 25, 28, 45,
46, 47, 62, 63, 64, 67-8, 76, 80-1,
88-9, 91, 95-6, 97, 98, 105, 111-12,
113, 123, 128-35, 137, 138, 142, 145

flowers, plants and shrubs 3, 19, 54, 60,
74, 78, 80, 81, 88-9, 93, 99, 110,
118-20, 122, 139-40
flutes 80, 140
frames and framing 3, 7, 57, 76, 86, 103,
110-11, 128
fruit (see also individual entries) 35, 37,
118-19, 122

Galatea, see Polyphemus and Galatea
Gallus 17, 43-4, 45, 49, 56, 62, 64, 65-72,
74, 75, 77, 79, 81, 131, 133, 135,
136, 137, 160
genres and literary forms 23-5, 28, 41,
46, 57, 64-6, 70-9, 83, 99, 115, 138,
140
gifts and giving 15, 17, 27-8, 53, 54, 64,
79, 81, 91, 119-20, 124, 125, 138,
146-7
goatherds 17, 24, 83, 106-9, 109-12, 121,
143
goats and kids 15, 16, 20, 39, 45, 53, 65,
78, 84, 87, 91, 94, 95, 100, 106, 107,
112-15, 139, 140-5, 150
gods (see also individual entries, and
readers) 9, 10, 13-14, 16, 22, 26, 34,
37, 43, 45, 47-9, 62, 66, 68-70, 80-1,
86, 87, 89, 98-9, 110, 113, 115, 119,
121, 131, 135-9, 141, 145-7, 149-51
golden age 1, 44, 54, 109, 131, 147-8,
150-1

hazel 22, 29, 112
Hebrus 43, 158
hedges 93, 112, 127
Helicon 60-1, 74, 137, 159-60
herding 94, 128-30, 139, 141
herds, flocks and pasture animals (see
also individual entries) 12, 15, 25,
27, 28, 39, 45, 48, 51, 55, 76, 78, 91,
92, 93, 94-5, 100, 127, 128-9, 131,
138, 139-43, 145, 148, 151
herdsmen (see also individual entries) 2,
5, 7, 11, 20, 70-1, 76, 77, 78, 79, 81,
82, 87, 91-2, 94-5, 99, 103, 112, 113,
114, 121, 128, 135, 140, 141, 143
Hesiod
Theogony 28, 63, 64, 156, 159, 160;
Theog. 5-8: 160; *Theog.* 30-1: 28,
155; *Theog.* 62: 63; *Theog.* 68-71: 63;
Theog. 77: 159
Works and Days 48, 107, 157; *WD* 197-
200: 48, 157; *WD* 256: 157
home 45, 52, 53, 75-6, 78, 94-5, 98, 129,
138, 142, 143, 150-1
Homer 24, 57, 74

179

www.ingramcontent.com/pod-product-compliance
Lightning Source LLC
Chambersburg PA
CBHW071515100726
47908CB00004B/1172